WITHDRAWN

Forms of Reflection

Forms of
Reflection

Genre and
Culture in
Meditational
Writing

David Hill Radcliffe

The Johns Hopkins
University Press
Baltimore and London

© 1993 The Johns Hopkins University Press
All rights reserved
Printed in the United States of America
on acid-free paper

The Johns Hopkins University Press
2715 North Charles Street
Baltimore, Maryland 21218-4319
The Johns Hopkins Press Ltd., London

Library of Congress Cataloging-in-Publication Data

Radcliffe, David Hill.
Forms of reflection : genre and culture in
meditational writing / David Hill Radcliffe.
p.   cm.
Includes bibliographical references and index.
ISBN 0-8018-4500-9 (acid-free paper)
1. English literature—Early modern, 1500–1700—
History and criticism.   2. Literature and society—
Great Britain—History—18th century.   3. Literature
and society—Great Britain—History—17th century.
4. English literature—18th century—History and
criticism.   5. Didactic literature, English—History
and criticism.   6. Meditation in literature.
7. Literary form.   I. Title.
PR438.S63R33   1993
820.9′005—dc20   92-31654

A catalog record for this book is available from the
British Library.

In memory of Robert Marsh

Contents

Contents

viii

Preface and
Acknowledgments

Good historical writing should reflect fairly on the past and reflect—as well—the concerns of its own place and time. But *reflection* itself has a history, a portion of which is the subject of this study. From premodern mirrors for magistrates to postmodern speculative fiction, writers have used forms of reflection to correlate literary with social structures in a bewildering variety of ways. *Reflection* has come to refer to the processes of thought, kinds of writing, and relations between the two. In this book I discuss continuities and discontinuities between forms of reflection used in the seventeenth and eighteenth centuries and forms of reflection used by contemporary critics. Because earlier writers address issues of concern to us using critical practices different from our own, a study of their writing can help us to see what is most historical about our criticism and suggest alternatives to our habitual ways of doing things. Many, perhaps most, of these differences stem from the invention, toward the end of the eighteenth century, of forms of reflection that locate differences within a *culture*. Writers began to discuss literature and society as a whole in ways that held out the promise of greater unity and coherence, while at the same time limiting the ways in which difference, and in particular historical difference, could be understood. One indication of this limitation is the rhetoric of crisis that has marked discussions of culture from the start.

The holism implicit in several senses of *reflection* limits understanding of difference, especially when these are combined or identified with each other. Modernists employed reflection in different and sometimes opposing senses: to relations between imaginative writing and the world fiction imitates, or to the relation of literature to modes of production, or to self-referential relations within literature itself. Postmodernist cultural historians draw upon all of these senses, extending them from literature narrowly conceived to relations within a much more inclusive notion of culture. This extension restores to literary criticism the broad scope it enjoyed before nineteenth-century writers restricted literature to imaginative writing, but a commitment to what may variously be described as theory, method, or science often circumscribes the ways in which difference can enter into critical writing and consequently into the ways in which differences in earlier writing may be understood.

The writers I discuss were usually much less committed to method than academic critics of culture; their writings resist closure in the belief that differences fostered in and by heterogeneous forms of reflection would lead to refinement, and refinement to useful forms of literary and social change. They described this process as civilization or cultivation, gerundive nouns implying processes of differentiation later deplored by most Victorian champions of culture. To these later writers differentiation no longer seemed like such a desirable literary and social goal; they pursued culture as an antidote to historical and social differences that seemed to threaten social stability. Critics and educators are now reassessing the social value of differentiation but using forms of reflection developed in conjunction with culture. The result is often a kind of cognitive dissonance; the words *culture* and *contradiction* are becoming inseparable in contemporary critical discourse. In seventeenth- and eighteenth-century writing, I argue, we can find alternatives to an overly narrow sense of the literary—but also alternatives to the holism that disables many recent attempts to reevaluate literary and social differences.

For this to happen, however, we have not only to consider a different way of writing, we need to consider that writing in a different way—to bracket *culture* in order to reassess structures of difference that do not make sense within the terms culture holds out to us. Rather than adjusting existing forms of reflection to accommodate an increasing awareness of literary and social differences—adding wheels within wheels to an outdated and overburdened explanatory mechanism—we might use our awareness of those differences to challenge the mechanism itself. If we are seeking to understand difference, why pursue concepts of culture that can be applied to all literatures and societies indifferently? This seems to be the impetus behind discussions of method in recent criticism: while cultural practices are thought to vary, all literatures and societies are

≡

Preface and Acknowledgments

thought to behave as cultures. When applied to literatures and societies innocent of concepts of culture and the critical practices associated with them, will the methodologies we use to write about culture do more than affirm our own presuppositions? Are our procedures for historicizing literature and society capable of recognizing structures of difference other than those articulated by and as culture? The challenge is to develop ways of writing about difference different from those employed in cultural criticism, ways of describing relations between literature and society that allow us to perceive cultural criticism as one set of critical procedures among others. This is what I hope to do with the concept of forms of reflection.

Generally speaking—speaking very generally indeed—both traditional academic criticism and the emerging practice of cultural studies locate difference in a logically prior unity (in poststructuralist variants, a logically prior contradiction); common to both is the tendency to formulate structures of difference as oppositions within this containing structure, be it understood as an informing "imagination" or a deforming "ideology." In either case, culture is a prior order of reflection, which it is the work of a second-order critical reflection to disclose. Through processes of inference and reconstruction, critics locate differences as oppositions within a spirit, world view, ideology, economy, or discourse. While critics disagree vehemently over just what differences are significant and what kind of structure they reflect, there is consensus that this is the proper function of criticism, for this is the relation between criticism and its objects pursued in forms of reflection associated with culture. This book proceeds differently, inquiring into how writing has been used to formulate concepts of culture rather than how culture has constituted kinds of writing. My own procedures for discriminating differences often take their start from those used by the seventeenth- and eighteenth-century writers I discuss. While these writings can be (and have been) described as culture, I argue that they were something else again.

In formulating literary and historical differences in terms of genre rather than culture, I call attention to the diversity of critical kinds employed at a given time and to differences in how one kind functions at different times. This marks a departure from much contemporary criticism, since cultural critics, if not always indifferent to generic relations, represent them as reflections of a prior order located above, below, or behind literary structures. These paradigms may be epistemological (controlling ideas), figural (well-wrought urns), or political (hegemonic systems), or, in "powerful" methods, several in combination. Such procedures for relating kinds of writing to other structures of difference have undeniably revealed significant connections that heretofore have gone unnoticed; in cases where culture is understood as a conflict between contending disourses, they usefully complicate earlier, overly simplistic heuristic models. But even quite sophisticated conceptions of culture conceal significant differences and have difficulty accounting for change. Where differences appear within or between paradigms, these are commonly described as contradictions, gaps, or aporias—aberrations in the paradigm, not difficulties with a kind of criticism that subordinates differences within logically prior structures. A generic history, on the other hand, will begin with differences, not only between kinds of writing, but between social acts performed by writing, the social orders articulated by writing, and the functions of a particular kind of writing at different moments in history. Rather than locating a work within a paradigmatic (if self-contradictory) system of constitutive principles, a generic approach to literary studies will attend to continuities and discontinuities within and between literary kinds, construing works against the multiplicity of literary and social norms engaged by the author. By formulating differences in this way, we can recognize that a work may belong to multiple genres, that every instance of a genre differs from every other instance of the genre, and that each new work alters the genres of which it is a member.

To think of differences differently is not necessarily to depart from the larger aims of contemporary cultural studies that attempt to specify historical relations between literary and social formations and bring these to bear on our own critical practice. It is with these ends in mind that I take meditational writing as the subject of this generic history. The reasonable demand that we use literary history to reflect on our own situation as writers and critics makes meditational writing especially pertinent to current issues in criticism. To this end, I include contemporary writers among the literary and social critics discussed in this book. I introduce digressions on historians who discuss meditational writing, comparing the procedures of modern critics to the procedures they criticize. While a short digression cannot treat such complex procedures in the depth they deserve, it can underscore significant historical differences and serve polemical purposes; in any case, the criticism discussed is familiar enough to many readers. John Donne is paired with New Historicists on discourse, John Denham with John Barrell and Harriet Guest on commerce, Daniel Defoe with Michael McKeon on probability, the Hertford

=

Preface and Acknowledgments

circle with Nancy Armstrong on women's writing, and Lord Shaftesbury with Robert Markley on disinterestedness. If my discussions have a polemical edge, I hope that the extent of my sympathy with their historicizing projects is also clear. Their attention to problems of difference overlooked by an older generation of critics and historians obviously informs the project of this book, even as it tries to formulate differences in a different way.

But I also owe much to traditional literary history. This is not the first history of British meditational writing, though it is the first to handle the subject at large in an explicitly social and political context. My research has been greatly facilitated by prior work, especially Louis Martz's *The Poetry of Meditation*, Barbara Kiefer Lewalski's *Protestant Poetics and the Seventeenth-Century Religious Lyric*, and Maren-Sofie Rostvig's *The Happy Man: Studies in the Metamorphoses of a Classical Ideal*. Each of these books is concerned with a tradition—Ignatian meditation, Protestant hermeneutics, imitations of Horace—and each studies its tradition largely in isolation from other kinds of meditation and other kinds of contemporary writing. My own work differs from these by treating meditational genres as parts of a changing field of opposing and intersecting literary and social formations. I say meditational genres, because meditations were composed in a bewildering variety of forms: I discuss an elegy by John Donne, a georgic by John Denham, a menippean satire by Izaak Walton, sylvas by Ben Jonson and Abraham Cowley, a novel by Daniel Defoe, the correspondence of Elizabeth Rowe and the Countess of Hertford, country house poems describing Lady Hertford's estate, a treatise by Lord Shaftesbury, and a periodical paper written by Samuel Taylor Coleridge.

For my purposes, what is most significant about meditational writing are the differences within the genre: meditations were written in prose and verse, in sacred and secular genres, in fictional and nonfictional forms, in discursive and narrative genres, as parts of and as containers for other kinds of writing, including theology, philosophy, science, politics, economics, history, and literary criticism. By examining how these forms of reflection engage a wide and diverse field of literary kinds I hope to give due weight to both social and intellectual factors. An understanding of how writers have used generic strategies to alter critical practices not only will make us better critics of seventeenth- and eighteenth-century writing, it can suggest why and how we might change the way we practice criticism today. It is not that we could or should substitute their procedures for our own but that we need to remember what historicism tends

≡

Preface and Acknowledgments

xiii

to overlook: history is not a one-way street. To appropriate a favorite georgic metaphor, the river of time that separates us from earlier writers can also serve as an avenue of commerce between us. That such commerce is possible is amply demonstrated by the innovative uses seventeenth-and eighteenth-century meditators made of their own literary past. New critical methodologies have always been constructed from elements of older practices.

There are methods and methods; like most of the writers I discuss, I take a skeptical view of critical methods making pretensions to science. I do not begin with a concept of the author function, a definition of meditation, or a theory of genre; my interest is in how concepts of authority, reflection, and literary difference change over time. I have opted to float several key terms — *meditation, reflection, georgic, culture* — since their meanings change and context is required to make sense of them. But this book is not without structure; to represent the complexities of a variety of intersecting and opposing historical processes I have adopted the technique of repetition and variation so often used by georgic writers. Each of my chapters is concerned with a group of related but differing literary works. I use generic continuities and discontinuities among these works to set forth the critical issues confronting their writers, their differing responses, and the literary and social innovations these responses entailed. I use the georgic technique of digression to bring history to bear on current methodological concerns. My five chapters are themselves a set of repetitions and variations on themes handled in different ways by meditational writers at different moments in history. This procedure allows me to track changes taking place in forms of reflection as values of courtly deference yielded to values of civil refinement, and those to later values of genius and universal humanity — courtesy modulating into cultivation, cultivation into culture. If this is not a methodical book, it is nonetheless a book about method. Rather than discuss method in a separate introduction, I have elected to take up methodological issues as they arise in the course of the discussion, treating them contingently in particularized social and historical contexts.

My selection and combination of works is also somewhat contingent. The writers I discuss were well known to their contemporaries if not always to us; their writings, insofar as they make use of genres most popular in their own times, may be said to be representative. Since this is a book concerned with change, I have selected writers who modify those genres in innovative ways that often became normative for later writing.

=

Preface and Acknowledgments

But in this respect they are hardly representative at all, since few works are innovative and fewer still make innovations that become norms. The emphasis on innovation has led me to the works of polite and sophisticated writers, even though much meditational writing was of more humble origin. It is not that I consider popular homilies beneath the dignity of scholarship; but the concerns of this study led me elsewhere. I have sometimes chosen particular conjunctions of works for reasons that have as much to do with criticism in our own time as with their contemporary situations. No doubt future histories of meditational writing, responding to different critical imperatives, will select different works and draw different connections between them. If this book makes a contribution to the history of culture, plainly it needs to be supplemented and corrected by other literary histories lluminating other genres and by other genres of history. Literary history has its limits.

In the first chapter I describe how Donne alters discursive procedures in response to historical circumstances, making Donne's reflections on method an occasion for considering how a study of genre might address issues raised in recent theory: the need to reformulate relations between text and context, literature and history, and individual authors and institutional structures. The second chapter describes the different procedures used by three georgic writers—Denham, Walton, and Cowley—to undermine courtly deference and propose decentered communities in which differences of rank are subordinated to differences of manners. The third chapter considers how Defoe, in *Serious Reflections of Robinson Crusoe*, interprets his famous novel by combining meditational and narrative procedures that extend the maxims of commerce and probable inference to literary criticism, theology, and political economy. The fourth chapter, on the Hertford circle, considers how georgic writing changes as eighteenth-century writers adopt epistolary procedures to ground community in reciprocity, romance procedures to redefine commerce and refinement as feminine virtues, and lyric procedures to subordinate material and historical difference to universalizing concepts of psychology and imaginative writing. The final chapter, on Shaftesbury and Coleridge, considers the different ways in which meditators reflect on cultivation and culture, examining how these writers employ aesthetic meditation to redefine literary authority, respecify concepts of progress in history and literature, and to reconceive the relation of critical method to literary and social structures.

=

Preface and Acknowledgments

This book, which began as a dissertation, owes many debts to the teachers who introduced me to these authors—Ernest Gilman, William Kerrigan, James Turner, Douglas Patey, Leopold Damrosch, and Martin Battestin—and also to the many graduate students at the University of Virginia with whom I would knock heads, especially Michael Coyle and my friends in the Theory Group, and Ted Ruml and the Eighteenth Century Society. Those were good times. My wife, Margaret, financed my higher education, even coming through with a "Radcliffe" fellowship when the department let me down. My colleagues at Virginia Tech have all been supportive; Hilbert Campbell, Peter Graham, Ruth Salvaggio, and Bob Siegle have given me useful counsel. I'm especially grateful to Michael Coyle and Michael Prince for their valuable criticism. Three persons in particular are responsible for leading me to and through this project, three very different characters, though genre critics all. Alastair Fowler was kind enough to come aboard on my dissertation committee at a very late stage and to see me transatlantically through what must have been the most trying year of my life. Here is a man who elevates common sense to most uncommon heights; I have benefited enormously from his knowledge, assistance, and insight. I would describe my debts to Ralph Cohen as inexpressible were they not so clearly stamped on every page of this book. He is a magisterial teacher. I also remember Robert Marsh, who made time amid a painful and lingering death to interest me in georgic poetry and to set me on the path I still follow. This book is dedicated to him.

Parts of chapter 2 have appeared in *Papers on Language and Literature, ELH,* and *English Literary Renaissance;* part of chapter 4 in *Studies in English Literature.* I am grateful to the editors for permission to reprint that material here.

=

Preface and Acknowledgments
xvi

Forms of Reflection

Donne in Meditation

Method and the
Varieties of Discourse

T he newer historical criticism," writes Louis Montrose, "is *new* in its refusal of unproblematized distinctions between 'literature' and 'history,' between 'text' and 'context'; new in resisting a prevalent tendency to posit and privilege a unified and autonomous individual—whether an Author or a Work—to be set against a social or a literary background."[1] Critics have agreed to problematize such distinctions, but with little consensus about how writing should be historicized or history written. The newer critics, often with good reason, accuse one another of retaining questionable elements of older critical practices.[2] To the extent that critics resist the idea of autonomy, concepts of culture, ideology, and discourse lose explanatory force; consequently, concepts of closure being pushed out the door come creeping back through the window. How can we speak of *contradictions* in a discourse, for instance, without implying standards of closure, coherence, or autonomy against which to measure those contradictions? If recent criticism attends to new contexts, it is not always so new in the ways it approaches contextualization: generally speaking, *culture* still implies a totality, *ideology* a system, and *discourse* a set of fixed and exclusionary principles.

Montrose speaks of "the *relative* autonomy of specific discourses" (6, author's emphasis), oxymoronically expressing a difficulty with much recent literary history: how can a discourse be "relatively" autonomous? This is more than just a verbal quibble. Carolyn Porter, for instance, underscores the unintended consequences of Michel Foucault's "model of power" in Stephen Greenblatt's cultural poetics:

> If theatricality, or literature, or art in general, is understood as *either* "set over against power" or "one of power's essential modes," and if this either/or allies the first choice with a formalist belief in literature's autonomy, then only formalists can believe that literature might harbor any socially resistant or oppositional force. Meanwhile, to believe that literature might have social or political weight as a form of cultural agency entails also believing that such agency as it has is by definition already co-opted by "power." What is thus excluded is the possibility that literature might well—at least occasionally— act as an oppositional cultural agent in history. It is the kind of possibility that has been foreclosed by the reading of Foucault at work in Greenblatt's analysis. [3]

Foucault can be read differently, of course, as when Jonathan Goldberg stresses that "there is no single way to describe the relationship between power and representation. . . . No directly functional bond links authority to literature." Yet even Goldberg describes the relation between language and discursive practices as "mutually constitutive." If he emphasizes contingency rather than determinism, the notion of constitutive relations would still seem to locate contingency within a closed circuit: "I use the terms language and politics in large ways. I intend *language* to subsume such terms as *writing, discourse, literature,* and *presentation; by politics* I refer to those social processes in which relationships of power are conveyed." Given this constitutive relation, apparent differences between kinds of writing and kinds of politics might register at best as "the contradictions inherent in language and the power and limitations conveyed by ruling contradictions." [4] It is difficult to see how a "ruling contradiction" might become an agent of historical change.

The idea that discursive formations display contradictions ought to give us pause, for it extends ordering principles appropriate to certain kinds of writing, politics, and criticism to discursive formations as such. But not all discursive formations can convey ruling contradictions because not all are governed by the kinds of closure and subordination of parts that the notion of contradiction would seem to require. Like most other critical terms, *discourse* has multiple senses: it is applied both to forms whose parts are subordinate to governing principles and to less regular or even irregular forms. While it is true that during the seventeenth century writers began to apply the word *discourse* specifically to rule-

=

Forms of Reflection

2

governed uses of language, the discourse as such was still regarded as only one form of discourse. Only since the invention of culture have whole literatures, and indeed whole combinations of arts, sciences, politics, economics, and religion, come to be regarded as governed by constitutive principles.[5] In the nineteenth century such putative totalities become objects of the new discourses concerned with the play of the spirit or the logic of the marketplace, sciences whose procedures for resolving differences into totalities often carry over into cultural poetics and cultural materialism. But we do well to discriminate between the several kinds of seventeenth-century discourse and the methods contemporary critics use to constitute all of those kinds as discourse—especially if we wish to think critically and historically about our own relations to earlier writing. It seems patently obvious that most seventeenth-century discursive formations are not organized according to rules such that they can be governed by ruling contradictions. It is also true that not all kinds of New Historicism are equally committed to method. But since discourse has once more become a defining issue in criticism, relations between those early attempts at methodizing discourses and their modern equivalents are worth exploring.

The instance I pursue in this chapter and throughout the book is meditational writing. In the seventeenth century, writers like Francis Bacon and René Descartes turned to meditation as a means of establishing fundamentals. They composed methodical discourses to demonstrate fundamental principles and drew upon those same principles to validate their methods. The problems with this kind of circular reasoning did not go unremarked. The Marquess of Halifax (1633–95) demurs in *Political Thoughts and Reflections,* a typical later-century response to the large claims made for method:

> Every Party, when they find a maxim for their turn, they presently call it a *Fundamental.* They think they nail it with a peg of iron, whereas in truth they only tie it with a wisp of straw.
>
> The word soundeth so well that the impropriety of it hath been the less observed. But as weighty as the word appeareth, no feather hath been more blown about in the world than this word *Fundamental.*
>
> It is one of those mistakes that at some times may be of use, but it is a mistake still.[6]

Halifax contests the claims being made for constitutive principles by writing in a form of meditation that, by detaching sentences and observations, explicitly rejects the ordering of its parts according to rules. Does this difference make a difference? Not, of course, if this generic difference can be expressed as a function of constitutive principles governing the whole of meditational writing or Renaissance politics. But what do we do with seventeenth-century writing that rejects constitutive principles on principle? It can only be reduced to order by means of constitutive principles of the critic's own making, begging the question of whether the discourse in question is then a seventeenth- or a twentieth-century construction. In such cases, we might well inquire into how one kind of order becomes part of another. How does seventeenth-century writing enter into twentieth-century discourse about discourse?

On the face of it, it makes little sense to extend the ordering principles found in one kind of writing to the literary and social practices of a society as a whole; there are manifest differences not only between but within literary formations. Yet assumptions about culture have long led literary historians to identify Renaissance theater, eighteenth-century fiction, or romantic odes with the literary and social practices of an entire society. Recently, concepts of a dominant or constitutive discourse have lent a new rigor to this kind of reduction, since a "generic" (unspecified, not generic) notion of discourse erases even those generic differences. Once Renaissance drama, eighteenth-century novels, and romantic lyrics are construed as discourse, all of them appear to conform to a suspiciously similar kind of logic. I return to this issue several times in the course of this book. For now, I suggest that until someone convincingly demonstrates that the whole of literature is constituted by the principles we find in only some of its parts, we are entitled to speak of differences, but not contradictions. My argument is that generic differences do make a difference, many kinds of difference, in fact.

By thinking of works as instances of a genre or genres rather than as instances of a discourse, we can develop more historically nuanced ways of conceptualizing relations between literatures and histories, texts and contexts, authors and social formations. To situate a work in a genre is to assume difference from the start—genres are not autonomous or even relatively autonomous. A historical and noncategorical approach to genre observes both continuities and discontinuities within a form as it changes over time and also changes in the relation between that genre and other literary kinds. To consider a work as an instance of a genre, or a genre as an instance of a social formation, is to recognize that its structures are always relative—relative to prior and contemporary works and practices

≡

Forms of Reflection

4

but also to the practices used by later critics to specify those relations.

In this chapter I consider points of continuity and difference among seventeenth-century literary kinds and also between seventeenth- and twentieth-century critical discourses. I do this by comparing the genres John Donne uses to anatomize his society with the kinds of criticism some recent writers have used to anatomize that same society. Donne's meditational works illustrate how generic structures are used to combine and oppose literary formations and social institutions. One can hardly fail to be struck by how many of Donne's writings are meditational and by how various these writings are. Donne wrote meditations in prose and verse, in Catholic and Protestant forms, in sacred and secular genres, for public and private occasions. Donne's meditations are almost always tied to historical and social circumstances. In the *Anniversaries* and the *Essayes in Divinity* the occasion is the author's search for a vocation and a place. In these works Donne reflects methodically on the literary and social forces bearing on their own creation—conflicts between discursive and affective writing and between religious and secular authorities. Donne probes the sources of these conflicts to establish new beginnings for himself as a Christian and a courtier. In describing how Donne alters discursive procedures in response to historical circumstances, I make an analysis of these writings an occasion for considering how a study of genre might address the issue raised by Louis Montrose—the need to reformulate relations between text and context, literature and history, and individual authors and social collectivities.

Joseph Hall's "Various Forms of Discourse" and the Problem of Contexts

The problem of contexts, perhaps the defining issue for New Historicism, is implicit in the contention between Louis Martz and Barbara Lewalski over the historical sources of Donne's meditational writing. In *The Poetry of Meditation* Martz composes a narrative history that identifies the mainstream of British poetry with a tradition of meditational writing extending from the metaphysicals into the twentieth century. He is not concerned with relations between genres, schools, or periods, but with the "essential kinship" of a tradition:

> The "metaphysical poets" may be seen, not as Donne and his school,
> but as a group of writers, widely different in temper and outlook, drawn

Donne in Meditation

5

together by resemblances that result, basically, from the common practice of certain methods of religious meditation. The direct influence of
one of these poets upon another, though considerable, would thus
become secondary: individual mastery of the art of meditation would
lie behind the poetry and be the essence of their kinship. . . . In short,
the present study attempts to modify the view of literary history which
sees a "Donne tradition" in English religious poetry. It suggests instead
a "meditative" tradition which found its first notable example not in
Donne but in Robert Southwell.[7]

Since the meditative tradition orginiates in Catholic divinity, that, and not
the poetry of John Donne per se, should be regarded as the wellspring of
the tradition of English lyric poetry.

By contrast, Barbara Lewalski's *Donne's "Anniversaries" and the
Poetry of Praise* locates metaphysical poetry in native, Protestant traditions of meditation: "I suggest that the scope and function of Donne's symbolism in the *Anniversary* poems evidently derives from and can best be
illuminated from certain contemporary trends in Protestant hermeneutics."[8] Rather than composing a narrative account, Lewalski outlines a
structure of period norms she then uses to interpret the *Anniversaries* and
other seventeenth-century British poetry. As she later expresses it, "these
[major] poets and most of their contemporaries shared a broad Protestant
consensus in regard to doctrine and the spiritual life, grounded upon
belief in the absolute priority and certainty of scripture and upon paradigms afforded by the Pauline epistles, a consensus overarching the
Anglican-Puritan divide and having great significance for religious
poetry."[9] This consensus is manifest in the *conventions* of meditational
poetry. Lewalski defines norms that exclude Catholic practices on the one
hand and later meditational lyrics on the other. The two critics differ over
both what contexts are relevant and the procedures for using contexts (dia-
chronic narrative, synchronic structure); where one sees continuity, the
other sees difference.

Either procedure is open to the same criticism: by homogenizing the
context, the historian obscures manifest differences among the works.
Martz, for instance, overlooks ways in which English poets modify their
sources, introducing new kinds and divergent traditions. Lewalski, while
recognizing that meditations are mixed kinds, overlooks the differences
these mixtures articulate, and with them, deep divisions among Protes-

=

Forms of Reflection

6

tants over how scripture is to be interpreted and how the authority of scripture should be brought to bear on modern institutions. She shows how common features, such as typology and panegyric, unify a field of genres and consolidate social practices without considering how these same features were also used to exacerbate doctrinal differences. The convention metaphor obscures ways in which writers used common generic strategies to disrupt consensus and promote difference. Meditators use method, the chief generic strategy I consider in this chapter, both to divide and to unite. In discussing Donne's meditational writings, I underscore multiple and conflicting contexts, using the idea of a combinatory discourse to locate these opposing practices both within the work and in the field of genres that work articulates. When Donne methodizes his elegies for Elizabeth Drury, he is not just reproducing the conventions of epideictic rhetoric; he is engaging in a doctrinal dispute over kinds of authority. The Counter-Reformation practices noted by Martz become one of the contexts of the *Anniversaries* by means of their inclusion within the poems, as well as by virtue of Donne's reference to "mis-devotion." To grasp just how Counter-Reformation practice operates in the poems, both narrative and structural analysis must be incorporated into a consideration of contexts.

Before I turn to Donne's poems, I will consider a prime source: Joseph Hall's *Arte of Divine Meditation* and his sources. Hall is the quintessential example of a writer demoted to context. In the words of one of his biographers, Tom Fleming Kinlock, Hall "never expressed a single idea which some one greater than himself had not conceived long before he was born."[10] Hall may not have been an innovative thinker, but his status as an innovative writer is beyond question: no history of satire, meditation, character, or essay can be written without considering him. These are precisely the genres that came to dominate seventeenth- and eighteenth-century literature, forms whose very occasionality made them more effective vehicles for altering social practices than major kinds like tragedy or epic. Hall had an uncanny sense for what was to come; the *Arte* was reissued in 1607 and in 1609 and appeared in no fewer than thirteen collected editions prior to 1650. U. Milo Kaufmann regards Hall's treatise as beginning the "central tradition in formal Puritan meditation."[11] Hall's supposed failure to present "a single idea . . . not conceived long before he was born" would not have hindered his reputation among seventeenth-century readers, who, after all, were avid collectors of commonplaces. But

Hall does more than just incorporate what others have said: he methodizes their sayings in ways both original and controversial. His work is context but hardly background.

Hall entered into an ongoing controversy over method, a controversy that divided Protestants from Catholics and Anglicans from Puritans.[12] The Jesuit Robert Persons responded angrily to Edmund Bunny's Protestant adaptation of his *Christian Directory* (1585); not only had Bunny altered or omitted passages, he had restructured the *Directory* according to the principles of the (Protestant) reformer of logic and rhetoric, Peter Ramus. Persons accuses his translator of introducing method for "methodes sake" and "by order bring[ing] all into disorder." He draws an analogy between Bunny's interpolations—"divisions, subdivisions, euery thing running therin by couples"—and the Protestant reformations that divided the established Church.[13] Compared to Bunny's adaptation of the *Christian Directory*, Joseph Hall's *Arte of Divine Meditation* (1606) is a much more sophisticated attempt to make off with Egyptian gold. Hall avoids the taint of Counter-Reformation theology by backdating his source: "In this Art of mine, I confesse to have received more light from one obscure namelesse monke, which wrote some hundred and twelve yeeres agoe, than from the directions of all other Writers" (67, 91), but he probably has more recent writers in mind when he censures his monk for "a double fault at the least, *Darknesse* and *Coincidence:* that they [his divisions] are both too obscurely delivered, and that divers of them fall into other, not without some vaine superfluitie" (103–4, 88).[14] Like Bunny, Hall Protestantizes his Catholic sources by methodizing them.

Hall's definition of meditation exemplifies Ramist principles of definition and division:

> Our Divine Meditation is nothing else but a bending of the mind upon some spiritual object, through divers formes of discourse, untill our thoughts come to an issue: and this must needs bee either Extemporall, and occasioned by outward occurrences offered to the mind; or deliberate, and wrought out of our owne heart: which againe is either in matter of Knowledge, for the finding out of some hidden truth, and convincing of an heresie by profound traversing of reason: or in matter of Affection, for the enkindling of our love to God. (96, 72)

Method was not the exclusive property of Protestantism; St. Francis de Sales, for example, also predicates meditation on logic: "we consider a

=

Forms of Reflection

thinge attentively to learne its causes, effectes, qualities."[15] As Martz demonstrates, Protestant use of the topics has analogues in Catholic meditation, but the issue finally turns on how method is used. No Catholic author would suggest that a function of devotional meditation is to discover heresy "by profound traversing of reason." But if Hall opposes Jesuit "superstition," he likewise resists Puritan "controversy": "for if there be some that have much zeale, little knowledge, there are more that have much knowledge without zeale" (96, 72)—this from a Cambridge-educated divine. Hall's writings begin to define an Anglican position by incorporating and resisting both Catholic and Puritan modes of discourse.[16]

Hall's *Arte* is one of a series of methodical discourses codifying the several arts and sciences: logic (Ramus), rhetoric (Talon), poetry (Sidney), education (Ascham), history (Bodin), natural philosophy (Bacon), and metaphysics (Descartes). It shares with these works what Lisa Jardine describes as an "increasing emphasis on the *practical* virtues of dialectic as a means of organizing and displaying subject matter in any discipline. These dialecticians do not present the rules of dialectic as the universal rules of discursive reasoning, but consider it primarily as a tool for the teaching of curriculum subjects."[17] Such authors, reflecting humanist principles, regard dialectic as a strategy of literary presentation rather than as a form of demonstration: "the art of discoursing plausibly according to any set theme (Agricola), the art of discoursing well, and in the same sense it is called logic (Ramus)."[18] As it became a constituent of multiple disciplines, so dialectical method became a constituent of several kinds of writing. Hall, for instance, uses it both to order his handbook and in meditational discourse itself. He disposes his meditations according to sound Ciceronian precepts: an *exordio* consisting of prayer and "entrance into the matter, which is in our choice thereof"; for *narratio*, a "description of that we meditate of"; an "easy and voluntary division of the matter meditated" for the *divisio;* for *confirmatio* and *confutatio,* a consideration of "matter of knowledge" and "matter of affection"; followed by a *conclusio.* If method was common to different kinds of discourse, different kinds of discourse were incorporated as con-texts within methodical works themselves—in the *Arte,* one for "matter of knowledge" and another for "matter of affection." Because meditation "begins in the understanding, endeth in the affection," deliberate meditation juxtaposes demonstrative and affective discourses (103, 87).

=

Donne in Meditation

Traditional methods of contextualizing literature by means of periods, schools, and traditions de-emphasize differences between works and within works. Only by considering both kinds of difference together can we recognize the strategy behind Hall's inclusion of both Protestant and Catholic devotional methods within a combinatory discourse: Calvinist procedures are modified and applied to "matter of reason" and Catholic procedures are modified and applied to "matter of affection." These changes result in a work that is neither Catholic nor Puritan but Anglican. Both Puritan and Counter-Reformation works are contexts for the *Arte*, and both appear oppositionally as contexts within the *Arte*. Like other humanist scholars, Hall is a pragmatist: just as he rhetorically incorporates opposing kinds of writing to bring the meditator's thoughts to "some issue," so he attempts, pragmatically, to make an issue of the Anglican assimilation of opposing doctrines and discourses.

Critics have likewise disregarded differences within the *Anniversaries*, and, with them, differences in the larger contexts Donne engages. It is not particularly helpful to categorize the *Anniversaries* as elegiac or meditational, Ignatian or Protestant; the issue turns on what happens to diverse kinds of material when incorporated within a combinatory discourse. O. B. Hardison, for instance, uses source study to erase Donne's combinatory procedures: "devotional works of the period were usually topical. Donne may have been imitating their organization, but it seems more likely that the "Anniversaries" and the devotional tracts resemble one another because of a common source—epideictic formulae."[19] Insofar as the poems are elegies, they do, of course, follow classical precepts for rhetorical organization. But such an analysis does not account for why Donne would merge elegiac with devotional material or describe how these genres change when so combined. Louis Martz, of course, classified the work as Ignatian meditation, basing his judgment on the distribution of the topics into threes, fives, and sevens, significant numbers in Catholic devotions: "Thus the number five becomes associated with the celebration of the Virgin: the five-petaled rose becomes her flower" (223). This kind of formal analysis also fails to account for Donne's combinatory procedures, as Barbara Lewalski points out:

> Yet as useful as they are for establishing general attitudes about meditation and suggesting typical structural patterns, the analogues Martz cites do not, as he himself admits, resolve the central problem of the *Anniversary* poems. For in the traditional meditation the ideal pattern

=

Forms of Reflection

10

of virtue eulogized is Christ or the Virgin, and Martz does not find an adequate explanation for Donne's substitution of this unknown girl as the object of the eulogies.[20]

Lewalski goes some way toward resolving categorical difficulties with her acceptance of Rosalie Colie's proposition that these are mixed genre works: "poems of compliment . . . informed by a conception of meditation."[21] Taking typology as the common denominator of "Protestant poetics," she compares the *Anniversaries* to epideictic poetry, verse epistles, sermons, meditations, and other literary forms. Yet in the end she remains committed to categorical thinking: "It seems evident that the poems are in some basic sense epideictic or panegyric works. . . . Surely this context [Protestant typology] is more apt than any other to reveal what these poems intend to praise when they celebrate a human personage as the image of God."[22] But not everything in the poems is epideictic; indeed their general tenor is plainly satirical. Donne's titles, *Anatomy* and *Progres*, suggest that scientific contexts are as apt as epideictic ones, as Thomas Willard persuasively argues.[23] The understanding of context employed by these critics prevents them from considering how contexts might function oppositionally within the poems or how a combinatory discourse might alter the kinds of discourse it incorporates.

The combinatory procedures Hall uses in *The Arte of Divine Meditation* will serve as a useful starting point for considering the procedures Donne adopts in the *Anniversaries*. Lewalski concedes that "Donne was aware of, and perhaps directly influenced by, Hall's theories of meditation"; Tourney agrees, although he argues that the *Arte* "provides no code to the structure of the *Anniversaries*." Tourney thinks that the author of the "Harbinger" may have seen the second poem through the press while Donne was abroad, Huntley that Hall may have revised his 1614 edition of the *Arte* in response to Donne's poems.[24] While we do not know the precise nature of the biographical relationship, the intertextual relation is not difficult to establish: Hall's method appears as one of several forms of discourse incorporated into Donne's poems.

It does not enter into this new context unchanged, however. As Hall modifies Catholic materials for use in Protestant worship, so Donne modifies Hall's private devotions for use in a courtly satire. What use for "profound traversings of reason" (96, 72) that are no part of courteous conversation? Hall apologizes for such monkish barbarisms; Donne, whom we may assume was writing for much the same audience, clearly

relishes them for the spice they contribute to a satura of praise and dispraise. What better platform than scholastic logic to ridicule the pretensions of human wit? The generic incongruities of yoking formal disputation with epideictic rhetoric were not lost on John Donne: he collapses
the predicables into the places, merging terms appropriated from the dis-
secting room with topics borrowed from the pulpit. Hall's "matter of
knowledge" and "matter of affection" reappear, transformed, in Donne's
titles: *An Anatomy of the World, The Progres of the Soule.* The first title
puns on dividing matter to be meditated and dismembering a corpse, the
second on being moved emotionally and reforming the social order. Implicit in Hall's method, and explicit in Donne's poems, is the conflation
of logic and rhetoric that aroused such fury between humanists and logi-
cians. Hall finds his warrant for innovation in Ramus's dialectic, Donne
in Moses's vatic lawgiving.

If Donne uses a mixture of literary and scientific discourses to dissect his society, critics of seventeenth-century culture have become similarly eclectic when they assimilate terms and procedures from literary
criticism and the social sciences.[25] Drawing variously upon aesthetic and
anthropological senses of culture, the new historical critics have generated a wealth of discourses that define culture as discourse. As diverse as
it is, the newer historical criticism has consistently returned to two issues
in contextualization: how can the multiplicity of writing and social practices in a given place and time be rendered as a discourse (or sometimes
as two discourses competing for dominance)? How can or should earlier
discourses enter into the context of contemporary critical practice? For
instance, consider Michael McCanles's formulation of the problem as one
of constitution: "I would suggest, then, that instead of viewing the
scholar's enterprise as merely the recovery and explanation of an already
constituted Renaissance text, Renaissance studies should recognize that
its central task lies in the constitution of that text through an intertext-
uality whereby two texts are brought together and fused: the constituted discourse of the Renaissance and the constitutive discourse of the
scholar himself."[26] The question becomes how an intertextual relation
can be seen as a constitutive relation, or, as I prefer to state it, how one
con-text can become part of another. Metaphors of fusion or constitution
are not very helpful here, as they imply an autonomy that neither the
Renaissance nor the twentieth-century text is likely to possess.

In his classic essay, "Invisible Bullets," Stephen Greenblatt combines literary criticism and social history as parts of a method he calls

=

Forms of Reflection

"cultural poetics." Drawing analogies between plays and travel writing, Greenblatt represents Jacobean drama and colonialism as different aspects of one discursive practice. This reconstituted poetics interprets plays as political performance and politics as theatrical performance.[27] Rather than extending poetics to include politics, Michael McKeon's interpretation of typological structures in *Absalom and Achitophel* works the other way around, subordinating poetics to (political) science; he "demonstrate[s], within a brief compass, a Marxist method of literary criticism." McKeon's demonstration divides "the historicizing process into four separate stages," which become "inseparable parts of a greater whole." It is not exactly clear whether the whole in question is seventeenth-century culture or McKeon's own essay. In that respect, it is like McCanles's idea of a constitutive critical discourse. But there is no mistaking the two-way intertextual relation between Dryden's "aesthetic detachment . . . playfully entertain[ing] all possibilities," and McKeon's own playfully aestheticized Marxism.[28] In merging literary and social criticism into a reconstituted combinatory discourse, Greenblatt and McKeon also permit the discourses being constituted to enter actively into the discourse doing the constitution: Greenblatt stages history dramatically; McKeon demonstrates history figurally.

There are other elements in the context as well: both critics incorporate New Critical readings of Shakespeare and Dryden into their reconstituted critical discourse; where culture is understood as a discourse, the tensions, ironies, and control an older generation located in literary writing can reappear as attributes of culture itself.[29] Formalist procedures are present in postformalist criticism as surely as Ignatian procedures are constituents of Protestant meditation—which is not to say that Greenblatt and McKeon are formalists, or that Hall and Donne are Catholics; the newer critics use method to set asunder what earlier critics had united, and vice versa. But why retain these elements in a reconstituted criticism?

The answer would seem to be that closure and methodical coherence remain desirable qualities—if not in cultures, at least in critical essays about culture. The interpretative essay remains the dominant genre in postformalist literary history because New Critical procedures for resolving parts into wholes and multiplicity into unity remain normative in postformalist readings of history. The impetus toward representing discursive formations as closed systems remains strong in both the more aestheticizing and more scientific versions of cultural studies, resulting in statements like this: "Marxism would have us see all of history as 'unstable' and 'in

=

Donne in Meditation
13

crisis,' a contradictory unity divisible into antagonistic periods each of which replicates, in its 'own' domain, the tensions of dialectical process."[30] The single quotation marks indicate areas where assumptions about the relative autonomy of discursive formations render differences within and between discourses difficult to conceptualize: the assumption that cultures resist change leads to the characterization of all change as "crisis"; history is "unstable" when cultures prove not to be unitary structures; the idea that periods or cultures are their "own" domains becomes problematic when a constitutive role is accorded to the historian's own discourse. In discussing the problem of contexts for Donne's *Anniversaries*, I have begun to indicate how such difficulties might be avoided by regarding literary works as parts of mutable and combinatory structures, as instances of generic rather than cultural formations.

Like Michael McKeon, John Donne arrives at the paradoxical conclusion that history and literature are in a state of permanent crisis. In the *Anniversaries* he uses an eclectic mixture of discourses to demonstrate this proposition very methodically.

Literature in History, History in Literature: Method in the *Anniversaries*

The *Anniversaries* attempt to make history by altering relations between kinds of discourse and to authorize these changes by appealing to historical origins and philosophical first principles. In taking the unusual step of publishing these poems, Donne thus pursued something more ambitious than merely to bring his private thoughts to "some issue": he sought to enact social reforms by reforming discursive practices. This is the case I argue, while conceding from the start that the poet's intentions are none too clear and that this very lack of clarity marks the project for failure. I consider the poems in two lights, first examining how their meditational structure combines the various kinds of discourse Donne seeks to reform and then considering how Donne's poetic and typological figures combine literary and historical discourses in ways that attempt to validate his proposed reformations. I find that while parsing the *Anniversaries* is pleasant work, reading anatomies of Donne's anatomy can be a penitential business. But to grasp how method is being used, it seems best to consider the poems methodically.

Each poem begins with a two-part introduction labeled "The Entrance." The first laments the decay of the world and calls for an autopsy:

≡

Forms of Reflection
14

I (since no man can make thee live) will try,
What we may gaine by thy Anatomy. (ll. 59–60)[31]

In the *narratio* Donne presents himself as a physician performing a dissection, as a priest divining the future out of the entrails of a sacrifice, and as a satirist inhaling the rich stink of corruption. In the sections that follow, his diagnosis follows Galenic procedures for deducing causes from effects in a topically arranged discourse.[32] The Entrances also announce the choice of matter to be meditated. The *Anatomy* contemplates a "new world" created from the memory of Elizabeth Drury's virtue:

> . . . and though she have shut in all day,
> The twilight of her memory doth stay;
> Which, from the carcasse of the old world, free,
> Creates a new world, and new creatures bee
> Produc'd: the matter and the stuffe of this,
> Her vertue, and the forme our practice is. (ll. 73–78)

From this matter of memory the Galenic physiognomist deduces four causes: a material cause for the new world (her virtue), a formal cause (our practice), an efficient cause ("Her Ghost doth walke," l. 70) and a final cause (to "arme / These creatures, from home-borne intrinsique harme," ll. 79–80). The Entrance to the second poem describes how Donne will populate the newfound world of the *Anatomy* with "convertites" to virtue:

> Immortall Maid, who though thou would'st refuse
> The name of Mother, be unto my Muse
> A Father, since her chast Ambition is,
> Yearely to bring forth such a child as this.
> These Hymnes may worke on future wits, and so
> May great Grand children of thy prayses grow. (ll. 33–38)

The first Entrance engages scientific, the second erotic, discourse: virginal Elizabeth will father poetical children (hymns/hims) on Donne's chaste muse, children who will then reproduce their kind in reforming works by "future wits." The *Anniversaries* are meant to be models for imitation. Hall's distinction between "matter of knowledge" and "matter of affection" is implicit in the two conceits.

Donne divides the trunk of his anatomy into five sections (ll. 91–190, 191–246, 247–338, 339–76, 377–434), each further dissected into pieces Martz calls "meditation," "eulogy," "refrain," and "moral." Hardison discerns similar subdivisions, which he names, in accordance with the epideictic structure, "lament," "eulogy," and "consolation." The five laments (ll. 91–170, 191–218, 247–304, 339–58, 377–98) usually make no reference to Elizabeth Drury, although the remaining three subsections (ll. 171–90, 219–46, 305–38, 359–76, 399–434) follow the elegiac formula of praise, lament, and moral. Across these inset pairs of meditations and elegies are distributed Hall's list of topics (causes, fruits and effects, subject, appendances and qualities, what is diverse or contrary, comparisons and similitudes, titles and names, testimony, ll. 105–10, 90–100). The catalogue follows Ramus, with definition and division dropped as redundant, given the material covered in the Entrance. Donne has eight places to wedge into his five sections: cause and effects in section 1, subjects and adjuncts in section 2, likes and differences in section 3; section 4, perhaps to avoid an awkward cut, elides titles and names with a discussion of likes and differences, while section 5 handles testimony.

Donne's diagnostic method mimics procedures for "anatomizing" a patient with deadly accuracy, if this textbook example is any indication:

> Yf thou be a Phisition and willing to teache (as for example) of a
> feuer . . . come to the places of inuention, and shewe fyrst the causes
> of the feuer euery one in order, the efficient, as maye be hotte meates,
> the matter as malancholie, choler, or some rotten humor, and soforthe
> with the formale causes and finall. The second place is theffecte, shewe
> then what the feuer is able to bring forthe, whether deathe or no. The
> third place wishethe thee to tell the subiecte of the feuer, whether it be
> in the vaines, artiers, or els where. The fowrthe to shewe the signes and
> tokens which appeare to pretende lyfe or deathe: and to be shorte, thou
> shalt pase thoroughe the rest of the artificiall places [comparisons,
> similitudes, names], and do that which is requyred in euery of them;
> And last come to the confirmying of thy sayinges by examples, aucthor-
> ities, and (as Hippocrates and Galen haue done) by stories and long
> experience.[33]

Like modern theories of discourse, Ramus's theory is "powerful" in the sense that it could be used to methodize any discipline whatsoever. So Donne begins with the *cause* of death, man's fall in Eden:

=

Forms of Reflection
16

[Women] were to good ends, and they are so still,
But accessory, and principall in ill;
For that first marriage was our funerall:
One woman at one blowe then kill'd us all.   (ll. 103–6)

He next considers two *effects* of this cause, "shortnesse of life" and "small-
nesse of stature." Section 2 discovers the *subject* world to be out of kilter
with its *adjunct* parts:

The world did in her cradle take a fall,
And turn'd her braines, and tooke a generall maime,
Wronging each joynt of th' universall frame.   (ll. 195–97)

'Tis all in peeces, all cohaerance gone;
All just supply, and all Relation.   (ll. 214–15)

Section 3 meditates on *likes* and *differences,* noting how empirical fact
deviates from norms of reason: the heavens are not "spherical" or
unchanging; the world is not "round," or "solid." It follows that the subject is out of square with the adjunct: "But yet confess, in this / The
worlds proportion disfigured is" (ll. 301–2). Section 4 compares the put-
rescent corpse to the lustre of the "new-borne earth," conflating likes and
differences with *names* and *titles:*

'Tis now but wicked vanitie, to thinke
To colour vicious deeds with good pretence,
Or with bought colours to illude mens sense.   (ll. 374–76)

In section 5 the topic is *testimony,* portents of the world's approaching dissolution:

Th'Ayre showes such Meteors, as none can see,
Not only what they meane, but what they bee;
Earth such new wormes, as would have troubled much
Th'Aegyptian *Mages* to have made more such.   (ll. 387–90)

The elegies paired with these satirical meditations apply the places of
invention to Elizabeth's heart, eyes, symmetry, flesh (the missing cut), and
virtue.

The second poem amplifies Hall's seven topics for matter of affection
(ll. 45–510), pairing meditations with eulogies. Once again, Donne wittily mars his structure by introducing an element of disorder: sections 3
and 4 pair a "descending" description with an "ascending" description,

Donne in Meditation

followed by a simple eulogy; sections 1 and 2, pondering worldly corruption, lack the corresponding ascent and have complex eulogies. Hall's first place, a "Taste and rellish of what we have thought upon" (l. 45), we can compare to Donne's,

> Thirst for that time, O my insatiate soule
> And serve thy thirst, with Gods safe-sealing Bowle.
> Be thirstie still, and drinke still till thou goe
> To th'only Health, to be Hyproptique so.   (ll. 45–48)

For the second topic, "A Complaint, bewailing our wants and untowardnesse" (l. 85), Donne describes a deathbed scene in a kind of Ignatian composition of place:

> Thinke thy friends weeping round, and thinke that they
> Weepe but because they goe not yet thy way.
> Thinke that they close thine eyes, and thinke in this,
> That they confesse much in the world, amisse.   (ll. 107–10)

Hall's third topic is "an hearty Wish of the soule, for what it complaineth to want" (l. 157). Here begin the two-part meditations. In the satirical section Donne pairs the body "Bath'd in all his Ordures" (l. 171) with a passage in which the soul, new "hatch'd" (l. 184), hastens toward heaven and "At once is at, and through the Firmament" (l. 206). For "An humble Confession of our disabilitie to effect what we wish" (l. 251), Donne satirizes intellectual pride:

> Thou art too narrow, wretch, to comprehend
> Even thy self.   (ll. 261–62)

For the "earnest Petition for what we confesse to want" (l. 321), Donne considers "With whom wilt thou converse?" (l. 325). In the descending section Donne satirizes courtiers and "spongy slack Divines" (l. 328); in the ascending section directs our conversation toward heaven—to the Virgin Mary, the patriarchs, prophets, apostles, and martyrs. Hall's sixth place is "a vehement Enforcement of our petition" (l. 383); Donne is suitably vehement, concluding the section on "essential joyes" with the admonition, "Double on heaven thy thoughts on earth emploid" (l. 339). For the final place, "a cheerefull Confidence of obtaining what we have requested and enforced" (l. 471), Donne contemplates the "accidental joy" of a soul's arrival in heaven:

=

Forms of Reflection
18

Joy of a soule's arrival neere decaies;

For that soule ever joyes, and ever staies. . . .

This kind of joy doth every day admit

Degrees of growth, but none of losing it.   (ll. 489–90, 495–96)

The parallel elegies praise the dead in the voluptuous conceits of Petrarchan lyric. A summary glance at Hall's topics suggests that an erotic sequence may have been implicit in *Arte* all along: "a Taste and rellish of what we have thought upon," a "Complaint, bewailing our wants and untowardnesse," and so on (110–12, 100–105).

With the places of invention common to so many literary kinds, it was not difficult for Donne to bring one kind to bear on another. Writers on method, Ramus chief among them, sometimes argued for a universal method at might subsume within itself all arts and sciences.[34] Then as now, proposals for such a master discourse tended to generate more heat than light, if only because of the combinatory nature of discursive formations: what is a part in one art or science may be a whole in another. Hall, following Ramus, juxtaposes logical and rhetorical methods as subordinate parts of a more inclusive art. In turn, Hall's art of meditation undergoes reformation when subsumed as a part within Donne's *Anniversaries*. Translating Hall's method from prose into poetry entails a shift up the hierarchy of genres and new relations with the various forms of discourse. As several remarks in the poems make clear, Donne considers the art of arts to be poetry rather than logic or rhetoric. He bases this foundational claim on the historical priorty of poetry compared with rival arts. In *The Arte of English Poesie* (1589), George Puttenham makes a similar claim; indeed, his catalogue of discourses derived from originary poetic utterance—divinity, history, and natural, moral, and metaphysical philosophy—chimes rather neatly with the discourses that become objects of Donne's satire throughout the *Anniversaries*.

> So . . . the Poets were also from the beginning the best perswaders and their eloquence the first Rhetoricke of the world. Even so it became that the high mysteries of the gods should be reuealed and taught, by a maner of vtterance and language of extraordinarie phrase, and briefe and compendious, and aboue al others sweet and ciuill as the Metrical is. The same also was meetest to register the liues and noble gests of Princes, and of the great Monarkes of the world, and all other the memorable accidents of time: so as the Poet was also the first historiographer. Then forasmuch as they were the first obseruers of all naturall

=

Donne in Meditation

19

causes and effects in the things generable and corruptible, and from thence mounted vp to search after the celestiall courses and influences . . . they were the first Astronomers and Philosophists and Metaphisicks. Finally, because they did altogether endeuor them selues to reduce the life of man to a certaine method of good maners, and made the first differences betweene vertue and vice, and then tempered all these knowledges and skilles with the exercise of a delectable Musicke by melodious instruments . . . therefore were they the first Philosophers of Ethick, and the first artificial Musiciens of the world.[35]

In challenging the priority of sacred poetry, misguided moderns have reduced this originary science to a Babel of contending discourses, divisive attempts at method that have fragmented and disproportioned the "pure forme" of the world as it left the hands of the creator (*Anatomy*, 257). Donne's alternative is the comprehensive discourse Elizabeth "fathers" on his muse, a master method to pull together what other artists have pulled apart. As an interdisciplinary critique of the social order, the *Anniversaries* seek to reform society by means of a method founded on the primal discourse of the first poets and lawgivers.[36]

Donne's project is thus an attempt to reform the present by reinterpreting the past. Donne's historicism differs from modern varieties, however, by remaining grounded in humanist concepts of imitation: contemporary structures of discourse are to be reformed by incorporating an earlier mode of discourse. The models Donne imitates were themselves models of reformation, of course, since the prophetic role was to reform a wayward people by reading their destiny from their origins. In that sense, the prophets had been "protestants" all along. Lewalski's insistence on the Protestantness of Donne's figural interpretations is very much to the point: Ignatian meditators are not historicists; they apply their senses and imaginations to scriptural texts without implying a typological understanding of contemporary history. Donne, by contrast, vigorously injects scriptural hermeneutics into meditation, methodically bringing sacred history to bear critically on modern manners. Describing this procedure as "incarnational symbolism," Lewalski uses Protestant typology to account for the importance Donne accords Elizabeth Drury as a historical individual.[37] But if he explores the doctrinal significance of Elizabeth's life and death, Donne also and perhaps more importantly makes Elizabeth's life and death the occasion for exploring the doctrinal significance of modern cor-

$$=$$

Forms of Reflection

ruption, including the corruption of God's originary discourse by the modern arts and sciences.

The *Anniversaries* seek to stem corruption by reuniting society around a united discourse of discourses. Figural analysis of history is well suited to this purpose, for as Hans W. Frei argues, typology was invented for the purpose of reordering a heterogeneous field of discourses:

> The emphasis in figural interpretation of the Bible is on the whole putatively temporal sequence narrated, and on the fact that inclusion in it shapes into one story the whole set of independent biblical stories covering its chronological sequences. They become linked as segments of the same sequence by being placed in one chronological order and by being referred to one another. In the service of the one temporally sequential reality the stories become figures one of another without losing their independent or self-contained status.[38]

In the seventeenth century it became increasingly common for interpreters to extend typological interpretation to current events, so that contemporary history could be used to interpret the scriptures and the scriptures to interpret contemporary events. In Donne's poems, Elizabeth is represented as God's will in his works, a text to be interpreted and a text used to interpret scriptural history. As a typological figure, she contains the whole of the history and science first proclaimed by God's prophets and poets and now corrupted into contending factions and disciplines.

So it is that the figures in the *Anniversaries* link discursive argument to historical narrative, the five sections of the *Anatomy* corresponding to five books of Moses, the seven sections of the *Progres* corresponding to events in the life of Christ. In a second Genesis, the meditator attempts to revive the dead world by reenacting typologically the covenants made by God and broken by man—the Edenic (Gen. 1:28), Adamic (Gen. 3:15), Noahic (Gen. 9:1), and Abrahamic (Gen. 15:18)—a sequence leading to the establishment of the Law of Moses, the prophetic discourse Donne hopes to reinstate by means of the *Anniversaries*. To these covenants correspond the five dispensations under which men have lived: innocence (Gen. 1:28), conscience (Gen 3:23), human government (Gen. 8:20), promise (Gen. 12:1), and the law (Ex. 19:8). Elizabeth Drury is antitype to Eve, Noah, and Abraham; in the conclusion Donne identifies himself with Moses, whose "great Office" he dares "boldly to invade" (l. 468). The *Anatomy* is thus a palimpsest of the Song of Moses, itself an abridgment of the scriptures:

Vouchsafe to call to minde that God did make
A last, and lasting'st peece, a song. (ll. 461–62)

By integrating his types and figures with the logical and rhetorical structures of the two poems Donne boldly dramatizes the possibilities of poetry as the art of arts. His figural narrative begins by relating the "causes and effects" of the failed first dispensation:

Wee seeme ambitious, Gods whole worke t'undoe;
Of nothing hee made us, and we strive too,
To bring ourselves to nothing backe. (ll. 155–157)

The paired eulogy describes how Elizabeth attempted to reinstate the dispensation of innocence:

Shee tooke the weaker Sex; shee that could drive
The poysonous tincture, and the staine of *Eve*
Out of her thoughts and deeds. (ll. 179–81)

In the subject and adjuncts section Donne describes the world as "all in peeces" when the dispensation of conscience fails:

Prince, Subject, Father, Sonne, are things forgot,
For every man alone thinkes he hath got
To be a Phoenix, and that then can bee
None of that kinde, of which he is, but hee. (ll. 215–18)

The eulogy describes how Elizabeth "had all Magnetique force alone, / To draw, and fasten sundred parts in one" (ll. 221–22).
In the sections on similitudes and contraries Donne decries the lack of "proportion" in the world following the failure of the dispensation of government:

The worlds proportion disfigured is;
That those two legges whereon it doth rely,
Reward and punishment are bent awry. (ll. 302–4)

Noah/Elizabeth renews the contract:

Both Elements, and Passions liv'd at peace
In her, who caus'd all Civill war to cease. (ll. 321–22)

Section 4, which treats "beauties other second Element, / Colour" (ll. 339–40 – the first was proportion) extends the Noahic conceit, God's

Forms of Reflection

"various Rainbow" (l. 352) sealing the dispensation of government. Section 5, on testimony, concerns the dispensation of promise. The type is the Abrahamic covenant (Gen. 15:18). In that time of miracles God promised to make a nation of Abraham's seed, but now

> The father or the mother barren is.
> The clouds conceive not raine, or doe not powre
> In the due birth time, downe the balmy showre.   (ll. 380–82)

The present age is barren of miracles, though Sarah/Elizabeth was, almost, capable of such "fruits":

> She, from whose influence all Impressions came,
> But, by Receivers impotencies, lame.   (ll. 415–16)[39]

In the *Progres* Donne shifts to New Testament history, from matter of reason to matter of affection, from law and the mechanics of method to the mysteries of grace and the inner light. As in the traditional *itinerarium mentis ad deum*, the poem follows a sequence from sensual to rational to intuitive understanding. The satirical meditations in sections 1 to 3 discuss the world, the body, and the soul in relation to the faculty of imagination; sections 4 and 5 discuss the intellectual world (knowledge of men and knowledge of nature) in relation to the faculty of reason, and sections 6 and 7 consider highest things (accidental joys and essential joys) in relation to the faculty of the will. The inset eulogies amplify the same topics according to the places of epideictic oration: in sections 1 to 3 goods of nature (Elizabeth's person), in sections 4 and 5 goods of fortune (Elizabeth's wisdom), and in sections 6 and 7 goods of character (Elizabeth's deeds).[40]

Elizabeth Drury is now the "redeemer" who is to populate Donne's newly-created world by attracting converts. Playing John the Baptist to this second Christ, the prophet arouses a "taste and rellish" of the matter to be meditated. First, a strong sensual dis-relish:

> The world is but a carkasse; thou art fed
> By it, but as a worme, that carkasse bred.   (ll. 55–56)

In the eulogy Elizabeth is a "prince," a "glimmering light," and a star leading the meditator to the new birth (ll. 78–87). The second meditation amplifies the theme of bodily corruption: "Think thee laid on thy death-bed, loose and slacke" (l. 95). As the Word, Elizabeth's body is (almost) immune from dissolution: "None can these lines, or quantities unjoynt"

Donne in Meditation

(l. 133). The type is the mystery of God made man: "The purest blood, and breath, that e'r [a sickness] eate" (l. 148). Moving on to the rational faculty, Donne's meditations now divide into two parts. Section 3 compares the body, "bath'd in all his ordures" (l. 171), to a soul that "Dispatches in a minute all the way, / Twixt Heaven, and Earth" (ll. 187–88). In the eulogy, Elizabeth, "whose faire body no such prison was" (l. 221), "chides us slow-pac'd snailes who crawle upon / Our prisons prison, earth" (ll. 248–49). The type is the adoration (ll. 226–30), given a Petrarchan turn: "we understood / Her by her sight" (ll. 243–44).

In the sections eulogizing Elizabeth's knowledge of nature (4), and knowledge of men (5), the places punningly dispraise method:

> In this low forme, poore soule, what wilt thou doe?
> When wilt thou shake off this Pedantery
> Of being taught by sense, and Fantasie?   (ll. 290–92)

Piety trumps pedantry:

> In heaven thou straight know'st all, concerning it,
> And what concerns it not, shalt straight forget.   (ll. 299–300)

Elizabeth Drury, who had never been to school, was a prodigy of wisdom nonetheless: "Shee who all libraries had thoroughly read / At home in her owne thoughts" (ll. 303–4). The type is Christ in the temple, as in *La Corona* (4):

> . . . see where your child doth sit
> Blowing out these sparks of wit,
> Which himself on the Doctors did bestow.   (ll. 2–4)

Section 5 extends the satire to ministers of church and state:

> With whom wilt thou convers? what station
> Canst thou choose out, free from infection.   (ll. 321–26)

Elizabeth—though a woman and unskilled in policy—had the best credentials; as Christ triumphant

> . . . these prerogatives being met in one,
> Made her a soveraigne State; religion
> Made her a Church; and these two made her all.   (ll. 373–75)

Section 6 (Hall's "vehement Enforcement") asks us to "Double on heaven, thy thoughts on earth emploid" (l. 439). Elizabeth resists the

≡

Forms of Reflection
24

false joys Donne enumerates in the inset meditation—worldly beauty, honor, and happiness—reserving herself for her spiritual spouse: she

> Still heard God pleading his safe precontract,
> Who by a faithfull confidence, was here
> Betroth'd to God, and now is married there.   (l. 460–62)

In the concluding section (Hall's "a cheerful Confidence of obtaining what we have requested and enforced"), Donne contrasts the fatal consequences of accidental joy on earth with the paradoxical "accident" of Elizabeth's arrival in heaven, "Where shee receives, and gives addition" (l. 510). The type is Christ's resurrection.

If Donne's disposition of places across the two poems implies closure (there could hardly have been a third *Anniversary*), the poems themselves underscore discontinuity in a narrative history of permanent crisis: the covenants were all broken; Elizabeth died in the prime of her life. Juxtaposing opposing genres like satire and eulogy reinforces the sense of corruption and fragmentation Donne anatomizes in his types and figures. In the *Songs and Sonnets* Donne had visited the Inns of Court in order to establish and subvert the "laws" of love; in the *Anniversaries* he travels to the school of Paris to establish and subvert the "science" of divinity. Donne the apostate flirts with Counter-Reformation theology but undermines the devotional methods he appropriates. The concluding colloquy informs us that he writes from France:

> Here in a place, where mis-devotion frames
> A thousand Prayers to Saints, whose very names
> The ancient Church knew not, Heaven knows not yet:
> And where, what lawes of Poetry admit,
> Lawes of Religion have at least the same,
> Immortall Maide, I might invoke thy name.   (ll. 511–16)

He might invoke Elizabeth, but he does not. Treading carefully the path to preferment, Donne disassociates *his* virgin from She whose cult was the acme of idolatry.[41] Elizabeth is not an idol to worship but a sacred text to explicate and proclaim:

> Since [God's] will is, that to posteritie,
> Thou should'st for life, and death, a patterne bee,
> And that the world should notice have of this,
> The purpose, and th'Authoritie is his;

Donne in Meditation

Thou art the Proclamation; and I am
The Trumpet, at whose voyce the people came. (ll. 523–28)

The "patterne" being figural, Donne could claim that his poem falls within the pale of Protestant divinity and the "authoritie" of scripture. Not all have agreed. Lewalski excepted, critics have never felt comfortable with Donne's mixture of secular eulogy and satire with sacred meditation. Drummond records Jonson's opinion "That Done's Anniversarie was profane and full of blasphemies: that he told Mr. Done, if it had been written of the Virgin Marie it had been something" – a sly insinuation that the poem is more Romish than the author might care to admit.[42]

Donning the mantle of scriptural prophecy, the poet methodically interprets historical texts in ways that lend authority to his own critical procedures. Donne uses his logical-typological structure to demonstrate how apparent ruptures in literature, society, and history are necessary parts of a grand design, subversive moments that finally confirm the unity made manifest by the critic's interdisciplinary method. This was a common enough strategy among seventeenth-century divines and is curiously similar to strategies adopted by New Historicists like Greenblatt and McKeon, who anatomize the operations of an ideology every bit as witty (if not so benevolent) as the providence in Donne's poems. New Historical critics are also like Donne in the ambivalence of their attitudes toward science, recognizing the rhetorical efficacy of a powerfully theorized discourse while remaining highly skeptical about the pretensions of the discourses they appropriate. Like Donne, they draw upon the resources of generic mixture to create a discourse of discourses that can represent literary and social difference and disorder as products of a controlling totality. Like Donne, they bracket their claims to science in quotation marks while drawing authority from the very kinds of discourse their criticism seems to discredit. One has only to compare Donne's or Dryden's typology to McKeon's Marxist demonstration of how four separate stages become "inseparable parts of a greater whole" to recognize similarities between otherwise very different critical projects.[43]

They are different: Donne's criticism is sacred rather than secular; he champions unity, discipline, and hierarchy rather than heterogeneity, transgression, and decentralization. But the presence of the past in these otherwise very different projects points to similar critical dilemmas for writers who combine opposing discourses. It was not unreasonable for Donne's contemporaries to suspect that Counter-Reformation devotional

≡

Forms of Reflection

practices undermine the institutional values the *Anniversaries* profess; nor is it unreasonable for our contemporaries to suspect that the presence of New Critical or old Marxist practices in recent writing about culture upholds institutional values that such writing professes to undermine. The way in which reconstituted discourses sustain and oppose prior discourses further undermines the idea that works and authors can be relatively autonomous.

This Office Boldly to Invade:
Interpretation and Institutional Structures

The word *culture* has always been used in multiple and contrary senses; critics in the arts have emphasized individual initiative, while critics in the social sciences have emphasized collective restraint. Much of what is new in New Historicism stems from attempts to redefine culture in ways that erase or reformulate distinctions between arts and sciences as commonly understood. In discussing Shakespeare, for instance, Jonathan Dollimore and Alan Sinfield pursue an understanding of culture as "used in the social sciences and especially anthropology: it seeks to describe the whole system of significations by which a society or a section of it understands itself and its relations with the world."[44] Not only does their emphasis on a *whole* system of significations carry over a concern for unity already present in literary usages of *culture*, it implies a totality of signifying practices while insisting on differences, at least between literary critics and social scientists. Late twentieth-century attempts to redefine the relation of culture to the arts and sciences thus encounter difficulties analogous to those of sixteenth-century attempts to redefine the relation of method to rhetoric and logic. In either case, we need to consider not only the status of individuals and collectivities as given within the theories but the status of the theories themselves as individual and collective structures.

Attempts to define a cultural poetics or cultural studies that incorporates elements of both literary criticism and social science have produced the predictable institutional divisions, including what Dollimore describes as the "most significant divergence within cultural analysis": the emphasis British Cultural Materialists place on the powers of resistance exhibited by the oppositional cultures as opposed to the emphasis American New Historicists place on the autonomy and containment of the dominant culture: "The former allows much to human agency, and tends to privilege human experience; the latter concentrates on the formative power of

=

Donne in Meditation

27

social and ideological structures which are both prior to experience and in some sense determining of it, and so opens up the whole question of autonomy" (3). Common to both cultural poetics and cultural materialism is, of course, the notion of culture, the belief that what historians have to do with is "a whole system of significations." But the issue of whether culture is located in experience or is prior to experience may be of less importance than the issue of whether or not literary and social formations should be construed as whole systems. The Americans, perhaps, have had the best of the argument, since they can demonstrate how constitutive structures render meaningful differences impossible, or at least unthinkable. The British, arguing that differences do make a difference, are left in the unhappy situation of trying to explain historical change through subcultures operating as constituent parts of the totality they oppose, or (worse) how change might originate within the subcultures themselves (subsubcultures?). But dispense with defining culture as a whole system of significations and the entire question of autonomy appears in a new light.

To account for change, it seems necessary to retain the idea of individuals and to allow to individuals—be they authors or works—the ability to differ from their peers and to alter the collectivities in which they participate. Individuals need not be regarded as autonomous. This is an area where the study of literary genres can prove very helpful, since it is in the act of generation that individuals and collectivities intersect and interact. It is not particularly difficult to discover in generic changes evidence of both individual and collective agency, nor is it difficult to see how generic strategies are a prime means by which social institutions are established or subverted, modified or replaced. This would be easier still were we to dispense with handbook definitions of genre as template, container, or category. It is worth recalling in this connection that as genres change, so concepts of genre change. The seventeenth-century term for genre was *kind*, a word closely related to *kin*. If modern concepts of genre emphasize categorical relations, the concept of kind often emphasizes genealogical relations, as in Dryden's designation of tragedy and epic as competing kinds of heroic poetry: "If it signifies any thing which of them is of the more Ancient Family, the best and most absolute Heroique Poem was written by Homer."[45]

Thinking of genres as families made sense in a patriarchal society, just as rejecting the idea of classes of literature made sense within the confines of liberal thought. Recovering the historicity of concepts of

=

Forms of Reflection

genre has obvious benefits not only for understanding earlier literature but also for the larger project of rethinking our own ways of conceiving of identity and difference. Genealogical analysis has returned and with it an emphasis on historical rather than categorical affiliations.[46] The notion of family resemblance is useful for conceptualizing differences within and between literary kinds, which can then be regarded not as essential types but as mutable sets of relationships among relatives: thematic, stylistic, intertextual, political; relationships between writers and works, relationships between works and readers. Like families, genres consist of individuals and grow and change by processes of accretion. Like families, genres have histories; they combine, divide, and enter into contestatory relationships, rise to prominence and decline into insignificance. While the analogy between kinds and kin has obvious limitations, it does help us to understand how mixture and change can be normal aspects of literary production, a possibility that would seem to be foreclosed by modern understandings of genre, informed as they are by modern understandings of culture.

Donne is thinking genealogically when he proposes that Elizabeth Drury "father" on his muse a new literary kind. But while the *Anniversaries* were not without imitators, neither Donne nor any other "future wit" reproduced the poems in kind.[47] If nothing else, the reception of Donne's poems illustrates the limits institutional constraints place on the autonomous actions of individuals. Arthur Marotti's assessment that Donne had failed to project a public persona in the poems helps to explain the response:

> The technique of autobiographical self-reference customary in [Donne's]
> manuscript-circulated coterie verse was, strictly speaking, quite out of
> place in a printed work. But then so too were the witty idiosyncracies
> of style and content that especially baffled a general readership unused
> to Donne's poetry and its peculiar communicative matrix. Donne
> resisted making the necessary adjustments demanded by the more pub-
> lic circumstances of print and suffered the consequent misinterpreta-
> tions and unsympathetic criticism.[48]

If Donne's self-references baffled his contemporary general public, the modifications he did make in his coterie style (in magnitude and complexity the *Anniversaries* are quite unlike the other elegies) proved equally baffling to courtly insiders like Jonson. Clearly, Donne was aiming very high — but at what? In addressing a general public, he may have been pur-

≡

Donne in Meditation

29

suing the kind of public office that would enable him to institute the reforms his poems demand—a high preferment indeed. The *Anniversaries* resemble the other epideictic works enough for us to surmise that these too are patronage poems. If so, they violate generic decorum to such an extent that they remain difficult to interpret: patronage poems ought to be addressed to a patron, not to the public at large. Donne's rather reckless juxtapositions of elegy, satire, and divinity failed to win the author a place and he himself seems to have regarded them as a misstep.[49]

The best evidence for this interpretation is to be found in the *Essayes in Divinity; being Several Disquisitions, Interwoven with Meditations and Prayers.*[50] Returning to the themes and structures of the *Anniversaries*, Donne reacts to constraint by yielding up his claims as a prophet in order to gain hearing as a divine. The *Essayes* retain the topical disposition of the *Anniversaries* and the conceit of creating and populating a new world through meditational discourse, but they drop the epideictic elements, curb the satire, return to manuscript circulation, and, returning to prose, yield up the claims of vatic inspiration. For matter on which to meditate, Donne turns to the account of creation in Genesis and the founding of the Jewish nation in Exodus—the anatomy/progress conceit without the intermediary figure of Elizabeth. Donne thus avoids several issues of social decorum and theological orthodoxy raised in the elegy. Pulling in his horns (as it were), he presents himself to potential patrons as the expositor of Moses rather than as the lawgiver himself. Donne does not, however, drop his contestatory aims. These generic modifications point to the constraints society places on authors but also to the resources available to authors who would challenge constraint. Rather than parse the typological structure in the *Essayes* as I did the *Anniversaries* (it is similar), I compare Donne's critical procedures to the discursive strategies he contests in both works. In different ways, each makes a bid for preferment by opposing the art of meditation to competing discourses handling similar material. The *Essayes* take aim at "lawyers," "casuists," "criminists," "civilists," and "schoolmen" (all of whom practice opposing arts of interpretation), but Donne's chief targets are natural philosophers and scientific divines, the subjects of his reflections on Genesis and Exodus, respectively.

For conflicts to arise, there must be points of continuity underlying the differences. Francis Bacon exemplifies the kinds of claims being made for natural philosophy that Donne challenges in the *Anniversaries* and the *Essayes*. Like Donne, Bacon seeks to authorize a new discursive

=

Forms of Reflection

practice by meditating on origins. *The Great Instauration* (1620) calls for reformation:

> And thus I conceive that I perform the office of a true priest of the sense . . . and a not unskilful interpreter of its oracles. . . . Such then are the provisions I make for finding the genuine light of nature and kindling and bringing it to bear. . . . But since the minds of men are strangely possessed and beset, so that there is no true and even surface left to reflect the genuine rays of things, it is necessary to seek a remedy for this also.[51]

To wean the faithless from the Golden Calf of neo-Aristotelian philosophy, the prophet returns to the original sources of knowledge. His method encompasses both matter of reason ("the genuine light of nature") and matter of affection ("kindling and bringing it to bear"). Bacon promises "to try the whole thing anew upon a better plan and to commence a total reconstruction of sciences, arts, and all human knowledge, raised upon the proper foundations" (4:8). The resemblance to the *Anniversaries* is unmistakable: "For I am building in the human understanding a true model of the world, such as it is in fact, not such as a man's own reason would have it to be; a thing that cannot be done without a very diligent dissection and anatomy of the world" (4:110). Both Donne and Bacon present themselves as vatic lawgivers, inventors of a comprehensive art of arts.

Along with Hall and Donne, Bacon explored several kinds of meditational genres over a period of decades. A set of devotional meditations was published with the *Essayes* of 1597, one of the earlier Protestant efforts in the form. Drafts of the "Novum Organon" show Bacon tinkering with several meditational kinds, including the "resolve" in *Cogitata et visa* (1607).[52] Each essay combines a cogitata section contemplating matter of knowledge with a visa section enforcing this matter on the affections. Resolves and aphorisms were small, occasional forms gathered by tens or hundreds into large collections such as Joseph Hall's *Meditations and Vowes Divine and Morall* (1605). Such is the structure of the "Novum Organon," the part of *The Great Instauration* concerned with invention. The opus magnus is itself a methodical work, a monumental discourse, with whole books occupying the several places of the Ciceronian oration. It is significant, therefore, that Bacon eschews methodical arrangement in the part of the work concerned with invention. Bacon explains his innovation:

=

Donne in Meditation

31

He thought that knowledge is uttered to men, in a form as if every thing
were finished; for it is reduced into arts and methods, which in their
divisions do seem to include all that may be. And how weakly soever
the parts are filled, yet they carry the shew and reason of a total; and
thereby the writings of some received authors go for the very art:
whereas antiquity used to deliver the knowledge which the mind of
man had gathered, in observations, aphorisms, or short and dispersed
sentences, or small tractates of some parts that they had diligently meditated and laboured; which did invite men, both to ponder that which
was invented, and to add and supply further.   (3:398)

Bacon writes methodically when he is refuting others, but he presents his
own inventions according to the order of nature rather than art. Since
experience is a cumulative process, literary forms that are to convey experience should depart from the closed structures of demonstrative reasoning.[53] So while the larger structure of *The Great Instauration* corresponds
to the methodical disposition of parts in the *Anniversaries*, Bacon's inset
meditations, unlike Donne's, are not topically arranged and do not give
the misleading impression of demonstrative closure.

As meditational works, *The Great Instauration* and the "Novum Organon" correspond to the two kinds Joseph Hall describes as deliberate and
extemporal meditation.[54] *Deliberate* implies methodical invention, while
extemporal implies occasionality, as in Hall's essays "Upon the Smell of a
Rose," "Upon the Sight of a Harlot Carted," "Upon the Sight of a Man
Yawning." Joining what Hall would sunder, Bacon reformulates deliberate
meditation by substituting occasional observations, where Hall and
Donne turn to the places of invention. He also seems to distinguish *contemplation* of outward occurrences from *meditation* on inward thoughts; in
the "Novum Organon," *meditation* almost always bears a pejorative con-
notation: "Those however, who aspire not to guess and divine, but to discover and know, who propose not to devise mimic and fabulous worlds of
their own, but to examine and dissect the nature of the world itself, must
go to the facts themselves for everything. Nor can the place of this labour
and search and worldwide perambulation be supplied by any genius or
meditation or argumentation" (4:28, my emphasis).

Bacon speaks of "specious meditations, speculations, and glosses"
(4:48), or "meditation and agitation of wit" (4:64). Contemplation, on
the other hand, is drawn not from "the depths of the mind but out of the
very bowels of nature" (4:24). Meditation besets the mind with idols, but

=

Forms of Reflection

"the very *contemplation* of things as they are, without superstition or imposture, error or confusion, is in itself more worthy than all the fruit of inventions" (4:115, my emphasis). Bacon opposes his art to wit and to logic, to both courtly poetry and academic pedantry. By elevating lesser kinds, like the essay and occasional meditation, to the status of science ("to discover and to know") Bacon succeeded where Donne failed: he and his many imitators altered the hierarchy of literary genres. As we shall see, contemplative writing became the chosen form for generations of writers seeking to initiate social change through new discursive practices.

Both Donne and Bacon were acutely aware of the institutional implications of their meditational procedures. While representing himself as both priest and prophet, Bacon tries to neutralize the objection that New Science "cals all in doubt" by presenting natural philosophy and divinity as discrete and incommensurable discourses:

> This . . . I humbly pray, that things human may not interfere with things divine, and that from the opening of the ways of sense and the increase of natural light there may arise in our minds no incredulity or darkness with regard to the divine mysteries; but rather that the understanding being already purified and purged of fancies and vanity, and yet not the less subject and entirely submissive to the divine oracles, may give to faith that which is faith's. (4:20)

Natural and moral philosophy are grounded in experience, divinity in "divine mysteries." Donne, who will have none of this, insists that matter of reason and matter of faith should be handled as two parts of one interdisciplinary discursive method. There is only one truth, he argues in the *Essayes in Divinity*, although it appears in different ways to different understandings. Donne does not share Bacon's view that reading the Book of Nature presupposes no other art; there is in the Book of Creatures only "enough to make us inexcusable, if we search not further. And that further step is the knowledge of the Bible" (8). Each book is required to gloss the other: "God himselfe is so much a Circle, as being everywhere without any corner, (that is, never hid from our Inquisition;) yet he is nowhere any part of a straight line, (that is may not be directly and presently beheld and contemplated) but either we must seek his image in his workes, or his will in his words, which, whether they be plain or dark, are ever true, and guide us aright" (38–39).

Revelation and the natural light are not parallel discourses but interdependent parts of one discursive method. Donne holds to the Augustinian view that we study the creatures not to gain power over the world (as in Bacon's "art of interpretation") but to prevent the world from gaining power over us.[55] Donne's meditations on causes and effects, essences and attributes, likes and opposites, are all invented out of the Book of Genesis — God's informing word, which is at once the source of nature and the authority for its interpretation.

Although Donne was not necessarily opposed to natural philosophy (he does, after all, compare Elizabeth Drury to Gilbert's magnet), he resists the idea that method should begin in observation and experience:

> When wilt thou shake off this Pedantery,
> Of being taught by sense, and Fantasie?
> Thou look'st through spectacles; small things seeme great
> Below; But up into the watch-towre get,
> And see all things despoyl'd of fallacies:
> Thou shalt not peepe through Labyrinths of eares, nor learne
> By circuit, or collections to discerne.
> In heaven thou straight know'st all, concerning it,
> And what concernes it not, shalt straight forget.[56]

Meditators have little need for Galilean "spectacles" or Baconian "collections." Donne invents his *Anniversaries* out of God's threefold book: Elizabeth as God's creature, his word incarnate, and his revealed will:

> . . . for shee rather was two soules,
> Or like to full on both sides written Rols,
> Where eyes might reade upon the outward skin,
> As strong Records for God, as mindes within.   (503–6)

In defense of the poems Donne claimed that he had never seen the object of his descriptions at all: "For no body can imagine, that I who never saw her, could have any other purpose in that . . . It became me to say, not that I was sure was just truth, but the best I could conceive."[57] This is the idol-ridden meditation Bacon opposes to contemplation: an "exercise of thought," a flexing of the "strength and excellency of the wit." In both the *Essayes* and the *Anniversaries*, Donne invents his arguments in accordance with Protestant divinity — of a certain persuasion.

The second of the two *Essayes* turns to matter of affection, the means by which the Word is propagated. On this point Donne grapples with the divines — defenders "of a well provided castle" — already singled out for dispraise: "To reverend Divines, who by an ordinary calling are Officers

Forms of Reflection

and Commissioners from God, the great Doors [of scripture] are open. Let me with *Lazarus* lie at the threshold, and beg their crums. *Discite a me*, says our blessed Saviour, *Learn of me*, as Saint *Augustine* enlarges it well, not to do Miracles, nor works exceeding humanity; but *quia mitis sum*; learn to be humble" (5). The "threshold" at which Donne begs his crumbs can be taken as the boundary between misspent youth and productive adulthood, between banishment and preferment, or as the boundary between lay and professional status. Excluded from the universities, he makes a "humble" petition for "such as I, who are but Interlopers, not staple Merchants, nor of the company, nor within the commission of Expositors of the Scriptures" (27). The *Essayes* extend an open palm to James but brandish a closed fist toward the guild. Before examining Donne's art of divinity, we need to consider the professional practices to which it is opposed.

A *Learned Treatise* by John Stoughton (d. 1639) exemplifies divinity as practiced by many "within the commission." Stoughton, later a Puritan lecturer at an important London parish, practices a kind of divinity better appreciated in the universities than in the courtly circles to which Donne aspired.[58] Like the *Essayes in Divinity*, Stoughton's oration is the masterpiece of a journeyman divine, making ostentatious displays of rhetoric, logic, and the authorities. Stoughton recommends methodical divinity to a peer audience of young professionals: unlike other arts, divinity "is the generall calling of all men. . . . Some are employed in Magistracy, some in Merchandise, some in Agriculture, or otherwise, but from the highest Statesman to the lowest craftsman, all should be divines, all should be imployed in this" (48). But this calling is particularly recommended to those in the *schooles of the Prophets* . . . whose gates will scarce admit of any, but such as are at the least welwillers to Divinity" (50). These are the gates at which Donne begs his crumbs, gates that exclude as well as give admittance. Divinity, Stoughton notes, is a proud profession, elevated above the other arts for the "nobility of its object," "for the necessity of its end," for the antiquity of its discipline, and for the authority of its "author . . . God himself" (55). But first and foremost, the dignity of the discipline resides in its status as foundational science:

> Whereas all other Arts, the skill of which we are to attain unto by naturall reason upon observation and experience are so uncertaine for the most part that a man when he hath done his best may remaine a Sceptick or Academick: by reason of the weakness of our understanding,

> proceeding from the wound of original sin; it is not so with this where
> we receive all our light and information from God himself, who being
> the fountain of wisdom is not subject to the least ignorance. (55)

As one might expect, Stoughton prefers demonstrative, "artificial" methods of exposition to "prudential" or rhetorical ones. Speaking to a lay audience, God was thrown upon the latter course: "For though the word of God aime not at the laying down of artificiall and notional truths; but bears almost altogether upon fundamentall in a method of divine wisdom and prudence: yet even those must have the ground and substantialls, from thence, though Art may put a form and modification upon them" (32). The science of divinity reformulates rhetorical artifice as logical artifact, translating scriptural heterogeneity into a coherent, monological discourse.

While Donne also swipes at "observation and experience," he takes strong exception to the idea that the function of divinity is to reduce scripture to term and topic. As an interpreter of the Bible, he engages three opposing traditions: cabalism (9, 13–14), Catholicism (49–50), and Calvinism. All have their attractions; Donne admires the learning of the syncretists, though not Pico's "incontinent wit"; he admires the solidity of the mother church, though not its "idolatry"; he admires the Puritan's power of demonstration, though not his choplogic. Donne incorporates elements from these suspect kinds into the *Essayes*, just as he had elements of Ignatian meditation in the *Anniversaries*. But toward neo-Aristotelian divinity, Donne is openly hostile:

> They therefore which stub up these severall roots, and mangle them
> into chips, in making the word of God not such . . . they, I say, do what
> they can this way, to make God, whose word it is pretended to be, no
> God. . . . So have they which break these Sentences, *importuna ingen-
> ium*; a wit that would take no answer nor denyal. So have they which
> break these Sentences, yea Chapters, rather then not have enough to
> break to their auditory, they will attempt to feed miraculously great Con-
> gregations with a loafe or two, and a few fishes; that is with two or three
> incoherent words of a Sentence. (39–40)

Like Persons censuring Bunny, Donne fulminates against undue reformation: "there are some things which the Author of light hides from us, and the prince of darkness strives to shew to us; but with no other light, then his fire brands of Contention, and curiosity" (13). Divinity should inspire

≡

Forms of Reflection

affection, not inflame contention. By breaking the Scriptures, scientific divinity divides the Church.

Donne believes the one sense of scripture is to be taken on faith rather than demonstrated by art. This leads him to oppose his own methods to those "who for ostentation and magnifying their wits, excerpt and tear shapeless and unsignificant rags of a word or two, from whole sentences, and make them obey their purpose in discoursing" (39). Rather than reduce scripture to a tree of syllogisms, divines ought to reproduce its figural structures in their own discourse: "The meditation upon Gods works is infinite; and whatever is so is Circular, and returns into its selfe, and is every where beginning and ending, and yet no where either" (38). The paradigm for his art is thus scripture itself: "But I do not at this time transgress this rule [against breaking the scriptures] . . . because [my verse] is not so unperfect, but that radically and virtually it comprehends all the book" (41). Imitating both the generic heterogeneity and figural unity of his "original," Donne interrupts his figural exposition with descriptions and apostrophes, conceits and colloquies.[59]

The meditator spins out his discourse in looping, snakelike trains of affective interpretation: "Only to paraphrase the History of this Delivery [in Exodus], without amplifying, were furniture and food enough for a meditation of the best perseverance, and appetite, and digestion, yea, the least word in the History would serve a long rumination" (74). Rather than break his text, the expositor swallows it whole, digesting its one sense while "incorporating" its figural strategies. The inset meditation from which this passage is taken, like the verse of Exodus it expounds, contains the whole of which it is a part. Wrapping a fourfold coil of exegesis around Moses' text, Donne applies the moral sense to his own liminal circumstances:

> Go one step lower, that is higher, and nearer to God, O my soul, in this Meditation, and thou shalt see, that even in this moment, when he affords thee these thoughts, he delivers thee from an Egypt of dulness and stupiditie. As often as he moves thee to pray to be delivered from the Egypt of sin, he delivers thee. And as often as thou promisest him not to return thither, he delivers thee. Thou hast delivered me, O God, from the Egypt of confidence and presumption, by interrupting my fortunes, and intercepting my hopes; And from the Egypt of despair by contemplation of thine abundant treasures, and my portion therein; from the Egypt of lust, by confining my affections; and from the mon-

strous and unnaturall Egypt of painfull and wearisome idleness, by the necessities of domestick and familiar cares and duties. (75)

Donne's contemplations differ from Ignatian meditation by substituting figural interpretation for composition of place and application of the senses, and from Puritan exegesis by collapsing interpretation into application. Incorporating elements of opposing methods, Donne's writing enacts the synthetic principles his doctrine expounds.

Nonetheless, the kinds of unity Donne pursues in the *Essayes* are nothing if not divisive—the emphasis on "one sense" divided Protestants from Catholics even as the emphasis on affective rhetoric divided Anglicans from Puritans. If the author presents himself as an outsider, the *Essayes in Divinity* nonetheless preach authoritarian doctrines to courtly readers in a flamboyantly courtly style. In his *Form of Wholsome Words, or an Introduction to the Body of Divinity* (London, 1640), Stoughton exhorts dissenting preachers to avoid such tinseled language: "but then besides the soundness of the matter, there is the *soundnesse of the manner* or *form of words*, in which these things are delivered; they must not be delivered in an affected language" (25). Delivering this sermon in the 1630s, Stoughton was likely warning his London parishoners to avoid the honey-tongued, licentious dean of Saint Paul's.[60] If, after the *Anniversaries*, Donne confined his public utterances to prose, he never doubted the congruence between the art of poetry and the art of divinity. The *Essayes* insist that poetry is a fit medium for lawgiving:

> And God himself in that last peice of his, which he commanded *Moses* to record, that Heavenly Song which onely himself compos'd (for though every other poetick part of Scripture, be also Gods word, and so made by him, yet all the rest were Ministerially and instrumentally delivered by the Prophets, onely inflamed by him; but this which himself cals a Song, was made immediately by himself, and *Moses* was commanded to deliver it to the Children; God choosing this way and conveyance of a Song, as fittest to justifie his future severities against his children, because he knew that they would ever be repeating this Song). (92)

Donne models his art of divinity on the imputed unity of God's theological-historical-philosophical-critical art of poetry, the "first Rhetoricke of the world." Donne says as much, though more boldly, in the elegy for Elizabeth Drury:

Forms of Reflection

Vouchsafe to call to minde, that God did make
A last and lastingst peece, a song. He spake
To *Moses* to deliver unto all,
That song: because hee knew they would let fall
The Law, the Prophets, and the History,
But keepe the song still in their memory.
Such an opinion (in due measure) made
Me this great Office boldly to invade.[61]

If the *Anniversaries* demonstrate the necessity of Donne's prophetic vocation, the court apparently had no office available for a vatic poet. Donne's
poems would only have confirmed the views of those who regarded the
writer as a great wit but an unsound individual. Perhaps because he was
willing to forget Donne's "lastingst peece," James eventually presented to
the divine the position of authority he was unwilling to grant the poet. It is
difficult to estimate just how much the *Essayes in Divinity* contributed to
Donne's preferment, but we may believe that tempering his position did
nothing to hurt his cause. The tables turned: Donne became dean of St.
Paul's, while Stoughton eked out a tenuous existence as a Puritan lecturer.

I have argued that the emphasis literary historians place on autonomy renders relations between literary and social change difficult to conceptualize and that the opposition between a literature "set over against power"
or literature as "one of power's essential modes" results from concepts of
culture that place an undue emphasis on autonomy. As an alternative, I
have described literary works as instances of genres rather than of cultures, arguing that oppositions within and between genres reflect and generate significant literary, social, and historical differences. To make this
case, I have situated Donne's *Anniversaries* and *Essayes* in a dynamic
field of intersecting and opposing literary kinds: elegy, satire, deliberate
meditation, occasional meditation, natural philosophy, Petrarchan lyric,
essay, resolve, sermon, scriptural commentary, controversial tract, literary criticism, medical textbook, sacred history, and so on. The variety
and complexity with which these literary kinds combine results from the
variety and complexity of seventeenth-century social institutions.
    This chapter has shown how a generic approach to literary history
might address the three problematics Louis Montrose uses to define a
new literary history without invoking the problematic notion of relative
autonomy. First, by thinking of works as complexes of genres, we can see

=
Donne in Meditation
39

how different and often opposing kinds of literary and social practices appear as contexts within a work—Protestant and Catholic devotional methods, for instance, or medical and erotic treatments of physiognomy. Second, literary works can make history by differing from the genre or genres in which they participate, as Donne alters meditational writing by fitting Hall's method to a different set of literary and social imperatives. Third, by treating literary works as generic structures we better understand the joint participation of individuals and collectivities in structures of difference that can make a difference in the way literature is produced and received.

If there is a conclusion to be derived from the debates over method discussed in this chapter, it might be Halifax's reflection that the appeal to fundamentals "is one of those mistakes that at some times may be of use, but it is a mistake still." Appeals to method and constitutive principles sometimes exert great suasive power, even when—or is it especially when?—institutional lines are changing or not clearly drawn. Making good use of such arguments, Hall and Donne rose to important positions in the established church. As a seventeenth-century writer, Donne was innocent of the idea of culture but was not without resources for representing literature and history as constituent elements of a methodically ordered discursive totality. But even as writers like Hall and Donne subsumed opposing discourses within Anglican doctrine, the established church was speaking for an ever-diminishing segment of the population. Demands for order, reform, and a more comprehensive science of discourse did little to rectify the situation. If appeals to fundamentals advanced careers, they also contributed to irreconcilable differences— such, at least, was the opinion of Halifax and many others who lived through the endless series of political, religious, and intellectual broils of the era. One result of those contentions was a meditational literature that came to accept heterogeneity and change as facts of literary and political life. This literature deserves attention if only because it tackles the kinds of issues that most concern us, without being tangled up in our received ideas about culture.

≡

Forms of Reflection

Seventeenth-Century Georgic

Denham, Walton, Cowley, and the Decentered Society

Seventeenth-century meditators generally preferred Baconian short and dispersed sentences to Aristotelian divisions by term and topic; they produced few deliberate meditations but shelves of essays, observations, aphorisms, proverbs, characters, and resolves. Writers came to avoid fundamentals for both epistemological and political reasons. With some notable exceptions, British writers from the seventeenth century onward rejected the rationalism of Descartes and the Port-Royal, at first because of the association with French absolutism and later because of the association with French Jacobinism. Instead, liberal reformers in Britain cultivated literary forms that stressed heterogeneity, reciprocity, and toleration—forms that substituted standards of politeness (and later sensibility) for courtly rituals of display and deference. Cultivation and refinement were pursued as alternatives to subordination; in the words of Shaftesbury, "All politeness is owing to liberty. We polish one another, and rub off our corners and rough sides by a sort of amicable collision."[1] Refinement implied heterogeneity, the heat and light produced by rubbing different substances together. Looking back on the last age, Whig and Tory writers alike could regard the civil wars as refining fires that changed the ways in which literature was written and politics practiced. More than one of them regarded their preference for short and dispersed literary forms over methodical writing as analogous to the political diffusion of authority that settled the long contest between king and Parliament. In this chapter I consider how seventeenth-century meditational writing worked to foster civility and decenter the social and literary principles of Renaissance absolutism.

The three authors I discuss all ring changes on retirement themes, presenting alternative versions of community in variations on georgic strategies. In *Coopers Hill* (1642) John Denham responds to the constitutional crisis by proposing a republican concept of mixed government. In *The Compleat Angler* (1653) Izaak Walton envisions an enclave of pious friends capable of forming an alternative community by tempering their differences. Abraham Cowley's *Essays in Prose and Verse* (1668) rejects political structures of patronage and deference in favor of a retired life of autonomous solitude. Few seventeenth-century works were more widely read and imitated than these, yet Denham, Walton, and Cowley have received relatively little attention from scholars and critics. Reasons for this neglect are perhaps not difficult to identify: the literary and social structures in georgic writing pursue norms of cultivation that have not seemed desirable to nineteenth- and twentieth-century critics of culture. Such critics have been slow to recognize that decentering was considered a positive literary and political value in the seventeenth century or to recognize how a poetics of refinement might promote social change. Unwilling to acknowledge heterogeneity as a principle of order, only recently have critics begun to discriminate between the varieties of variety seventeenth-century writers used to promote their political objectives. One purpose of this essay is to recover the literary and historical procedures informing meditational writing in the georgic mode; another is to exemplify how similar procedures of discrimination can be used to resist the holism characteristic of modern concepts of culture. The *cultivation* pursued by georgic writers should be carefully distinguished from the *culture* later writers used to reject refinement and discrimination as social and literary values.

Coopers Hill and the Poetics of Change

The author of the most significant georgic poem since Virgil was a true cavalier, more likely to lose an estate at play than to plant a grove or prop a vine. *Coopers Hill* is less about agriculture than politics; Denham's subject is the structure of British history from Plantagenet times down to the recent attainder and execution of the Earl of Strafford.[2] The poem begins with an augury of foul weather and concludes with a prophecy of deluge:

≡

Forms of Reflection

42

when *Coopers Hill* appeared in August 1642, troops were already being mustered. Denham casts his meditation as a georgic, the form used by Virgil to celebrate the arrival of peace and prosperity following the wars of Augustus. The poem adapts the georgic devices of prophecy, allegory, and description, situating the present conflict prospectively in history and the landscape by reformulating procedures Virgil used to merge politics with natural philosophy.

If Denham did not succeed in reforming the political process, he did succeed in reforming poetical processes; his poem assembles the repertoire of English georgic – history, politics, religion, natural science, character, encomium, allegory, *ecphrasis,* and epigram. These are by and large the constituent elements of Donne's *Anniversaries*. What has changed are procedures of combination and concepts of change: for Donne heterogeneity signifies corruption, the "all cohaerence gone" of a stinking world indifferent to transcendental virtues. Denham, on the contrary, regards heterogeneity as the source of harmony and the basis for future stability: in the aggregative structure of *Coopers Hill* friction among contending parts becomes a positive social and literary value. Critical responses that seize upon the irregularity of the *Anniversaries* or the smoothness of *Coopers Hill* tend to overlook the larger purposes to which satire and georgic are being bent: Donne mounts an argument for social subordination, Denham an argument for social interdependence. Attempts to impose closure on Denham's differential structures – by literalizing the concept of perspective, overlooking the *discors* in Denham's *concordia,* or disregarding his combinatory procedures – all obscure the ways in which Denham combines opposing points of view, contrary values, and a variety of literary kinds.

Earl Wasserman's formalist analysis of *Coopers Hill* argues that "total poetic success must lie in the transformation of all the other topographical features in the poem into metaphoric relevance." Denham's metaphors exhibit a unity of "expression and concept . . . so contained in each other as to imply a single all-controlling mode of thought."[3] James Turner's materialist interpretation also pursues an all-controlling mode of thought: "Denham's task is to establish a single viewpoint equally free from flattery and idiosyncrasy; his opinions will then appear as natural and irrefutable as sight itself"; "Every perspective device has a 'subtile Philosophy' of this kind, an exclusive viewpoint which claims to reveal the true form of appearances. Landscape is the subtlest form of prospective, for its trickery is unobtrusive and the resulting image overwhelmingly clear." The poet's "visual realism" describes things not as they are but as they appear in a distorting political perspective.[4] Not surprisingly, both critics discover contradictions in the poem. Wasserman describes these as aesthetic flaws: "Unfortunately for the artistry of the poem, at this point there is an abrupt and apparently unmotivated redefinition of the images. . . . But now, with another unmotivated substitution of image values. . ." (70, 71). The contradictions Turner discovers result from ideological distortions: the comparison of Windsor Castle to Chertsey Abbey "is rather a dishonest one; since St. Anne's hill is visually less prominent than Windsor and lies in the opposite direction, the eye is obviously led by a political argument and not vice versa." Departures from monocular perspective indicate "trickery" and "sleight of hand" (51, 53).

Neither interpretation takes generic matters into account; as a georgic poem, *Coopers Hill* would not turn on one controlling metaphor, as a lyric would; nor, since the georgic was an avowedly political genre, should its landscape metaphors be considered attempts to conceal a political program. In an age when civil authority resided in tradition and divine right, Denham could not have expected an appeal to nature to be taken as self-evident; the evidence of the senses was often rejected, as in Donne's slighting reference to "lattices of eyes" (*Progres*, l. 296). Denham does not offer a single perspective or an "overwhelmingly clear" point of view; in fact he takes pains to avoid such a practice. In addition to describing what lies before him, the poet recalls the past: "Here have I seene . . . " (l. 263); anticipates the future: "But if . . . No longer then within his bankes he dwels" (ll. 337–39); and invents out of "a quicke Poeticke sight" (l. 254).[5] He describes Windsor as it appears from Coopers Hill, but London from a God's-eye perspective:

> Exalted to this height, I first looke downe
> On *Pauls*, as men from thence upon the towne. (ll. 13–14)

Allusions to Narcissus and the "emptie, ayrie contemplations" of the monks at Chertsey (l. 170) remind readers that reflections may be deceitful. While he certainly makes nature and material causes the basis for his political philosophy, Denham insists that our faculties are limited; like a good Baconian investigator, he tries to circumvent the idols of the mind by examining his subject in different lights. Rather than insisting on one point of view, *Coopers Hill* dramatizes the problem of bringing diverse outlooks together.

The much-discussed doctrine of *concordia discors* would have led

≡

Forms of Reflection

critics to such an understanding, had not *concordia discors* been pressed
into service as a world view. As it is, the history-of-ideas analysis only but-
tresses the one-perspective interpretations. Brendan O Hehir finds in the
"classical and Renaissance cosmological principle of 'balanced opposition' or *concors discordia* . . . the outlines of a particular world view—
both a means of interpreting and an assumption about the nature of the
apprehensible universe—which controlled Denham's writing." Like Wasserman and Turner, O Hehir describes deviations in point of view as
contradictions: "the doctrine is emotional rather than intellectual . . .
[and] not susceptible of rigourous analysis or capable of strict logical
exposition" (*Expans'd Hieroglyphics*, 165). While all these critics offer valuable local insights, the poem as a whole resolutely refuses to correspond
to their monological interpretations. If Denham frequently invokes the
principle of *concordia discors*, he also invokes the concept of hierarchy.
He might apply both to the same object, as when he describes Windsor
Hill first as a balance of opposites, "A friend-like sweetnesse, and a King-
like aw" (l. 62), and then as an instance of just subordination:

> So *Windsor*, humble in it selfe, seemes proud
> To be the Base of that Majesticke load.   (ll. 65–66)

Were Denham really proposing a "single all-controlling mode of thought,"
as Wasserman suggests, this would indeed be an "unmotivated substitution of image values."

Sometimes the poet deliberately avoids invoking the principle of
balanced opposites, as in the opening lines:

> Sure we have Poets, that did never dreame
> Upon *Pernassus*, nor did taste the streame
> Of *Helicon*, and therefore I suppose
> Those made not Poets, but the Poets those.
> And as Courts make not Kings, but Kings the Court;
> So where the Muses, and their Troopes resort,
> *Pernassus* stands; if I can be to thee
> A Poet, thou *Pernassus* art to mee.   (ll. 1–8)

Romantic aesthetics leads us to expect a balanced synthesis of perception
and imagination, or, as Wasserman puts it, "coherently organized symbols generated by the friendly struggle between eye and mind" (51). But
Denham announces that he will subordinate perception to fancy: as

=

courts do not make kings, so landscapes "make not Poets, but the Poets those." No *concordia discors* here:

> Through untrac't waies, and airie paths I flie,
> More boundlesse in my fancie, then my eie. (ll. 11–12)

The differences between Denham's procedures and those of romantic poetry are not the least interesting aspects of the poem. In his classic essay, "Structure and Style in the Greater Romantic Lyric," M. H. Abrams underscores the difference between georgic poetry and romantic lyric: "We are a long way . . . from the free flow of consciousness, the interweaving of thought, feeling, and perceptual detail, and the easy naturalness of the speaking voice which characterize the Romantic lyric." We are indeed, if only because we are concerned with different *kinds* of meditation. But distinctions of kind are the first casualty of a romantic aesthetic that implicitly takes the concerns of romantic lyric as norms for poetry as such:

> The process of vital artistic creation reflects the process of this vital crea-
> tive perception. Unlike the fancy, which can only rearrange the "fixities
> and definites" [Coleridge] of sense-perception without altering their
> identity, the "synthetic and magical power" of the secondary imagina-
> tion repeats the primal act of knowing by dissolving the elements of per-
> ception "in order to recreate" them, and "reveals itself in the balance
> or reconciliation of intellect with emotion, and of thought with object."[6]

Like most georgic poets, Denham is not interested in a higher synthesis; he is interested in how material forces acting in history combine, oppose, and correct one another.

Finally, critics have pursued unity as a function of genre. George Sherburn, concerned lest the poem "falls into fragments and does not make a unit," takes exception to Samuel Johnson's definition of local poetry as that which takes as its subject "some particular landscape, to be poetically described, with the addition of such embellishments as may be supplied by historical retrospection, or incidental meditation."[7] Writing before the invention of culture, Johnson is not concerned with what Wasserman calls "organic wholeness" (47); he describes local poetry as a combination of largely discrete elements in which some parts stand in a subordinate relation to others. O Hehir regards some of the elements listed by Johnson as essential, others as accidental: "Since by virtue of the very novelty of the new work its essential nature may not be under-

=

Forms of Reflection

stood even by its creator, prominent superficial characteristics are almost inevitably seized upon as definitive of the new kind, and spurious new genres then arise based upon imitation of the accidents rather than the essence" (*Expans'd Hieroglyphics*, 7). O Hehir lists three generic constituents of Denham's poem that he regards as essential to later instances of the genre: that the poem be named after a hill, describe a particular landscape, and narrate an allegorical stag hunt. On this basis he discriminates between proper members of the genre, such as Waller's *Upon His Majesties repairing of Paul's* and Pope's *Windsor Forest,* and inferior imitations such as Dyer's *Grongar Hill.* But such taxonomic procedures are really not very helpful: Waller's poem meets only one criteria, while *Grongar Hill* meets two. The argument grows more tangled when O Hehir describes *Coopers Hill* as "a special sub-species of political-didactic poetry" (14) that includes works as various as Jonson's epigrams, Marvell's *Horatian Ode,* and Dryden's *Annus Mirabilis.* What differentiates the process of selection that defines a subspecies from that which defines a pseudogenre? Who decides which features are essential and which accidental?

Categorical thinking makes generic mixture and generic change difficult to comprehend. It creates difficulties for Abrams, who argues that the greater Romantic lyric "displace[s] what neo-classical critics had called 'the greater ode.'" But Abrams does not discuss eighteenth-century odes; he discusses eighteenth-century georgics: "For many of Denham's successors [landscape description] displaced history and politics to become the sole meditative component in local poems, and it later evolved into the extended meditation of the Romantic lyric."[8] Instead of a disjunction in the lyric ode, Abrams describes a process by which locodescriptive poetry sheds its excrescences and evolves into the purity of Romantic lyric.

The evolutionary model implied in Abrams's developmental narrative presents difficulties because he is concerned with changes in not one but several genres. The concepts of organic unity and identity that Abrams appropriates from Coleridge do not map neatly onto the relations of continuity and discontinuity operative within a field of genres that includes lyric ode, locodescriptive poetry, the conversation poem, and many other kinds. The substantial differences within and between eighteenth-century genres are just too complex for the model of organic development to accommodate. Genres change and new genres appear not only because new material is added or taken away but because procedures of combination change. Denham introduced new combinations of descrip-

=

Seventeenth-Century Georgic

47

tive, historical, and didactic writing; so, for that matter, did Wordsworth. Their work is of the greatest import for any literary theorist or historian concerned with problems of conceptualizing identity and change. Given the concerns of contemporary criticism, procedures for conceptualizing difference found in georgic poetry offer a useful alternative to the forms of reflection twentieth-century critics have adapted from the meditational procedures of Coleridge and his contemporaries. But to understand those procedures we need to approach georgic poetry on something like its own terms.

Alastair Fowler notes the growing importance of epigram in a variety of genres: "Major works of the seventeenth and early eighteenth century can sometimes seem bound together by catenas of epigrams. This might be said of works as different as Denham's 'Coopers Hill' and Pope's *Essay on Man.* One obvious sign of this is the integrity of quotable distichs, which in some cases have actually been detached and printed separately."[9] Much of *Coopers Hill* is epigram: the opening lines on poets and Parnassus, the sequence of topographical emblem-epigrams, an epigram on a Rubens portrait of Charles, an epigram on the flow of rivers and the flow of verse, and so forth. The style and often the substance of these epigrams is Jonson's. O Hehir notes the source of Denham's Garter emblem for the two kingdoms in Jonson's "Epigram V, 'On the Union'":

> The world the temple was, the priest a king,
> The spoused paire two realmes, the sea the ring. (ll. 3–4)

Denham's exclamation

> Oh happiness of sweete retir'd content!
> To be at once secure, and innocent. (ll. 47–48)

while it has sources in Horace and Virgil, can also be found in Jonson's "The Praises of a Country Life":

> Happie is he, that from all Business cleere,
> As the old race of Mankind were. (ll. 1–2)

The device of moralizing Windsor Palace obviously derives from Jonson's "To Penshurst," itself an imitation of an epigram of Martial's.

Seventeenth-century epigrams are often meditations in verse, just as many meditations are epigrams in prose. Herbert's *The Temple* and Herrick's *Noble Numbers* are examples of the former; examples of the latter include collections of resolves by Hall (1605), Tuke (1614), Feltham

=

Forms of Reflection

(1623), and Fuller (1645).[10] As meditations became more epigrammatical, their subjects likewise began to include all things great and small:
moral topics in Feltham's *Resolves*, philosophical issues in the "Novum
Organon," folk wisdom in Herbert's *Jaculem Prudentum*, and politics in
Quarles's *Observations concerning Princes and States Upon Peace and
Warre* and in Fuller's *Good Thoughts in Bad Times*. These works consist
of large collections of small observations, variously expressed as epigrams, aphorisms, essays, or proverbs. All these topics appear in *Coopers
Hill*. Compare, for instance, Fuller on landscape and politics:

> In Merionethshire in Wales there be many mountains whose hanging
> tops come so close together that shepherds sitting on several mountains
> may audibly discourse one with another. And yet they must go many
> miles before their bodies can meet together, by the reason of the vast
> hollow valleys which are betwixt them. Our Sovereign and the mem-
> bers of this Parliament at London seem very near agreed in their gen-
> eral and public professions. Both are for the Protestant religion; can
> they draw nearer? Both are for the privileges of Parliament; can they
> come closer? Both are for the liberty of the subject; can they meet
> evener? And yet, alas! there is a great gulf and vast distance betwixt
> them which our sins have made, and God grant that our sorrow may
> seasonably make it up again.[11]

The sentiments are Denham's, as is the meditational structure: an emblematic image followed by a sequence of observations or rhetorical questions leading to a moral point. Hall's *Occasional Meditations* contains
reflections on a ruined abbey, concluding: "Happy is that cottage that
hath an honest master and woe be to that place that is viciously inhab-
ited."[12] Denham's Chertsey episode points a similar moral about Henry's
avarice:

> Is there no temperate Region can be knowne,
> Betwixt their frigid, and our Torrid Zone?
> Could we not wake from that Lethargicke dreame,
> But to be restlesse in a worse extreame?
> And for that Lethargy was there no cure,
> But to be cast into a Calenture?   (ll. 173–78)

The lazy monks are no more hypocritical than the king who destroyed the
abbey in the name of reform. The same point is made in Quarles's *Enchy-
ridion* (1641): "It is an infallible signe of approaching ruine in a Repub-

lic, when Religion is neglected, and her established Ceremonies interrupted: Let therefore that Prince that would be potent, be pious; And that he may punish looseness the better, let him be religious: The joy of Jerusalem depends upon the peace of Sion."[13] Quarles follows the resolve formula, the "Let therefore" signaling the move from an observation to the resolution. Compare the original ending of *Coopers Hill*:

> *Therefore* their boundlesse power *let* Princes draw
> Within the Channell, and the shores of Law. (ll. 351–52, emphasis
> added)

These are antimethodical works but not without philosophical and literary rationale. The force of a maxim is keyed to local application; we say "He who hesitates is lost" but also "Look before you leap." Collections of epigrammatical wit and wisdom give pleasure by their comprehensiveness and variety; thus the argument of Herrick's *Hesperides*:

> I Sing of *Brooks*, of *Blossomes, Birds*, and *Bowers:*
> Of *April, May*, of *June*, and *July*-Flowers.
> I sing of *May-poles, Hock-carts, Wassails, Wakes,*
> *Of Bride-grooms, Brides*, and of the *Bridall-cakes*. (ll. 1–4)[14]

In Herbert's *The Temple* or Vaughan's *Silex Scintillans* the poets take equal pride in varying the meter, rhyme, and subject matter of their meditations. These collections were sometimes termed *sylvae*, connoting rural subjects, unformed matter, and formal diversity. Denham implies all three senses in the section of *Coopers Hill* labeled "The Forrest":

> Here Nature, whether more intent to please
> Us or her selfe with strange varieties,
> (For things of wonder move no lesse delight
> To the wise makers, then beholders sight.
> Though these delights from severall causes move,
> For so our Children, thus our friends we love.)
> Wisely she knew the harmony of things,
> Aswell as that of sounds, from discords springs;
> Such was the discord, which did first disperse
> Forme, order, beauty through the universe. (ll. 223–32)

In this statement of the *concordia discors* theme, Denham places his emphasis resoundingly on variety, strangeness, and heterogeneity.

But if Denham finds a place for strangeness and discord in his

Forms of Reflection

satura, he is likewise concerned to temper differences among constituent elements in his poem. *Coopers Hill* is not a disjointed collection of occasional pieces; if many of the epigrams can stand alone, they are also combined in ways that permit them to stand together. Denham's sylva differs from similar collections by situating its several constituents within a containing frame, a formal strategy obviously related to the political doctrines the poem espouses. These political concerns are implied by Thomas Fuller in the preface to *Mixt Contemplations on these Times* (1660). The author still stresses the variety of material he has to present, but a new note is sounded:

> I confess myself subject to just censure, that I have not severally sorted these contemplations, setting out such which are 1. of Scripture, 2. historical, 3. occasional, 4. personal, distinctly by themselves, which now are confusedly heaped, or rather huddled together. . . . However, such a confused medley may pass for the lively emblem of these times, the subject of this our book. And when these times shall be reduced into better order, my book, at the next impression, may be digested into better method.   (26)

Fuller promises to reform his contemplations, "confusedly heaped, or rather huddled together," when society proves able to reform itself. While Denham does not dispose his parts by "method," he does knit his contemplations on the times into a continuous fabric, tempering variety of matter with a continuity of manner. The literary procedures he develops to temper order and variety were a major innovation in seventeenth-century writing.

Coopers Hill turned English poetry toward Augustan poetics, introducing sweeping changes in relations between figural language and literary representation. Where the epigrammatical mode had favored metaphor, idealism, and closure, georgic poetics stressed metonymy, materialism, and mutability. The longer format encouraged narrative investigations of cause and effect and bold experiments in representing temporal processes in participial adjectives, compound epithets, and an elaborately varied couplet syntax. As poets invented new ways of representing history, the turning of the seasons and the flow of rivers replaced mirrors, portraits, and well-wrought urns as favorite figures: identity was reconceived as continuity amid change. With the new interest in change came a new interest in materialism. The attitudes toward cosmology and politics against which Denham was innovating are exemplified in *The Faerie*

=

Queene. The Knight of Justice confronts a plebeian giant seeking to redress inequalities by weighing matter in a balance. Such arguments can be easily dismissed when justice is understood as hereditary right and stability as fixed identity:

> But if thou now shouldst weigh them new in pound,
> We are not sure they would so long remaine:
> All change is perillous, and all chaunce vnsound.
> Therefore leaue off to weigh them all againe,
> Till we may be assur'd they shall their course retaine.[15]

The giant and his balance are cast into the abyss. In *Coopers Hill*, georgic poetics supplants allegory in order to argue that rejecting change is more perilous than embracing it. For similar reasons, Milton rejects Spenserian epic in favor of a georgic presentation of human history. In *Paradise Lost* he draws upon Spenserian allegory to represent chance and discontinuity in the brilliantly archaic and incoherent figures of Chaos, Sin, and Death.

Much of the new poetics could be found ready to hand in Virgil's poetry, in which prophetic utterance links human affairs to material causes:

> Ye sacred Muses, with whose Beauty fir'd,
> My Soul is ravish'd, and my Brain inspir'd:
> Whose Priest I am, whose holy Fillets wear;
> Wou'd you your Poet's first Petition hear,
> Give me the Ways of wandring Stars to know:
> The Depths of Heav'n above, and Earth below.
> Teach me the various Labours of the Moon,
> And whence proceed th'Eclipses of the Sun.[16]

Denham imitates this passage, but shifts the emphasis from occult knowledge to empirical science. His *auspex* is unmistakenly a Baconian investigator:

> As those who rais'd in body or in thought
> Above the Earth, or the Aires middle Vault,
> Behold how winds and stormes, and Meteors grow,
> How clouds condense to raine, congeale to snow,
> And see the Thunder form'd, before it teare
> The aire, secure from danger and from feare;

Forms of Reflection

So rais'd above the tumult and the crowd
I see the City. . . .   (ll. 21–28)

Virgil is reread through Lucretius:

Such was the discord, which did first disperse
Forme, order, beauty, through the universe.   (ll. 231–32)

Denham's meditator contemplates physical processes of cause and effect. Ralph Cohen describes Denham's use of the prospect device as "innovative in dealing with man's relation to nature in the georgic poem" and argues that the poem "is based on a perceptual rather than allegorical scheme."[17] While the poem does contain an allegorical hunt, Denham's materialism clearly introduces changes into emblematic representation. In the Fuller meditation above, for example, the Welsh mountains have no literal connection with the English parliament, whereas in *Coopers Hill* Saint Paul's not only represents the church, it is the church, and so likewise for Windsor Palace and the monarchy, Chertsey Abbey and the destruction of religion, and so forth. Synecdochical relations supplant metaphorical relations; as Virgil represents history by the empty helmet and half-hidden inscriptions uncovered by the plow, so Denham construes his castles and cathedrals.[18]

The meditational procedures in *Coopers Hill* also modify elements of Virgilian georgic. In his "Essay on the *Georgics*" prefacing the Dryden translation, Joseph Addison comments that the poet "must take care not to encumber his Poem with too much business; but sometimes to relieve the subject with a Moral Reflection, or let it rest a while for the sake of a pleasant and pertinent digression."[19] In *Coopers Hill* and later English georgic this relation is inverted; the precepts become ornamental, while the substance of the argument is conveyed by the digressions on moral, historical, philosophical, and literary affairs. Agriculture remains a constituent, but from Denham onward writers understand cultivation primarily as commerce, which enters into the poetry as a theme, in figures and metaphors, and in relations of exchange between writers and readers. In Addison's term, commerce is the "business" of English georgic. This new emphasis alters the status of epideictic material in the poem; Denham follows Virgil in praising the reigning monarch but situates his compliments as part of a series of retrospective digressions on how various monarchs have managed or mismanaged the political economy. Denham was surely familiar with Donne's combinations of description, history, and medita-

=

tion in the *Anniversaries*, yet he favors the digressive method for an obvious reason: closed, hierarchical structures were simply inappropriate for
representing the complexity and volatility of the mercantile state. While
Denham was as much a courtier as Spenser or Donne, his meditational
procedures decenter the court within the poem and the landscapes it
describes.

J. G. A. Pocock describes the "Machiavellian moment" as the attempt by Renaissance writers to reconceptualize political history "for the
purpose of dealing with particular and contingent events and with time as
the dimension of contingent happenings."[20] Guicciardini and Machia-
velli propose innovative theories of republican government, governments
whose mixed structures would enable a balanced and dynamic response
to historical change and the varieties of local customs and climate. With
Coopers Hill the "Machiavellian Moment" arrives in British literature.
Denham's historical retrospections recount how, by failing to respond to
the dynamics of commerce and historical change, English monarchs
have been blindly swept up by fortune:

> Thus Kings by grasping more then they can hold,
> First made their Subjects by oppressions bold,
> And Popular sway by forcing Kings to give
> More, then was fit for Subjects to receive,
> Ranne to the same extreame; and one excess
> Made both, by striving to be greater, lesse;
> Nor any way, but seeking to have more,
> Makes either loose, what each possest before.   (ll. 343–50)

To avoid Fortune's revolving cycle, the constituent elements of government need to be put on a different footing. If mixed monarchy could be
established in England, time would flow like a river rather than turn like
a wheel.

The enduring popularity of *Coopers Hill* had as much to do with its
republican principles as its related refinements of syntax and versifica-
tion: the poem became more rather than less popular after the establishment of the Commonwealth; after 1688 its principles became the law of
the land. In the summer of 1642 Charles had already agreed in principle
to the concept of mixed monarchy in his *Answer to the Nineteen Propositions*. The framers of this document, Sir John Colepeper, Lucius Vis-
count Falkland, and Sir Edward Hyde, employ Denham's figures and
may have seen his poem in manuscript:

≡

Forms of Reflection

There being three kinds of government among men, absolute monarchy, aristocracy and democracy, and all these having their particular
conveniences and inconveniences, the experience and wisdom of your
ancestors hath so moulded this out of a mixture of these acts as to give
this kingdom (as far as humane prudence can contrive) the conveniences of all three, without the inconveniences of any one, as long as
the balance hangs even between the three estates, and they run jointly
on in their proper channel (begetting verdure and fertility in the mea-
dows on both sides) and the overflowing of either on either side raise
no deluge or inundation.[21]

The talk about balance indicates the extent to which Spenser's reforming
giant had become an active participant in British politics. In the event,
however, Charles's concessions did little to satisfy parliament. Observing
the foul weather forming over London, Denham's contemplative ventures
a prognostication:

> Thus all to limit Royalty conspire,
> While each forgets to limit his desire,
> Till Kings like old *Antaeus* by their fall,
> Being forc't, their courage from despair recall,
> When a calme River rais'd with sudden raines,
> Or Snowes dissolv'd o'reflowes th'adjoyning Plaines,
> The Husbandmen with high rais'd bankes secure
> Their greedy hopes, and this he can endure.
> But if with Bays, and Dammes they strive to force,
> His channell to a new, or narrow course,
> No longer then within his bankes he dwels,
> First to a Torrent, then a Deluge swels;
> Stronger, and fiercer by restraint, he roars,
> And knowes no bound, but makes his powers his shores.   (ll. 329–42)

If events did not turn out quite that way, the subsequent history of the
rebellion and its aftermath lent great credence to Denham's arguments.
Well into the next century georgic writers represented political husbandry
as the fruitful commerce between heterogeneous elements — as gardeners
must know when to prune and when to graft, so governors should know
when to subordinate and when to coordinate.

Denham's use of genre illustrates seventeenth-century understandings of commerce and cultivation and the seventeenth-century belief

that such processes would institute progressive rather than merely fortuitous changes in manners and literature. In *Coopers Hill* elemental strife
among constituent parts results in what Shaftesbury calls an "amicable
collision"; while differences remain, the several genres enter into reciprocal and dynamic relations. Denham's combinatory strategies stand in a
curiously syntagmatic relation to the larger literary and social transformations in which they participate. In the earlier episodes degrees and boundaries are sharply observed:

> So having tasted Windsor, casting round
> My wandring eye, an *emulous* Hill doth bound
> My more *contracted* sight . . .   (ll. 145–47, emphasis added)

Each section closes with a point: "O Happinesse of sweete retir'd content!" (l. 47), "Here could I fix my wonder . . . " (l. 141), "Parting
thence, 'twixt anger, shame, and feare" (l. 183). These more epigrammatical episodes express courtly values in a courtly genre, but the more georgic passages that follow deliberately erase the boundaries between kinds
and episodes; the reader glides through the "Thames," "Forrest," and
"Egham Meade" sections like the metonymic river itself.

Such is the transformative work of commerce, whose powers of displacement Denham represents syntactically: the river

> Finds wealth where 'tis, and gives it where it wants,
> Cities in Desarts, woods in Cities plants.   (ll. 213–214)

So also in the poem at large: before our eyes (as it were) *Coopers Hill* modulates from the epigrammatical closure of courtly deference to the epigrammatical fluidity of georgic cultivation. Addison underscores the
mutability of Virgil's verses: "As in a Curious Brede of Needle-Work, one
Colour falls away by such just degrees, and another rises so insensibly,
that we see the variety, without being able to distinguish the total vanishing of the one from the first appearance of the other" (146). Denham
believes that commerce can work just such an effect on the social fabric.
Coopers Hill does not call for social leveling or dissolution of literary
kinds but for a new conception of how these might be made integral parts
of a differential whole changing with the times.

Refinement presupposes continuity amid change; georgic poetics
presuppose a literature of process and progress. Denham introduces continuity into his digressive structure by means of repetition and variation:
readers are called upon to discriminate parts of the poem, even as the

poet discriminates parts of the landscape. The poem itself instances progress and refinement: in successive versions Denham honed his verse and altered his argument: Charles becomes the hunted rather than the hunter.[22] The opening lines set up a parallel between Parnassus and Coopers Hill that calls attention to Denham's procedure of repeating classical literature with a difference, as do allusions to Virgil and Lucretius. Readers are expected to notice not only that the poem is written in a classical genre but that the poet modifies that genre to fit his local circumstances and that literary commerce alters Virgillian georgic, even as Virgilian georgic modifies English poetics. The text itself is understood to engage in the processes of transformation it represents.

In this respect *Coopers Hill* differs from the *Anniversaries*, where the poet rehearses the song of Moses without, presumably, altering its substance. Apart from political considerations, one reason that Donne's poem failed to reproduce its kind was its very emphasis on closure: having demonstrated the necessity of his procedures, Donne could hardly have provided an encore without adding to or altering those procedures in ways that would call that very necessity into doubt. It was otherwise with Denham's georgic, of course, which founded a kind that would reproduce itself in meditational verse down to Wordsworth's time and beyond. *Windsor Forest, An Essay on Man, The Seasons, The Pleasures of Imagination, Night Thoughts, The Task,* and *The Minstrel* all grew by georgic processes of accretion, alteration, and refinement. As each was a repetition and variation of earlier instances of the genre, so each altered constituents and relations of combination within georgic poetry. As a result, literary commerce altered the norms of progress and refinement themselves. By the end of the eighteenth century, very little of Denham's program remained: authors came to identify poetry with spiritual rather than material causes; private insight displaced public civility as the measure of literary worth; intensity came to be valued over refinement, and an emphasis on universal truths supplanted local and historical insight. In a later chapter I discuss eighteenth-century imitations of *Coopers Hill* in which cultivation begins to mutate into culture.

If readers today are more likely to share Denham's materialist convictions than readers a generation ago, the New Critical attack on commerce has by and large been continued by New Historicist critics. There have been changes: modernists often condemned commerce as a divisive and fragmenting force, while their successors are more likely to condemn commerce as a totalizing and hegemonic force. Social values have changed, but the terms of the discussion have not changed, insofar as modernist conceptions of culture and postmodernist conceptions of ideology are founded on similar ways of resolving parts into wholes. A good instance is John Barrell and Harriet Guest's critique of georgic poetics, "On the Use of Contradiction: Economics and Morality in the Eighteenth-Century Long Poem," which both attacks and reproduces New Critical procedures. They write:

> The article of faith in much twentieth-century criticism that the value of a poem is a function of the unity it exhibits, produced a considerable volume of writing about Pope and Thomson which argues that such contradictions [as result from generic mixture] are only apparent. We want to suggest that these efforts may be as misconceived as they have been unsuccessful, insofar as they are predicated upon the assumption that the concern with unity and consistency, was as important to Pope and Thomson as it was (for example) to Wasserman. We are arguing that the concern for method and unity in eighteenth-century poetry was accompanied by a tacit permission for long poems of mixed genre to contradict themselves. (135)[23]

This recognition that georgic poems are generically complex departs from New Critical thought, but to describe these differences as contradictions is to invoke something very like New Critical standards of poetic closure. That modern critics are more concerned with consistency than georgic poets were is certainly true—true of New Critics, but true of New Historicists as well. For as I argue above, to represent differences as contradictions is to import a standard of coherence to which not all kinds of writing aspire. Barrell and Guest speak of contradictions in long poems because they see poems as instances of a single structure of thought. While they discuss generic differences, it is clear that these differences fail to make a real difference: "'the disparate hegemonic discourses' of which [the ensemble of discourses] is composed are 'knotted together . . . into an apparently self-reinforcing, limiting structure of thought'—nature, as delivered up to us by ideology" (123). But do the contradictions reside in the poetry or in the procedures used to articulate it? How, in any meaningful sense of the terms, can a discourse be at once disparate and hegemonic?

If it is true that "a criticism that legitimates the employment of a variety of discourses within a poem is one that legitimates a new notion of what makes a work coherent," it does not follow "that a poem of mixed

=

Forms of Reflection
58

genre should be, as a whole, *consistent*, that each topic, as it is elaborated, should exhibit a discursive unity, and that the separate topics should *cohere*, should be glued together in such a way that we can see the join, but are not offended by its abruptness" (136, emphasis in original). Georgic poetry did introduce a new notion of what makes a work coherent; but it was a notion of continuity amid change, not the internal consistency implied by "discursive unity." To describe such a poetics as hegemonic is misleading; the English georgic not only endorsed substantial social changes: georgic itself changed substantially over the course of its long career. This was new. By contrast, Barrell and Guest do not introduce a new notion of what makes a work coherent. When they describe the long poem as a "hybrid discourse" (124) lacking discursive unity, they invoke standards of coherence quite similar to those of Wasserman and Abrams. Since they discover the same contradiction between theodicy and economic amoralism in every part of every poem discussed, their reading would appear to demonstrate that the long poem and its ideology are unified (in contradiction) after all. That "nobody in the [eighteenth] century seems to comment upon the contradictions these transitions [between genres] produce" (136) may point less to ideological blindness than to an understanding of generic differences that does not make sense to modern critics.

"Study to Be Quiet": Satire in *The Compleat Angler*

A useful way to begin discriminating between kinds of discourse is to think of the discourse as one genre among others, various in itself and variously related to other kinds. Izaak Walton's *Compleat Angler; or, the Contemplative Man's Recreation*, for instance, is a discourse that combines genres in ways that undermine closure, coherence, and consistency. The "compleat" in Walton's title points to inclusiveness, the "or" to a combinatory strategy: while angling cannot be reduced to contemplation, nor contemplation to angling, Walton treats both disciplines in one discourse.[24] As we shall see, his reasons for adopting this strategy are as much political as piscatory. Published in 1653, the *Angler* appeared at a time when the limits of discourse must have been painfully obvious to anyone engaged in political life: clear and distinct arguments were met with opposing arguments equally clear and distinct; the most scabrous satires (the common recourse where reason fails) were never quite scabrous enough to shame an opponent into submission. Discourses produced factions; factions pro-

duced discourses. If the "brotherhood of the angle" (96) is one such faction and *The Compleat Angler* one such discourse, Walton's work differs
from contemporary satires, sermons, and treatises that handle similar
political material. Like *Coopers Hill*, it upholds toleration and inclusiveness while resisting closure and conformity.

The brotherhood is an early instance of a social formation that came
to dominate the intellectual landscape of the English Enlightenment: the
community of private individuals pursuing social change through reforms
of language and manners. Later examples include the Royal Society, the
Society for the Promotion of Christian Knowledge, the Kit Kat Club, the
Scriblerians, and the salon. Such institutions responded to the limitations
of centralized authority by diffusing power and knowledge among citizens and the gentry. Diffusion encouraged tolerance, and tolerance
encouraged diversity. Both qualities appear in much of the literature celebrating the public role of private life: conduct books and essays, newspapers, tracts, and, above all, polite conversation. While not democratic,
such communities, like the genres that articulated their differences, were
heterogeneous and interpenetrating. Writers such as Walton understood
very well that in order to reform society it would be necessary to make
over the kinds of discourse on which community was based. This was a
contestatory enterprise, though in the case of the *Angler* not a violent one.
Walton situates his discourse on angling and contemplation amid a whole
range of literary forms, appropriating them, opposing them, transforming
them. In retrospect, we can see that Walton's work prefigures much of
later literature. In founding virtue on manners rather than rank, he renders satire polite and transforms the conduct book into prose fiction. In
making natural processes rather than sacred texts the basis of civic and
religious education, he was among the first to popularize the georgic
mode. In expressing social harmony through lyric song, he brought the
hymn down to earth and recognized the significance of ballads and popular song for national life. The *Angler*'s peculiar mixture of politeness, politics, and poetry makes distinctions and recognizes limits, while remaining
a very open structure.

These discursive procedures have not been recognized for what they
are. John R. Cooper's valuable study notes the trouble with categorical
approaches: "With the domain of literature divided neatly by critics and
librarians alike between the imaginative and the useful, fiction and non-
fiction, the case of *The Compleat Angler* presents special difficulties" (5).
To circumvent these difficulties he turns to Renaissance genres for a

≡

Forms of Reflection

different set of distinctions. Yet Cooper is unable to find a Renaissance genre against which to judge the merits of Walton's work: pastoral "elements are certainly in *The Compleat Angler*, but it is equally true that there are long passages in which Piscator discourses on the art of angling, or on social, moral, or religious questions, and which, if these narrative passages of the *Angler* are its only source of interest, must be considered aesthetic flaws" (3). Cooper makes astute use of genre in tracing Walton's sources, but the idea that genres should be kept discrete leads him to wonder how georgic, pastoral, and dialogue might be integrated into a "unified whole" (99). While it contains georgic and pastoral themes, Cooper argues, *The Compleat Angler* cannot be a member of these categories because it is a prose dialogue. "Is there a design that comprehends both the rhetorical development of georgic instruction and the satirical pastoral drama about society?" (99). Cooper thinks not and concludes that the work must be considered something of a failure: the mixture of genres "is a somewhat mechanical arrangement, however, and we are less conscious of this process in reading the *Angler* than of the fact that passages of instruction alternate with passages of natural description or of pastoral play" (100). But Walton promises *compleat*ness, not unity. We should not be surprised that *The Compleat Angler* cannot be reduced to a single genre. It is a very heterogeneous work, containing not only georgic, pastoral, and dialogue, but proverbs, lyrics, recipes, illustrations of fish, and a musical score. If the *Angler* does not exhibit formal unity or logical coherence, it is because Walton is concerned with other kinds of order.

Like Denham, Walton turns to georgic to make the case for a more inclusive social order. But circumstances had dramatically changed for royalist writers. In Denham's poem the Order of the Garter's "Azure round" (l. 131) signifies both the circulation of commerce and the political unification under the Stuart kings. Denham also translates its motto, "Who evill thinks may evill him confound" (l. 128). A decade after *Coopers Hill* was published the gentry were hopelessly divided, the court was in France, and parliament was reduced to the Rump. *The Compleat Angler* is thus insular in a very different sense: it abandons the comprehensive vision of the prospect view and attempts to reconstruct an oppositional community within the confines of a local and temporary enclave. Walton does not identify his landscapes with royal authority; his own motto is much less threatening: "Study to be quiet." Walton defines his brotherhood by means of differential social values expressed in combin-

=

atory and oppositional uses of genre. The political context of the *Angler* has been given little attention by readers who have taken Piscator as an everyman figure in a timeless, idyllic landscape. While not wholly unjustified, such readings are partial and incomplete: pastoral is but one genre among several. The work is in fact quite georgic in its historical and geographical specificity: its green world is contained within and defined by the political drama that was Cromwell's Britain. For Walton, retirement is a political posture: he advocates withdrawal and introspection at a time when religion was being aggressively pursued as an instrument of state policies.

Walton calls his work a *recreation*, a generic term that requires unpacking. *Recreation* had more meanings in the seventeenth century than it has today. It could mean a pastime (OED, "recreation" 1:3), but also culinary "refreshment" (recreation 1:1). Punning on satura, or "dish of various ingredients," Walton's preface promises a chowder of heterogeneous kinds of writing: "And I wish the Reader also to take notice, that in writing of [angling], I have made a recreation of a recreation; and that it might prove so to thee in the reading, and not to read *dull*, and *tediously,* I have in severall places mixt some innocent Mirth; of which, if thou be a severe, sowr complexioned man, then I here disallow thee to be a competent judg" (59).[25] Walton's "recreation" is menippean satire in the tradition of Lucian's dialogues, Boethius's *Consolation of Philosophy*, Erasmus's *In Praise of Folly*, and Burton's *Anatomy of Melancholy*. While diversity is characteristic of most genres, menippean satire is unusual in that it makes diversity a mark of belonging. The hallmarks of the genre, such as they are, are inclusiveness and heterogeneity; with its mixture of dialogue and narrative, poetry and prose, songs and proverbs, dinner parties and discourses, and catalogues of fishes and flowers, the *Angler* is in many ways a paradigmatic menippean satire on contemplative themes.[26]

Walton keys his mixture of kinds to his concept of temperament; if "sowr complexioned" men reject his interdisciplinary art of angling and contemplation, the author still insists on mixture, because he regards good humor as both the means and the end of the disciplines he practices. Hence the third pun on recreation ("recreation" 2): a re-creation of character by remixing the temperament. Re-creating a self presupposes a mutable disposition rather than a fixed constitution. As Walton goes on to say, "The whole discourse is a kind of picture of my owne disposition, at least of my disposition in such daies and times as I allow my self, when

≡

Forms of Reflection

honest Nat. and R.R. and I go a fishing together" (59). Walton thinks of the "complexions" of self, book, and community as aggregate mixtures and mutable dispositions. These several senses of *recreation* are all implicated in the generic strategies Walton uses to present the *Angler* as a conduct book, meditation, and lyric evocation of social order.

Not the least of Walton's objections to interregnum society was the bad manners displayed by "Covenanters, Confusion, Committee-men, and Soldiers. . . . You may be sure Dr. *Sanderson*, who though quiet and harmless, yet an eminent dissenter from them, could not live peaceably."[27] Much of the noise disturbing the likes of Sanderson took the form of menippean satire. Eugene P. Kirk's bibliography of the genre lists some 150 surviving examples from the period 1640 to 1653. With titles such as *The Schismatick Stigmatized* (1641), *The Arminian Haltered* (1641), and *A Case for Nol Cromwell's Nose and the Cure of Tom Fairfax's Gout* (1648), these motley pamphlets were written by factionalists of all political persuasions and employed the whole battery of Lucianic devices: symposia, dialogues of the dead, and voyages to imaginary worlds. If the *Angler* is modeled on the contemplative satires of Boethius and Burton, its menippean satura also parodies and refines the prime controversial genre of his time. Lest this point be missed, Walton opens his discourse with a pair of characters pointedly alluding to Lucian: "Sir, There are many men that are by others taken to be serious grave men, which we contemn and pitie; men of sowre complexions; mony-getting men, that spend all their time first in getting, and next in anxious care to keep it. . . . We enjoy a contentednesse above the reach of such dispositions" (64). The bad manners of the London Puritans are matched by their Cavalier counterparts:

> I pray bid the Scoffer put this Epigram into his pocket, and read it every morning for his breakfast. . . . Hee shall finde it fix'd before the Dialogues of *Lucian* (who may be justly accounted the father of the Family of all *Scoffers*:) . . .
>
> *Lucian* well skill'd in *scoffing*, this has writ,
> Friend, that's your folly which you think your wit:
> This you vent oft, void both of *wit* and *fear*.
> Meaning an other, when your self you jeer.   (66)

Parliamentarians may be pious, but their sour dispositions forbid making proper use of the goods the world has to offer. Scoffers are well acquainted with worldly pleasures, but their libertine ways make them

=

Seventeenth-Century Georgic

reprehensible. Walton's good-humored satire combines the desirable elements in both characters.

In seeking to correct bad manners through recreation rather than raillery, Walton produced one of the most worldly contemplative manuals ever written. Pleasure was a political issue in 1653; in opposition to official values, Piscator is quick to defend "honest pleasures"—the printed ballads and lavender-scented rooms of "Trout Hal" (83), singing and storytelling (88), "shovelboard" (147), and wholesome meals (passim). He goes so far as to draw a favorable comparison between the use of cosmetics and the spots on a trout, which give the trout "such an addition of natural beautie, as I (that yet am no enemy to it) think was never given to any woman by the Artificial Paint or Patches in which they so much pride themselves in this age" (121).[28] Yet there are limits to what gets included in the *Angler:* compendious as it is, the satura excludes intemperate forms of discourse such as sour sermons and bawdy epigrams; they are engaged only to define contrary values through generic difference.

By definition, *temperate* citizens are complex characters. We are simple, Piscator argues, only "if by that you mean a harmlesnesse, or that simplicity that was usually found in the Primitive Christians, who were (as most Anglers are) quiet men, and followed peace; men that were too wise to sell their consciences to buy riches for vexation, and a fear to die; men that lived in those times when there were fewer Lawyers" (66–67). Angling is not to be confused with the summertime activities of country louts: "But if by simplicitie you meant to expresse any general defect in the understanding of those that professe and practise Angling, I hope to . . . remove all the anticipations that Time or Discourse may have possess'd you with, against that Ancient and laudable Art" (67). By art, Walton means a science or discipline whose precepts can be codified in a discourse. Like fencing (60), angling is a gentlemen's art, practiced not for sustenance or financial gain but for higher purposes: it is, like *"vertue, a reward to it self"* (68). Men of leisure—or citizens on holiday—pursue angling as a liberal art.

As a conduct book, *The Compleat Angler* defines the character of a proper citizen through piscatory metaphors. Manners were necessarily a prime concern—under a republican form of government.[29] Citizens should combine learning with practicality, action with contemplation: "Both these meet together, and do most properly belong to the most honest, ingenious, harmless Art of Angling" (69). Walton, who made his liv-

=

Forms of Reflection

ing in trade, was sensitive about such matters: "I would rather prove my self to be a Gentleman," Piscator remarks, "by being *learned* and *humble, valiant* and *inoffensive, vertuous* and *communicable,* then by a fond ostentation of *riches;* or (wanting these Vertues my self) boast that these were in my Ancestors" (68). The new dispensation required men of talent as much as men of rank. Jesus sought out men in the lower occupations, fisher-disciples elected to be founders and leaders. Litigious parliamentarians are condemned not as upstart proles but as bad citizens; they might learn from the patient art of angling:

> None do here
> use to swear,
> oathes do fray
> fish away,
> we sit still,
> watch our quill
> Fishers must not rangle.   (149)

Watching one's quill is a mark of good character—one that is gentle as well as genteel. As an angler and as a satirist, Walton takes care not to trouble the waters in which he wishes to fish.

During the interregnum, of course, Anglicans had few practical alternatives to patience. Walton supplies a Biblical type for their situation:

> The very sitting by the Riverside, is not only the fittest place for, but will invite the Angler to Contemplation: That it is the fittest place, seems to be witnessed by the children of *Israel,* who having banished all mirth and Musick from their pensive hearts, and having hung up their then mute Instruments upon the Willow trees, growing by the Rivers of *Babylon,* sate down upon those banks bemoaning the *ruines of Sion,* and contemplating their own sad condition.   (70)

One must not forget the old ways. But unlike the Jews, Anglicans should string their harps and sing lustily of better times. Walton regards the art of poesy as an integral part of both the disciplines he professes. His interpolated songs have a complex political resonance. In the republican thought of the time, hierarchy was not regarded as incompatible with equality under the law; nor does Walton's participation in elite culture require him to exclude popular literature. While they observe distinctions of rank, the anglers incorporate popular songs into their discourse, just as they mix on familiar terms with country folk. Piscator admires "the

=

good old Song of the *Hunting in Chevy Chase*" and enjoys the broadside ballads pinned to the walls of an "honest alehouse" (145). At the same time, he can recite a copy of verses accessible only to the elite. The *Angler* includes inset lyrics by a number of courtly poets: Herbert, Donne, Wotton, Marlowe, and Raleigh. The alliance of polite poetry with popular song—Marlow's and Raleigh's lyrics are sung by two milkmaids, who believe they are old ballads—underscores the hedonistic values common to both court and populace.

If the *Angler* offers pleasure as a bait to fellowship, it also offers song as bait to contemplation. Walton's capacious regimen of rural meditation finds a place for both. While the satura contains didactic poems and jolly poems, the key lyrics in the anthology, including the first and the last, are devotional meditations. These verses, along with occasional meditations in prose, operate as contrary genres to sour sermons and tomes of controversy; they are interdenominational, noncontestatory means of devotional discipline. The inset poems and essays eschew the methodical exposition favored in Puritan discourses; addressing themselves to "God's other book" they seek an uncontroversial text for exposition; substituting wit for logic, they aim at winning conviction through pleasure. Bishop Hall describes the occasional meditation as a form of recreation, a way "to improve those short ends of time which are stolen from . . . more important avocations."[30] Walton, of course, accords recreation a higher status.

While it is a prose work, the *Angler* is typically georgic in combining contemplation with praxis. Addison describes how this form "raises in our Minds a pleasing variety of Scenes and Landskips, whilst it teaches us: and makes the dryest of its Precepts look like a Description. *A Georgic therefore is some part of the Science of Husbandry put into a pleasing Dress, and set off with all the Beauties and Embellishments of Poetry.*"[31] Like Virgil's famous digressions, the "characters" of the fish are inserted as recreations for readers who might find unadorned precepts dull. Like Denham, Walton alters the form of occasional meditation by weaving his poems and essays into a continuous narrative—a georgic device. Much of the literary art in *The Compleat Angler* lies in the subtle modulations Addison describes as "unforc'd Method": "We see the variety, without being able to distinguish the total vanishing of the one from the first appearance of the other" (146). Though it lacks the clear and distinct partitions of a treatise, Walton's discourse is not without a method of sorts. But while Walton consulted halieutic poems in Latin and Neo-Latin poetry, he does not quote from the georgic poets (Du Bartas excepted). He includes a cata-

=

Forms of Reflection

logue of rivers, a georgic device, but his recreational theme excludes celebrations of labor, and his oppositional stance precludes celebrating national prowess or progress. Like Denham, though in different ways, Walton re-creates georgic to fit the disposition of time and place.

Walton's concern with manners and his desire to entertain his readers lead him to personify several of his subjects. The occasional meditations sometimes veer toward politics, as in case of the pike: "All Pikes that live long prove chargeable to their keepers, because their life is maintained by the death of so many other fish, even those of his owne kind, which has made him by some Writers to bee called the *Tyrant* of the Rivers, or the *Fresh-water-wolf,* by reason of his bold, greedy, devouring disposition" (122). In this case the "character" grows into a narrative in which we are told how a particular pike, overreaching himself, was dragged ashore by the mule to which he had attached his rapacious jaws. The "natural history" closes with an epigrammatic point: "It is a hard thing to persuade the belly, because it has no ears" (122). It would be difficult to establish whether or not the bad character of the pike glances at the Protector, although beast fables were often used for just such a purpose.[32] This episode is typical of the fluidity with which Walton interweaves themes (angling, manners, science, politics) and genres (character, fable, natural history, meditation, proverb).

Often Walton weaves pastoral themes into his meditations on the creatures. Viator notes the lyrical pull of Piscator's discourse: "Sir, take what liberty you think fit, for your discourse seems to be musick, and charms me into attention" (73). In a passage where fishing and flowergathering become metaphors for rural meditation, Walton opposes culling flowers of reflection to material possession:

> I thought this Meadow like the field in Sicily (of which Diodorus speaks) where the perfumes arising from the place, makes all dogs that hunt in it, to fall off, and to lose their hottest sent. I say, as I thus sate joying in mine own happy condition, and pittying that rich mans that ought this, and many other pleasant Grove and Meadows about me, I did thankfully remember what my Saviour said, that the meek possess the earth; for indeed they are free from those high, those restless thoughts and contentions which corrode the sweets of life. (150)

By comparing his own contemplations to the rich man's "Law Suites," Viator's meditation underscores a contrast between kinds of discourse and modes of appropriation. In this artful passage pastoral trumps georgic: the perfumes overpowering the hunt represent the effect Walton's lyric prose was intended to have on his listeners, drawing them away from a material world of money and business and care. In this and other passages, pastoral acts as an oppositional genre. Pastoral allegory was well suited to articulate the alienated sentiments of those taking refuge in retirement; Walton employs it to preach Anglican values to those at either extreme of the social hierarchy. As it begins to rain, Piscator and Viator prop their rods and retire under a tree:

> And let me tell you, this kind of fishing, and laying Night-hooks, are like putting money to use, for they both work for the Owners, when they do nothing but sleep, or eat, or rejoice, as you know we have done this last hour, and sate as quietly and as free from cares under this *Sycamore*, as *Virgils Tityrus* and his *Meliboeus* did under their broad *Beech* tree: No life, my honest Scholer, no life so happy and so pleasant as the Anglers, unless it be the Beggers life in Summer; for then only they take no care, but are as happy as we Anglers. (112)

The passage reflects on Cromwell's policy (akin to that of Augustus) of financing war by confiscating property and making beggars of owners.[33] But by making good work of their leisure, the new class of beggars can turn material loss to spiritual profit.

In describing the apprenticeship Viator must serve before becoming a master singer of the Anglican rite, Walton dramatizes the discipline required for membership in the sylvan community. Discipline is not imposed from above but established dialectically by juxtaposing kinds of discourse. Because Walton is aware of the subversive power of anacreontic song, he is careful to delimit its use. If he pits song against sermon, he also offers a sermon against the abuses of pleasure. There must be no snakes in the garden; the host of the Thatched House is condemned for his lascivious jests, "for which I count no man witty: for the Divel will help a man that way inclin'd, to the first, and his own corrupt nature (which he alwayes carries with him) to the latter. . . . Such discourse as we heard last night, it infects others; the very boyes will learn to talk and swear as they heard mine Host" (82). Improper forms of mixture—corruption—come in for censure, although the anglers usually avoid such pointed reflection. Contemplative discipline encourages citizens to avoid controversy; rather than learning to debate, the initiate is taught to harmonize differences. The degree of civility is the measure of belonging; as Piscator remarks, "Trust me, brother Peter, I find my Scholer to be so suit-

=

Forms of Reflection

able to my own humour, which is to be free and pleasant, and civilly merry, that my resolution is to hide nothing from him" (93). The republican emphasis on civility should not be construed as social leveling: anglers may be citizens, but they are always gentlemen.

Pastoral song acts as a regulative principle within the sylvan community; as Piscator comments: "I love civility, yet I hate severe censures: I'll to my own Art" (82). In speaking of art, Walton underscores the equivalence and opposition between controversy and his own generic strategy. As a discourse, *The Compleat Angler* aims at comprehensiveness, yet its parts generally intersect rather than coalesce. This relation is dramatized in the three singing contests, which emblematize the harmony of literary and social formations that Walton strives to re-create. There is potential agon as Maudlin sings Raleigh's "Come live with me and be my love," and her mother responds with Marlowe's knowing "If all the world and love were young" (90–91). Yet conflict is averted when "parts" are allowed to differ; the elder milkmaid comments, "I learned the first part in my golden age, when I was about the age of my daughter; and the later part, which indeed fits me best, but two or three years ago" (89). In the second episode, Corydon underscores reciprocity by insisting that all must take part in pastoral singing: "I wil sing a Song if any body wil sing another; else, to be plain with you, I wil sing none. . . . 'Tis merry in Hall when men sing all" (93). The final contest is no contest at all; "Come, we will all joine together . . . and then each man drink tother cup and to bed, and thank God we have a dry house over our heads" (151). Walton prints the tune to Viator's catch, inviting readers to participate. In contrast to the "hodge-podge of business and money, and care" censured in the song, the catch's intertwining parts represent social harmony expressed through difference. In response, Peter apostrophizes music:

> With what ease might thy errors be excus'd
> Wert thou as truly lov'd as th'art abused. (151)

Walton's tolerance is quick to seize upon such possibilities: he knows that the force of a genre depends upon its local context and disposition. As the meaning of one of the embedded forms turns on its place in the satura, so the meanings of the work itself turn on reciprocal relations between its parts.

Such concepts of order go unrecognized when critics equate "hybrid" works with internal contradiction or regard them as products of a "fragmenting and fragmented world."[34] The *compleat*ness Walton advocates is better understood as a complex assemblage of social differences articulated in a diversity of literary forms. Walton and his contemporaries were well aware of the ill consequences following from demands for conformity, from either end of the political spectrum. In addressing problems of difference, the *Angler* deploys generic strategies almost as various as the materials it contains: accretion (natural histories, lyrics, occasional meditations), modulation (georgic and pastoral), inversion (sacred parody, Lucianic dialogue), alterity (menippean satire). This willingness to entertain multiplicity while insisting on the social value of discrimination sets the *Angler* apart from most recent discussions of discursive communities. Walton refuses the utopian fantasies of free play and dystopian fantasies of absolute control that figure so prominently in many recent discussions of discursive formations. Consider the difference between Walton's critical procedures and Stanley Fish's discussion of the limits discourse supposedly imposes on the groves of academe. In a lecture presented to the Modern Language Association of America, "Being Interdisciplinary Is So Very Hard to Do," Fish pursues the logic of incommensurablity and contestation to its paradoxical extreme, arguing that disciplinary communities cannot respond to

> questions one might put from the outside, questions like (for teaching) "why is it that you want your students to learn?" or (for criminal law) "why should we be interested in the issue of responsibility at all?" or (for history) "why would anyone want to know what happened in the past?" You can't be seriously asking these questions and still be a member of those communities, because to conceive of yourself (a phrase literally intended) as a member is to have forgotten that those are questions you can seriously ask.[35]

Since few professional organizations are more preoccupied with such questions than the body to which Fish was speaking, the issue clearly turns on what one understands by "seriously" and "community." If one accepts Fish's assumptions about what constitutes a discipline, there is the end of the matter. But as the *Angler* indicates, not all disciplines are founded on constitutive principles. Refusing to take himself seriously, Walton conceives of identity as a variable mixture of humors; defining *community* through norms that tolerate difference, he also recognizes pragmatic limits to toleration. To contest contestation, Walton pursues the idea of an interdisciplinary discourse predicated on heterogeneity and civility. He avoids the paradox of unspeakable questions by establishing

=

Forms of Reflection

norms through a dialectical play of differences; the result is a critical discourse in which difference and historical change are not inconceivable.[36] Moreover, Walton's interdisciplinary discourse did the unthinkable and changed with the times: in successive editions, the narrative altered as new characters and new material were added; the work was continued by another hand; after the Restoration, manners, religion, and republican politics received rather less attention and natural history rather more. As in *Coopers Hill*, the coherence of *The Compleat Angler* is a matter of process rather than logical consistency.

One can agree with Fish that an interdisciplinary criticism without disciplinarity is no discipline at all, without concluding that discipline as such implies closure and foundational principles. A more inclusive concept of discursive formations would permit literary historians to consider alternatives to disciplinary closure and undisciplinary confusion, in the works we read as well as in the works we write. To lay hold of these possibilities, one need only think of discourse as a kind of writing rather than as a categorical imperative. Euclidean geometry is not the paradigm for modern academic discourses; these disciplines, like the combinatory genres that articulate their differences, can and do change. As Walton's contemplations remind us, the issues at the heart of interdisciplinary criticism need not be foundational principles but may be kinds of limits, kinds of mixture, kinds of change. Contemporary criticism might benefit from a reconsideration of georgic writing and the techniques georgic writers developed to take into account the local dispositions of a mixed community amid the flux of history.

Sylvan States: Jonson's *Forrest* and Cowley's *Essays*

In the last two sections I considered how seventeenth-century authors combined genres into a single, continuous work; in this section I consider the combining of single works into a discontinuous whole. The principles that go into arranging an anthology can be very similar to those that go into composing a poem or an essay: authors choose between hierarchical or decentered arrangements of parts. We have already seen how Denham invokes the principle of sylva in the part of his poem labeled "The Forrest"; in this concluding section I consider two works in which the sylva is the containing genre rather than the thing contained: Ben Jonson's *The Forrest* (1616) and Abraham Cowley's *Several Discourses by way of Essays, in Verse and Prose* (1668). All three works use the sylva form to comment

=

on principles of order in a mixed state; but the disposition of parts in the sylvae, as much as the authors' programmatic statements, indicates changing attitudes toward retirement, the relation of poets to the court, and the relation of the court to the state. In Cowley's *Essays* rural meditation settles into the largely oppositional role it would maintain throughout the next century.

The term *sylva* was a metaphor for principles of generic constitution predicated on mixture and heterogeneity. As Jonson explains in the preface to *Under-Woods*: "the Ancients call'd that kind of body *Sylva*, or *Hyle*, in which there were works of divers nature, and matter congested; as the multitude call Timber-trees, promiscuously growing, a Wood, or Forrest" (8:126).[37] Jonson does not regard promiscuity as confusion or contradiction but as an ordering principle opposed to exclusion. He applies the same generic designation to his collection of prose essays, *Timber*: "*silva*, the raw material of facts and thoughts, *hyle*, timber, as it were, so called from the multiplicity and variety of the matter contained therein" (8:562).[38] The raw materials going into the sylva, whether essays or poems, are neither autonomous entities nor mere functions of the larger structure of which they are parts. Like the social orders they represent, the genres included in the sylva oppose and interpenetrate one another in a dense thicket of relations. At issue in the Jonsonian sylva is more than a simple choice between pure or mixed forms or between open and closed forms: heterogeneity itself is variously conceived in *The Forrest*, *Under-Woods*, and *Timber*, which include different collections of genres disposed according to different principles of order. Jonson expected his readers to discriminate; in his hands an apparently disorderly form becomes an instrument for promoting manners, taste, and refinement.

As we have already noted, the concept of refinement implies not only heterogeneity, but change. Cowley understands this: imitating Jonson, he includes a sylva in his *Works* to document the vicissitudes of his own various career and also to refine Jonson's form according to the georgic strategy of repetition and variation discussed above in connection with *Coopers Hill*. The displacements Cowley introduces into Jonsonian sylva indicate changes in the social circumstances of professional poets: unable to succeed at court like Jonson, Cowley and the muses retire in good earnest.

The Forrest contains private reflections, lyrics from *Volpone*, verse epistles to patrons, and satires of the sort that in Jonson's time required the protection of a patron. The anthology is a palimpsest of Jonson's

=

larger oeuvre and a documentary history of his twenty-year rise to the position of laureate. Generic differences are immediately felt (libertine poems rubbing shoulders with sober reflections on chastity and religious love), while more subtle and contrary tendencies toward unity emerge only on reflection. Sequence is Jonson's prime means of regulating the collection: one can discern a series of poems attacking courtly vices and praising exemplary peers winding irregularly up the hierarchy of genres to the penultimate heroic ode, a sequence framed by a contrary but related sequence of private poems on poetry in which Jonson expostulates with Cupid, the muses, and God.[39] Since the virtue of praise or censure depends upon the status of the speaker, Jonson underscores his sincerity in these three liminal poems. *The Forrest* is an anthology of poems on poets and peers, a study of patronage relationships in which rank, family, and reputation are articulated in the appropriate genres of occasional verse. In keeping with its themes, *The Forrest* is a more tightly ordered and hierarchical work than *Under-woods* or *Timber*.

Cowley's *Essays* attack the social values Jonson celebrates: courtly pleasures, treasures, and ambitions. Truly good men, he argues, value moderation over indulgence, autonomy over display, and obscurity over power.[40] While Jonson tempers his praises of public life with a dignified respect for domesticity, Cowley prefers private life altogether. *The Forrest* is suffused with epigrammatical material; poems of whatever genre mete out praise and blame in measured points. Since Cowley disparages the very notion of fame, what was a major constituent in Jonson's work now becomes much less important. Like Donne, Jonson makes his poems of compliment occasions for moral reflection; these poems themselves are disposed in a hierarchical arrangement, terminating in a colloquy with God. Cowley devalues the compliment genre and reorders the sylva by arranging the parts as detached essays, in the best Baconian manner. Indeed, the shift from odes and epistles addressed to patrons at court to essays addressed to common readers marks a social displacement. Cowley, as well as Jonson, had patrons; by excluding them from his sylva he underscores the high value retirement poetry traditionally places on autonomy.[41] This point is reiterated in the concluding memoir, "Of Myself," which sums up the lessons of the preceding essays and applies them to Cowley's own career. Failing to win the patronage he felt he had deserved for services to the king, the man who had once thought of himself as "the Muse's Hannibal" dissevers his vocation from public life: he "was thus made a Poet as immediately as a Child is made an Eunuch"

=

Seventeenth-Century Georgic

(2:458). As in *The Compleat Angler*, poetry is seen as a contemplative activity removed from the centers of power and opposed to active participation in public affairs. Cowley, however, reduces his sylvan society to a community of one. Presenting himself as a hermit scorning the society that has scorned him, he adopts the postures of retirement writing to reflect on deferential relationships between peers and commons, patrons and poets.[42]

Sylvan landscapes represent dispersed societies, though the kind of dispersion varies from work to work; while only peers are mentioned by name in *The Forrest*, the more promiscuous *Under-woods* ranges widely among the saplings, shrubs, and weeds of society. Cowley's *Essays* praise the life of the gentleman-commoner in prose and verse saturated with georgic themes and figures. In the country, vices are "pruned away like suckers that choak the Mother-Plant, and hinder it from bearing fruit" ("The shortness of Life and uncertainty of Riches" 2:449); city life, by contrast, "will bear nothing but the Nettles or Thornes of Satyre" ("Of Agriculture," 2:406). While georgic was already a significant element in Jonson's generic mixture, Cowley's *Essays* amount to a line-by-line redaction of the key passages in Latin literature concerning rural virtue. The sway of georgic is so strong that it all but subsumes the heterogeneity of sylva into the even temper of the middle style. In georgic writing, topographical distances signal moral differences. Jonson compares Durrants, "with unbought provision blest," to London, where wealth is "Purchased by Rapine" ("To Sir Robert Wroth," 8:96). Cowley lays the fault for the late war at the doorstep of the court and city: "In our late mad and miserable Civil Wars, all other Trades, even the meanest, set forth whole Troopes, and raised up great Commanders. . . . But, I do not remember the Name of any one Husbandmen who had so considerable a share in the twenty years ruine of his Country, as to deserve the Curses of his Countrymen" ("Of Agriculture," 2:402).

While both sylvae present versions of country politics, the two poets delineate rural virtue differently.[43] While Jonson seldom misses an opportunity to take a dig at the court, he praises a rural England populated by peers of the realm and pacified by deferential values. The social order elaborated in his odes, epistles, and country-house poems is organized from the top down. Driven by status, deference, and compliment, it is opposed to acquisitiveness and social climbing. Jonson tells Rutland that the present is a gilt (guilty) and not a golden age, a time when money gives "pride fame and peasants birth" ("Epistle to Elizabeth Countess of Rutland," 8:114). He praises Aubigny's beauty, character, and family—not her dowry—because

> Some alderman has power,
> Or cos'ning farmer of the customes so,
> T'advance his doubtful issue, and ore-flow
> A Princes fortune. . . . ("Epistle to Katherine, Lady Aubigny," 8:117)

Fully aware that a money economy was displacing deferential relations of exchange, Jonson smites the status quo by conjuring up a largely counterfactual order of feudal ties and rural innocence. At a time when baronetcies were put up for sale, most readers would have recognized Jonson's vision of Merrie England as something of a fancy.[44]

Fifty years and a civil war later, Cowley imagines a rural society thriving on liberty rather than patronage. Jonson trumpets fame, family, and responsibility; Cowley whispers obscurity, solitude, and independence. Where Jonson relishes the country pleasures of a wealthy peer, Cowley situates happiness in the more humble establishments of the lesser gentry. Given a choice, says Cowley, "I should pitch upon that sort of People whom King James was wont to call the Happiest of our Nation, the Men placed in the Country by their Fortune above an High-Constable, and yet beneath the trouble of a Justice of Peace, in a moderate plenty, without any just argument for the desire of encreasing it by the care of many relations" ("Of Liberty," 2:386). This rejection of the Jonsonian hierarchy is both a personal response to recent history and a traditional stance in georgic poetry. An income of five hundred pounds would be ideal—enough to liberate a gentleman from labor but not enough to support a large family of servants and retainers ("Of Greatness," 2:431). Turning the deferential order on its head, Cowley describes the peer as the greatest servant of all: "Nothing seems greater and more Lordly then the multitude of Domestick Servants. . . . [Yet] the trouble and care of yours in the Government of them all, is much more then that of every one of them in their observance of you" ("Of Liberty," 2:383). He takes ironic aim at "To Penshurst" and poems where the poet sings for his supper:

> Hail, old Patrician Trees, so great and good!
> Hail ye Plebeian under wood!
> Where the Poetique Birds rejoyce,
> And for their quiet Nests and plentious Food,
> Pay with their grateful voice. (2:395)

In a truly sylvan state, poetic birds would sing because they are happy, not because they are hungry. In imagining such a primitive scene, Cowley refines "To Penshurst" and overgoes the whole genre of estate poems that deprecate grand houses. Unable to build a house for himself, Cowley imagines an estate with no house at all:

> Here Nature does a House for me erect,
> Nature the wisest Architect,
> Who those fond Artists does despise
> That can the fair and living Trees neglect;
> Yet the Dead Timber prize.   (2:395)

Cowley's interest in living timber is typical of English georgic. In "Of Agriculture" he proposes colleges to instruct gentlemen farmers in scientific land management, and he puffs Evelyn's research on the subject, soon to be published in a volume entitled *Sylva, or A Discourse of Forest Trees* (1664). Unlike Jonson's wealthy peers, Cowley's gentlemen improvers are expected to feather their own nests.

The Forrest testifies to the successes of Stuart patronage, the *Essays* to its failings.[45] Writing before the Civil War, Jonson looks for security in the greatness of his patrons; in the aftermath of rebellion, Cowley looks for security in personal autonomy. The "most Gentlemanly manner" of assisting someone, he declares, "is not to adde any thing to his Estate, but to take something from his desires" ("The danger of Procrastination" 2:453). Differing attitudes toward peers and patrons lead to differing formal and rhetorical structures in the two sylvae. Jonson reminds Lady Aubigny that by praising virtue and censuring vice he puts himself at personal risk, as indeed he had. This very fact, he argues, confirms the value of his praises. I will not "feare to draw true lines," the poet says, "'cause others paint" (l. 20). Jonson's abilities as a limner—and a colorist—are displayed in a range of style that vary from the biting satire of "To Sickness," to the judicious deliberations of the epistles, to the raptured lyricism of the ode to William Sydney. Jonson arranges his sylvan matter into a monumental composition not unlike that he promises to erect for the Countess of Rutland:

> There like a rich, and golden pyramede,
> Borne up by statues, shall I reare your head,
> Above your under-carved ornaments,
> And show, how, to the life, my soule presents
> Your forme imprest there. . . .   (8:115)

Forms of Reflection

A golden pyramid is a good emblem for Jonson's aim in transforming the raw matter of occasional verse into a design that is more than the sum of its parts. Fifteen, as Fowler points out, is a "pyramidal number."[46] There are three divisions in *The Forrest*, marked by the liminal poems: a base of nine poems on duties to others, a midsection of five on duties to oneself, and a point of one on duties to God. But this formal design is only one among several. Where several pairs and sequences of poems intersect, oppose, and jostle for attention, any tendency toward hierarchical subordination must compete with countertendencies toward heterogeneous variety. Indeed, the several themes and functions of the "under-carving" tend to obscure any monumental design. The deference implied in Jonson's rustic monument is by no means absolute; the poet, not the patron, occupies the peak of the pyramid in a poem that is a private, not a public, utterance.

Cowley's sylva addresses similar problems of organization in an equally complex design that strives for order without subordination. In the *Davideis* Cowley used a heroic form to express resistance to heroic values; in the *Essays* he adapts another elevated genre to celebrate the virtues of a humble life:

> If Life should a well-order'd Poem be
> (In which he only hits the white
> Who joyns true Profit with the best Delight)
> The more Heroique strain let others take,
> Mine the Pindarique way I'le make.
> The Matter shall be Grave, the Numbers loose and free.
> It shall not keep one setled pace of Time,
> In the same Tune it shall not always Chime,
> Nor shall each day just to his Neighbor Rhime.   (2:391)

Freed from the restraint of patronage, the poet can sing his own tune his own way. Instead of Jonson's stately pyramid, Cowley raises a monument to sylvan liberty. The overall structure of the *Essays* reflects the "Pindarique way." The first and last essays frame nine others treating the subjects of ambition, greed, and luxury in three groups of three. The poems following the prose essays are grouped in a separate pattern forming a complex quasi-regular counterpoint: 5 1 1 5 1 1 2 1 1 2 3. The central twelfth poem, placed off-center behind the fourth of the eleven essays, tells the story of proud King Gyges, who mistakenly thought monarchy the pinnacle of human happiness. On being told of a happier man than he, Gyges sets out in pursuit of this mighty ruler, only to discover him to be a humble peasant far removed from any court. Cowley gets in another swipe at absolute monarchy in the midpoint of the central essay, entitled "Of Greatness." This, the "triumphal place" in traditional numerology, describes the foolish behavior of a variety of ancient emperors and modern kings (2:430). Cowley's displaced and inverted centers flatten Jonson's stately pyramid into a promiscuously Pindaric structure with centers everywhere and nowhere.

Cowley's "Pindarique way" is in fact the familiar georgic structure of repetition and variation; by composing poems and essays as variations on a theme Cowley supplies an orderly alternative to hierarchy. "Nor shall each day just to his Neighbor Rhime"—the several parts of the sylva rhyme in dispersed metaphors: society as a garden, retirement as a mistress, life as a journey. Consistency, as much as variety, is part of Cowley's conception of sylvan order, and this too has a political dimension. Cultivating refinement, Cowley erodes social distance by means of the familiar style:

> That I who Lord and Master cry'd erewhile,
> Salute you in a new and different Stile,
> By your own Name, a scandal to you now,
> Think not that I forget my self or you.   (2:388)

Where Jonson runs through a vertical hierarchy of poetic genres, Cowley never deviates from the middle style and conversational manner he deems appropriate to rural independence.[47] Aware that maintaining the same demeanor in all circumstances threatens dullness ("Of Solitude," 2:393–94), Cowley challenges himself to present country life in as many lights as possible and to fit his consistent style to as many forms as he can: no two of the eleven prose essays are constructed on the same plan; comparable refinements appear in subtle modulations in poetic genres and in subtle and not so subtle deviations from classical sources. Cowley writes in the georgic mode for much the same reasons as Denham and Walton do: tempering unity with variety, georgic suggests alternative possibilities for formal, thematic, and political coherence. Cowley's swan song survives in many eighteenth-century imitations; his program for retirement became a model for later writers, notably Pope, who knew the *Essays* well:

> Who now reads Cowley? if he pleases yet,
> His moral pleases, not his pointed wit;
> Forgot his Epic, nay Pindaric Art,
> But still I love the language of his Heart.[48]

≡

Forms of Reflection
78

In this discussion, I have shown how three georgic writers modified meditational writing in ways that decentered courtly literature and deferential values. In *Coopers Hill*, commerce is presented as the means by which society can turn heterogeneity and change to its own advantage. Denham exemplifies his theme by reconstituting classical georgic in ways that situate his own writing within the social and historical processes he describes. In *The Compleat Angler* Walton opposes conversational genres to swingeing sermons and scurrilous satires. Refinement becomes recreation, a means of tempering social differences through a mixed discourse combining pious and pleasurable literary forms. Cowley's *Essays* recreate the Jonsonian sylva by reordering its constituent elements. Rather than ordering his parts by hierarchical subordination, Cowley disposes his poems and essays by means of repetition and variation, a revisionary procedure that imitates what Jonson himself had done in refining the Latin sylva. Cowley's more thoroughly georgic meditations substitute a dispersed society of gentleman farmers for Jonson's courtly society of landed peers. As georgic works, all of these meditations underscore historical and material relations between social and literary formations. But unlike the contemporary criticism discussed here, they do so without defining coherence as closure or uniformity. While this inclusiveness was limited, we would be mistaken to label such works as hegemonic; indeed, they advocate and instantiate literary and social changes.

It would be more useful to see in them alternatives to the ways in which concepts of culture resolve parts into wholes. I have tried to illustrate how this might be done; rather than abstracting a georgic ideology from the works, a system within which their differences can be read as contradictions, I have represented those differences as continuities and discontinuities within a historically evolving field of genres. By attending to relations between genres, we can better grasp how difference could be a normative condition in English georgic; such works were expected to be internally various and different from earlier instances of the genre. These works make a point of dramatizing their conditions of production and the social and literary rationale for their innovations; if this has gone unrecognized, it is not the fault of the authors. To reduce the structures of difference within and between these works to surface manifestations of a putatively concealed ideology is to conceal just those literary and critical procedures potentially most valuable for anyone attempting to reconceptualize the relations of literature to history.

=

Seventeenth-Century Georgic

79

3

Providence or Prudence?

Fabling in *Serious Reflections of Robinson Crusoe*

A fter the Restoration, writers begin referring to contemplative works as *reflections;* this shift in terminology marks a change in relations between meditation and a whole field of genres reorganized around the new empirical psychology. Distinctions between history and fiction, for example, though not particularly problematic on ontological grounds, became very troublesome to writers trying to separate fiction from history as a distinct kind of representation. The new generic distinctions turned less on what stories are about than on how stories are told; readers needed to know about authors' intentions to judge whether representations are fictional, historical, or attempts at deception. But since authors' intentions are most often known only through their writing, the difficulties multiplied. Small wonder that deception, already a constituent of novel and romance, became an even more prominent theme in the "true histories" written by Congreve, Behn, Manley, and Defoe. Since one of the new tasks assigned to mental reflection was to distinguish between kinds of representation, reflection became a constituent of narrative, and vice versa.

Describing *Robinson Crusoe* as allusive allegorical history, Defoe's famous castaway calls attention to the ambiguous status of his creator's representations: how can a work be at once a history and an allegory? In *Serious Reflections of Robinson Crusoe*, Crusoe attacks problems of narrative representation by means of a probabilistic reinterpretation of typology. Robinson Crusoe's meditations encourage Defoe's readers to reflect on how, why, when, and to what narrative signs refer. *Serious Reflections* thus is a primer in procedures of probable inference, teaching readers to infer a literary design from narrative circumstances and a serious moral from that design. While Defoe's providential fiction has roots in traditional typology, it extends devotional hermeneutics by exploring the intersections between literary criticism, theology, and economics. The result is to change the functions of narrative within meditational writing and the functions of meditational writing within narrative. The extent and significance of Defoe's innovations becomes apparent when we compare his reflections to others by Gildon, Bunyan, and Mandeville.

Designing Arguments and Arguments from Design

Interpretations of *Robinson Crusoe* recall the old fable of the blind men and the elephant: each, grasping a different part of the body, receives a different impression of the object. Depending on their particular starting place, critics describe Defoe's work variously as a novel of individualism, an economic parable, a saint's life, and a colonialist fantasy. *Robinson Crusoe* is all of these things, yet reducible to none of them.[1] How can such an unlikely beast be said to exhibit what Defoe calls design? *Design* is a term much out of fashion with critics, many of whom associate it with an outmoded intentionalism, but it is a concept worth recovering if we are to understand the social and political significance of Defoe's narrative. In the eighteenth century, design was a key term in several kinds of writing, including theology, law, and literary criticism. Critical debate over *Crusoe* begins with a dispute over Defoe's extension of this term to the heterogeneous material included in his narrative. Charles Gildon, Defoe's first and most bitter critic, denies that the work has any coherent design at all. Gildon's *The Life and Strange Surprizing Adventures of Mr. D—— DeF——, of London, Hosier* (1719) attributes a lack of design in the work to a lack of character in its creator. Unlike most modern commentators, Gildon refuses to make Defoe a mouthpiece for any particular theme or ideology:

> The Fabulous Proteus of the Ancient Mythologist was but a very faint Type of our Hero, whose Changes are much more numerous, and he far more difficult to be constrain'd to his own Shape. If his Works should happen to live to the next Age, there would in all probability be a greater Strife among the several Parties, whose he really was, than

among the seven Graecian Cities, to which of them Homer belong'd;
The Dissenters first would claim him as theirs, the Whigs in general as
theirs, the Tories as theirs, the Non-jurors as theirs, the Papists as
theirs, the Atheists as theirs, and so on to what Sub-divisions there may
be among us.[2]

Gildon finds no design in *Crusoe*: "By the Rules of Art you have not
attain'd any one End and Aim of a Writer of Fables in the Tale you have
given us" (35).

Design is especially lacking in just those parts of the book where
Defoe instructs readers to look for it, in the "Moral Reflections, as you are
pleas'd to call them . . . put in by you to swell the Bulk of your Treatise
up to a five Shilling Book" (30–31). While twentieth-century critics eval-
uate those passages rather differently, they largely ignore Defoe's third
volume, *Serious Reflections During the Life and Surprizing Adventures of
Robinson Crusoe With his Vision of the Angelic World*–dismissing it, as
Gildon discusses the earlier reflections, as "Bulk." Thus Ian Watt: "The
Serious Reflections of Robinson Crusoe (1720) are actually a miscellaneous compilation of religious, moral, and thaumaturgic material, and cannot, as a whole, be taken seriously as a part of the story: the volume was
primarily put together to cash in on the *Surprizing Adventures*, and the
smaller one of the *Farther Adventures*." Watt makes no such objection to
the "religious, moral, and thaumaturgic material" that appears with
almost equal frequency in the previous volumes. Paul Hunter dismisses
both the second and the third volumes: "By *Robinson Crusoe*, I mean
only part 1. . . . The two sequels, *Farther Adventures* and *Serious Reflections*, were published later and seem . . . to have been separately conceived."[3] While critics have mined the third volume for what Watt calls
valuable clues, very few take *Serious Reflections* seriously. Nor, to judge
from the bibliographic evidence, was the third volume much read in the
eighteenth century.[4] Critical approaches to narrative have changed since
Watt and Hunter were writing twenty and thirty years ago, and we have
learned to pay greater heed to marginal writings. But *Serious Reflections*
should not be regarded as marginal, since it contains Defoe's most extensive discussions of narrative theory, and since the generic contexts in the
third volume are continuous with its predecessors. In "Robinson Crusoe's
Preface" Defoe asserts that the third volume completes a prior design:
"As the design of everything is said to be first in the intention, and last in
the execution, so I come now to acknowledge to my reader that the

=

Providence or Prudence?

present work is not merely the product of the two first volumes, but the first volumes may rather be called the product of this. The fable is always made for the moral, not the moral for the fable."[5] While there is every reason to doubt that the third volume was planned from the start, we should not dismiss the statement without inquiring into what Defoe means by "design," "fable," and "moral." For all its heterogeneity, *Serious Reflections* is thematically and formally related to its predecessors: the first parts journey to the West and East Indies, the third to Saturn; the first parts are concerned with the depredations of cannibals and pirates, the third with the depredations of atheists and the devil; the first parts interpolate meditations into narrative, while the third part interpolates narratives into meditation. All three volumes are concerned with problems of representation and truth telling, but especially the third, in which Crusoe's reflections on honesty and interpretation become the container rather than the thing contained.

Defoe probably published *Serious Reflections* less to capitalize on the popularity of *Crusoe* than to answer a "malicious and foolish writer" (x) — Charles Gildon.[6] By the time the third volume appeared, Gildon's *Life and Strange Surprizing Adventures* had run to three editions. The arguments in Defoe's seven essays — on solitude, honesty, freethinking, sectarianism, providence, evangelism, and apparitions — respond to the most serious charge Gildon levels at *Crusoe*:

> The Christian Religion and the Doctrines of Providence are too Sacred to be deliver'd in Fictions and Lies, nor was this Method ever propos'd or follow'd by any true Sons of the Gospel; it is what has been, indeed, made use of by the Papists in the Legends of their Saints, the Lying Wonders of which are by Length of Time grown into such Authority with that wretched People, that they are at last substituted in the Place of the Holy Scriptures themselves. For the Evil Consequences of allowing Lies to mingle with the Holy Truths of Religion, is the certain Seed of Atheism and utter Irreligion; whether, therefore, you ought to make a publick Recantation of your Conduct in this Particular, I leave to yourself. (48)

Gildon overstates his case, handing Defoe a golden opportunity to reiterate and amplify his earlier positions on lying and fiction, commerce and faith.

In the preface to *Farther Adventures* Defoe asserts that "the just application of every Incident, the religious and useful Inferences drawn from

≡

Forms of Reflection

every Part, are so many Testimonies to the good Design of making it publick, and must legitimate all the Part that may be call'd Invention, or Parable in the Story."[7] The literary design reflects the religious design, and
both testify to the good designs of its author. Responding to this passage,
Gildon's pamphlet denies design in any sense:

> But when it is plain that there are no true, useful or just Inferences
> drawn from any of the Incidents; when Religion has so little to do in
> any Part of these Inferences; when it is evident that what you call Reli-
> gion, is only to mislead the Minds of Men to reject the Dictates of Rea-
> son, and embrace in its Room a meer superstitious Fear of I know not
> what *Instinct* from unbodied Spirits; when you impiously prophane the
> very name of Providence, by allotting to it either contradictory Offices,
> or an unjust Partiality: I think we may justly say, that the Design of the
> Publication of this Book was not sufficient to justify and make Truth of
> what you allow to be Fiction and Fable; what you mean by Legitimat-
> ing, Invention, and Parable, I know not; unless you would have us
> think, that the manner of your telling a Lie will make it a Truth. (33)

Either the events happened, or they didn't; references to testimony, parables, inference, and instinct are beside the point. Responding to these
charges in *Serious Reflections*, Defoe refuses to be boxed into such a simple ontological distinction between history and fiction.

Having conceded that parts of the narrative are "fiction and fable,"
the statement in the third preface that "there is not a circumstance in the
imaginary story but has its just allusion to a real story" (xi–xii) becomes
problematic, to say the least. Apart from mocking Gildon's slighting identification of Crusoe with his "creator" ("Ho, ho, do you know me now?
You are like the Devil in *Milton*, that could not tell the Offspring of his
own Brain, *Sin* and *Death*," vii), why would Defoe make the unlikely
assertion that *Crusoe* is both an allegory and the history of his own life?
Critics regard allegory in *Robinson Crusoe* as a remnant of Puritan distrust of fiction; thus Paul Hunter describes the biographical realism of
Crusoe as a "further step" toward later fiction (120). But surely few of
Defoe's readers were antagonistic to fiction as such. Michael McKeon
describes *Crusoe* as a "next step": "In Defoe the balance between spirit-
ualization and the claim to historicity has been reversed [relative to Bun-
yan], and it is as though he has—not without the spiraling misgivings of
the *Serious Reflections*—taken that perilous next step and, in the name of
a 'positive' secularization, explicitly sanctioned our resistance to allegori-

=

cal translation."[8] But given the state of narrative fiction in 1719, Defoe's turn to pious allegory might just as easily be considered a step back to the last century; Gildon thought so: "There is not an old *Woman* that can go to the Price of it, but buys thy Life and Adventures, and leaves it as a Legacy, with the *Pilgrim's Progress*, the *Practice of Piety*, and *God's Revenge against Murther*, to her Posterity" (x). The understandable desire to represent change as progress has led critics to overlook the obvious fact that Defoe was sacrilizing genres already secularized: not demystifying Bunyan but "Puritanizing" Behn, not restricting but extending the reach of allegory.

What, then, of the claim that the allegory is founded on "a real story"? This seems to respond to Gildon's charge that *Crusoe* delivers sacred doctrines in "Fictions and Lies." Defoe does not make a Sidneyean apology for poetry because the issue between himself and Gildon is not just the relation of fiction to history (Gildon wrote "true" novels himself) but the relation of fiction to providence. The design of the work testifies not only to the good intentions of its creator but also to those of its creator's creator, so to speak. So Crusoe must cumbersomely declare that

> when in these reflections I speak of the times and circumstances of particular actions done, or incidents which happened, in my solitude and island-life, an impartial reader will be so just to take it as it is, viz., that it is spoken or intended of that part of the real story which the island-life is a just allusion to; and in this [present work] the story is not only illustrated, but the real part I think most justly approved.   (xii)

Defoe is willing to acknowledge that his fictions are fictions but not that his providences are invented. The shipwrecks and pirates were included only to attract readers to what is in fact a serious work. But there is more to the reply than this. By writing as Crusoe, Defoe complicates the issue of truth telling in a way intimately bound up with his own conceptions of providence. Since he withholds both his own name and the details that would allow us to confirm the "real story," we are left to judge on the basis of internal evidence or else to believe the narrator's assertion that his story is true. Either way, we are confronted with mere representations of the truth—the same representation in fact, since the man asserting the truth of the narrative speaks from within the narrative itself. And that is how it is, with providences as with fictions: we are left to infer a creator's intention from his design. Defoe would "have us think, that the manner of [his] telling a Lie will make it a Truth."

=

Forms of Reflection

86

Crusoe suggests that we might divine the truth of the matter by reflecting on the "circumstances" and "particular actions" of his (or Defoe's) life with impartiality and justice. Defoe, of course, had more than passing experience with the law, so it is perhaps not surprising to discover him introducing juridical rhetoric into the defense of his fiction.[9] In the most familiar passage in *Serious Reflections*, Crusoe testifies to his own existence:

> I, Robinson Crusoe, being at this time in perfect and sound mind and
> memory, thanks be to God therefore, do hereby declare their objection
> [that Crusoe is feigned] is an invention scandalous in design, and false in
> fact; and do affirm that the story, although allegorical, is also historical;
> and that it is the beautiful representation of a life of unexampled misfor-
> tunes, and of a variety not to be met with in the world, sincerely adapted
> to and intended for the common good of mankind, and designed at first,
> as it is now farther applied, to the most serious uses possible.
>
> Farther, that there is a man alive, and well known too, the actions of
> whose life are the just subject of these volumes, and to whom all or most
> part of the story most directly alludes; this may be depended upon for
> truth, and to this I set my name . . . Robinson Crusoe.   (ix–x, xiii)

Since the man in question is not called forth to testify, we are left to judge Crusoe's case on its merits. Defoe, in other words, expects us to extrapolate his good design from the evidence of his book.

As Maximillian Novak explains, "Defoe is obviously equivocating throughout this preface, but his statements are not without meaning. What Defoe is defending is the kind of moral fable which Le Bossu believed the basis of all good fiction, not allegory but symbolism" (655). However, this is symbolism of a rather specific kind. Douglas Patey cites John Dennis and Le Bossu as critics who use *fable* in a probabilistic sense that helps to explain what Defoe means in his appeal to circumstances and design. According to Le Bossu, an epic action "must be render'd *Probable* by the Circumstances of *Times, Places,* and *Persons.*" The poet must invent "such Circumstances as alter nothing of the Essence either of the Fable, or the Moral," the *"Ground-work* upon which all the rest is built." Patey describes this as a hierarchy of probable signs; poets move from moral down to circumstances; interpreters move upward, from circumstances to moral. Dennis extends this construct from epic to narrative in general: "I know of no difference that there is, between one of Aesop's Fables, and the Fable of an Epick Poem, as to the Natures, 'tho there be many and great ones, as to their Circumstances" (109–13).

=

Providence or Prudence?

When Defoe tells us that "The fable is always made for the moral, not the moral for the fable," he implies that his "beautiful representation" conforms to this kind of probabilistic structure: moral, fable, circumstances. While the circumstances of the island story are different from those in the real story, both fables point to the same moral: "Here is invincible patience recommended under the worst of misery, indefatigable application and undaunted resolution under the greatest and most discouraging circumstances" (xii). While Defoe's narrative in and of itself can be considered allegorical in Le Bossu's sense, it can be construed as allegorical in yet a different sense, as in James Beattie's distinction between the two kinds of modern romance: "In reading the *allegorical prose fable*, we attend not only to the fictitious events that occur in the narrative, but also to those real events that are typified by the allegory: whereas in the *poetical prose fable* we attend only to the events that are before us." Beattie lists *Robinson Crusoe* under the heading of pure or "poetical" fiction, either because he does not take Defoe's claims seriously or (more likely) because by midcentury the third volume was largely forgotten.[10]

Beattie's discussion of allegory is perhaps most pertinent, since neo-Aristotelian critics like Le Bossu had regarded epic fables as allegorical, without insisting on a basis in fact. But as Beattie suggests, fictitious events sometimes typify real events, so that a fable might be both historical and allegorical. During Defoe's lifetime, typology underwent important changes: typological procedures were extended to secular genres; figural readings of scripture were circumscribed by a new critical understanding of Biblical history; and *type* became assimilated with *character*. While he confines his discussion of *Crusoe* to Biblical types, elsewhere in *Typologies in England 1650–1820* Paul J. Korshin describes what he calls "abstracted typology" (34).[11] Defoe's contemporaries interpreted secular history as a structure of probable signs and types:

> The past is a series of chronicles scattered with significant events and characters which, if properly understood, would enable Englishmen to predict correct solutions for the present. . . . By the last half of the [seventeenth] century . . . typology becomes attractive to the practitioners of other literary genres [than sacred], especially to satirists, character writers, the authors of prose and verse fables, and, perhaps most important, the writers of prose narrative. (110–11)

Drawing upon innovative conceptions of character and fable, authors structured fictional narratives as "predictive structures" (114). Gildon charges

≡

Forms of Reflection

that *Crusoe* lacks such probability because its hero is so unpredictable: "The Fabulous Proteus of the Ancient Mythologist was but a very faint Type of our Hero, whose Changes are much more numerous, and he far more difficult to be constrain'd to his own Shape."

While Robinson Crusoe plays different roles, they are almost always roles of a predictable type. When Defoe represents his castaway as a solitary hermit conning scripture by candlelight and reflecting on the mysteries of providence, he locates his character in circumstances that readers will immediately recognize. Joseph Hall's "Characterism of the *Faithful man*" (1608), for instance, is a strikingly apt character for Crusoe:

> Examples are his proofes; and Instances his demonstrations. What hath God given, which hee can not give? What have others suffered, which hee may not bee enabled to endure? is hee threatned banishment? There he sees the Deare Evangelist in Pathmos cutting pieces; hee sees Esay under the saw. Drowning? hee sees Ionas diving into the living gulfe. Burning? he sees the three children in the hote walke of the furnace. . . . He is not sure he shall die, as that he shall be restored; and outfaceth his death with his resurrection. . . . In common opinion miserable, but in true judgement more than a man. (Korshin, 123)

Here, in germ, is Defoe's "beautiful representation of a life of unexampled misfortunes," both an instance of a type and an illustration of the whole structure of probable inference ("examples are his proofes; and Instances his demonstrations"). As both Hall and Defoe make clear, meditation is central to the interpretation of providential narratives: the hermit meditates by matching his own circumstances with the appropriate fables, a process of seeking out the corresponding types. L'Estrange's preface to the *Fables of Aesop* (1694) also exemplifies how fables were thought to function as probable narratives. By fables "we are brought Naturally enough, by the Judgment we pass upon the Vices and Follies of our Neighbours, to the Sight and Sense of our Own; and Especially, when we are led to the Knowledge of the Truth of Matters by *Significant Types and Proper Resemblances*" (Korshin, 128). As we shall see, this is just how Defoe's *Serious Reflections* "reflect." Character, fable, and allegory are both the objects and the means of reflection, parts of a narrative and the devices a reader uses to interpret that narrative. As a significant type, Crusoe in *Serious Reflections* is—reflexively—both interpreter and object of interpretation.

Robinson Crusoe differs from contemporary allegories, epics, fictions,

=

Providence or Prudence?

fables, and characters by a narrative circumstantiality which, according to McKeon, "explicitly sanctions our resistance to allegorical translation" (319). But as we have seen, to eighteenth-century readers circumstantiality might be considered an allegorical procedure itself. In *The Eclipse of Biblical Narrative*, Hans W. Frei describes how critical and historical readings of Scripture exerted pressure on traditional modes of interpretation: "Rather than inquiring simply into what had taken place (though this was also involved), 'historical understanding' sought to understand how the ancient writers had experienced and thought, in their own distinctive, culturally or historically conditioned consciousness."[12] Once theologians began to treat prophetic utterances as representations of a mental act instead of simple statements of fact, the familiar gulf opened up between narrative and intention. As probable reasoning was called in to close this gap, a detailed examination of circumstances became necessary:

> Embodied in the argument over the fulfillment of prophecy was the breakup of the old identity of literal explicative meaning with historical reference or estimation, and their reintegration under an independent criterion which identifies meaning with reference to independently establishable fact claims. An exegetical or hermeneutical argument about determining the meaning of certain narrative texts has become an argument about the status of the fact claims apparently made in them. (72)

To know whether an Old Testament type predicted a New Testament event, the prophecy had to be tested not only against the circumstances of the two events but against an intention inferred from the circumstances in which utterance was made.

While he may have enjoyed narrative particularity for its own sake, Defoe clearly had theological reasons for making his providential narratives probable. In this respect, his narrative practices differ not only from Bunyan's, but from those of Fielding, who did not think that *Joseph Andrews's* chastity need be probable to be providential. Defoe, like the critical interpreters of the Bible, demands more than merely formal resemblance; his notion of allegory requires a probable rendering of historical circumstances. Crusoe's life is not merely analogous to his own; "There is not a circumstance in the imaginary story but has its just allusion to a real story, and chimes part for part and step for step." The allegory would be nothing without such particularity, even though the particular circumstances have been translated halfway round the world:

=

Forms of Reflection

Thus the print of a man's foot, and surprize of the old goat, and the thing rolling on my bed, and my jumping out in a fright, are all histories and real stories; as are likewise the dream of being taken by messengers, being arrested by officers, the manner of being driven to shore by the surge of the sea, the ship on fire, the description of starving, the story of my man Friday, and many more most material passages observed here, and on which any religious reflections are made, are all historical and true in fact.   (x–xi)

We may doubt, yet independent evidence exists for several of the narratives in *Serious Reflections*.[13] Defoe probably did regard Crusoe's providences as his own; certainly he is serious in asking readers to accept them as testimony of divine intervention in history. While a formal story, or what Beattie calls a "poetical prose fable," is sufficient to point a moral, a providential narrative requires more. Defoe's allegory is circumstantial because the author desires his readers not merely to believe in his fiction but to believe in the reality of God's providences. His allegory is historical.

I hope this rather complicated discussion of the relation of fable to allegory helps to clarify the dispute between Defoe and Gildon. In "Robinson Crusoe's Preface" Defoe responds to his opponent by raising the critical stakes: it is not only Defoe's design that is in question but God's. "'What a wretch am I!,'" Crusoe/Defoe confesses, "at the same time [I] smile at the harebrained enemy, whose tongue, tipped with malice, runs ahead of his understanding, and missing the crimes for which I deserve more than he can inflict, reproaches me with those I never committed" (55). We would be naive to accept Defoe's designs at face value, in the novel as much as in the life. But my purpose is less to establish Defoe's true intention or to try his case for him than it is to establish what he is trying to prove. Juxtaposing *Crusoe* with stories of visions, apparitions, and strange providences seems an unlikely way to bolster probability or to lay claim to design. Yet "Robinson Crusoe's Preface" and *Serious Reflections* do allow us to make inferences about generic innovations in *Robinson Crusoe*. Throughout *Serious Reflections* Defoe's discussions of literary criticism, theology, and commercial ethics are related to the problems of faith and credit; throughout, faith and credit are measured according to new standards of probability. When Defoe asserts that the events on the island allude to a "real story," he deliberately raises the issue of narrative representation to undermine earlier distinctions between fiction and history; in the essays that follow, fables reflect on fables

=

Providence or Prudence?
91

until the work becomes a veritable hall of mirrors—serious reflections indeed.

In an astute essay on Defoe's personas, David Marshall writes, "In the *Serious Reflections* Defoe again puts on the costume of Robinson Crusoe in order to address the guilt generated by his posture."[14] Defoe may be anxious about his fictionalizing but only in the sense that the chairman of the Federal Reserve might be said to be anxious about money: it is not the illusoriness of credit that is troubling but the ethics of manipulating what Defoe refers to as "the economy of Heaven" (274). One of Defoe's purposes is to establish rules for the regulation of credit in the interrelated fields of literature, theology, and commerce.

The Interpreter's House and Probable Narrative

Most studies of *Crusoe* emphasize Defoe's fictional innovations, treating the religious material as a kind of survival from an earlier era. But Gildon was right: Defoe is more innovative as a devotional writer than as a novelist, no more so than when he delivers "the Doctrines of Providence . . . in Fictions and Lies" (48). As *Serious Reflections* makes clear, Defoe was not abandoning allegory for fiction, he was attempting to make fiction *serious*, which is to say religious. Defoe shared Bunyan's conviction that reading an allegory and spiritualizing a life are equivalent procedures, but he alters allegorical procedures in the process of extending them. Most of these changes result from the probabilism Defoe uses to bridge gaps between circumstances and intentions, appearances and reality, present and future states. Probabilism concerns itself with signs and seemings, in contrast to Bunyan's allegory, which subordinates signs and seemings to one or another kind of unconditional knowledge of absolute truth. Bunyan's more extreme skepticism is the counterpart of his unqualified faith; Defoe has greater confidence in human reason but less in our ability to achieve certainty. While *The Pilgrim's Progress* and *Robinson Crusoe* are both providential narratives, Christian and Crusoe pursue their pilgrimages through very different kinds of allegory.

In "Of Solitude," the first essay in *Serious Reflections*,, Crusoe alters and extends the character of which he is a type; the "strange surprizing adventures" he underwent on the island are no longer those of a character in a romance but types of a universal human condition:

≡

Forms of Reflection

I desire to be heard concerning what solitude really is; for I must confess I have different notions about it, far from those which are generally understood in the world, and far from all those notions upon which those people in the primitive times, and since that also, acted; who separated themselves into deserts and unfrequented places, or confined themselves to cells, monasteries, and the like, retired, as they call it, from the world. (3)

To "retreat from human society, on a religious or philosophical account" is a "mere cheat. . . . Man is a creature so formed for society, that it may not only be said that it is not good for him to be alone, but 'tis really impossible he should be alone" (10–12). Human converse (and commerce) are not at all opposed to solitude: "Men may properly be said to be alone in the midst of the crowds and hurry of men and business" (2). In fact, solitude is unavoidable: "Our meditations are all solitude in perfection; our passions are all exercised in retirement; we love, we hate, we covet, we enjoy, all in privacy and solitude. All that we communicate of those things to any other is but for their assistance in the pursuit of our desires; the end is at home; the enjoyment, the contemplation, is all solitude and retirement; it is for ourselves we enjoy, and for ourselves we suffer" (2–3). If our wants render us inherently social, our enjoyments render us inextricably private.

To illustrate this point, Defoe relates the story of a man, offended by his family, who maintains a silence for twenty-nine years (paralleling Crusoe's stay on the island). As his wife and family desert him, his willful silence lapses into literal solitude. Yet not quite; one daughter stays on to tend to her deranged father. Like Crusoe and Friday, they communicate "by signs" (4); meanwhile the metaphorical castaway "was often heard to pray to God in his solitudes very audibly and with great fervency" (5). He is saved in the end and "frequently talked with his daughter, but not much, and very seldom to anybody else" (5). The silent man performs a kind of Cartesian reduction; from his experience we learn the necessity for signification and exchange and, with them, the inexorability of representation. Crusoe infers from this example that all social commerce is theater: "Sometimes I have as much wondered why [solitude] should be any grievance or affliction, seeing upon the whole view of the stage of life which we act upon in this world it seems to me that life in general is, or ought to be, but one universal act of solitude." The difference between the "is" and the "ought" concerns our ability to regulate the signs that attach us to and separate us from the society of which we are a part. Since we apprehend others only as representations flitting before the mind's eye, a great deal hinges on our ability to interpret appearances by means of observation and reflection. "Of Solitude" demonstrates how solitude is (or "ought to be") a social state and extends the place of meditation from devotional life to all forms of social commerce. Our solitary condition is properly regulated when devotion and commerce act as checks on one another.

Defoe's identification of interpretation with commerce distinguishes his devotional writings from those of his predecessors. To apprehend the larger implications of this innovation, it will be useful to compare Defoe's procedures with those of John Bunyan. Bunyan's Christian carries out an experiment not unlike that of Defoe's castaway or Crusoe's silent man: abandoning family, calling, and citizenship, he pursues his own way. *Way* signifies method, of course, and it is worth recalling how similar Christian's experiment in enlightenment is to Descartes's meditations on first philosophy. *The Pilgrim's Progress* is, among other things, a meditational discourse on method. But to make the comparison is to underscore the difference: Christian's way is narrow but not, like Descartes's, straight. Not all ways lead to Heaven, but Bunyan makes clear that pilgrims are led there in an abundance of ways. The multiplicity of the way is underscored in the Interpreter's House episode, where Bunyan, like Descartes and Defoe, explores the relation of solitude to interpretation. Since this is perhaps the most obscure episode in part 1, we may suppose that Bunyan is attempting to make a point about obscurity.

What is being interpreted in this episode? U. Milo Kaufmann believes that "the house is the Word; and, in keeping with Puritan belief about its perspicuity, in it dwells its own sure interpreter, the Holy Spirit. Christian may be exposed to dark riddles in his exploration of the Word, but single authoritative interpretation is ever at his elbow in the person of his host." If that were true, we would find in treatises on scriptural hermeneutics our own sure guide to interpreting the interpreter. But Kaufmann hesitates when it comes down to cases: "All these scenes support a reading of the House as the Word, provided that the equivalences are not applied too rigorously. The identification served as a kind of model for Bunyan's fabrication of the episode, a model more or less embodied in its structure and detail, and the degree of embodiment conceded by the reader depends upon how persuasive he finds the evidence." Part of this evidence is "the fact that Interpreter presents Evangelist, whose picture Christian is shown initially, as 'the only Man, whom the Lord of the Place wither thou art going, hath Authorized, to be thy Guide in all difficult places thou mayest meet with in the way.'"[15] This reading, also made by Roger Sharrock, is fraught with difficulty. While the pun on *places* suggests Scripture, only one of the scenes is Biblical. Nor is Evangelist, who makes but one more inconsequential appearence, the pilgrim's guide in the episodes that follow. I suggest that in this episode Christian is being taught to walk by his own light, the candle of illumination lit by Interpreter.

This light illuminates the professor, not the Bible, and since he is being taught to reflect on himself, the Interpreter's House becomes a hall of mirrors. As in part 2, Interpreter introduces seven emblems, the number signifying fullness and closure: the picture of a very grave man, the dusty parlor, the fire against the wall, the two children, the stately palace, the man in the cage, and the man with a vision of judgment. The house is packed with "ways" of interpretation: Interpreter expounds the portrait by riddles, the dusty parlor by types, the fire by causes; the episode of the children is given a fourfold allegorical exegesis; Bunyan is prudently silent about the palace ("Then Christian smiled, and said, I think verily I know the meaning of this" 34); the man in the cage is a moral exemplum; and the dreamer makes a prophecy. Some of the scenes have later analogues (the man in the cage with Doubting Castle, the vision of judgment with crossing Jordan, and so on), but the sequence does not directly foreshadow the shape of the narrative. Rather, the design folds reflexively back onto itself, since the portrait supplies mottoes for the emblems to follow, which in turn refer back to the portrait itself. Here is the passage:

> Then said the *Interpreter,* come in, I will shew thee that which will be profitable to thee. So he commanded his man to light the Candle, and bid *Christian* follow him; so he had him into a private Room, and bid his Man open a Door; the which when he had done, *Christian* saw a Picture of a very grave Person hang up against the wall, and this was the fashion of it, *It had eyes lift up to Heaven* [1], *the best of Books in its hand,* [2], *the law of Truth was written upon its lips,* [3], *the World was behind its back* [4]; *it stood as if it pleaded with Men* [5], and a Crown of Gold did hang over its head [6]. (28–29)

In response to Christian's "What means this?" Interpreter explains that it is the portrait of a good professor: "The Man whose Picture this is, is one of thousand, he can beget Children, Travel in birth with Children, and

Providence or Prudence?

Nurse them himself when they are born" (29). The qualities I have num-
bered (1), (2), (3), and (5) "shew thee, that his work is to know, and unfold
dark things to sinners"; (4) and (6) "shew thee . . . he is sure in the world
that comes next to have Glory for his Reward." The six scenes following
the portrait of the grave way typify its character of a good professor, and
recall the emblems in the Interpreter's House: "eyes lift up" alludes to the
man in the cage "looking down to the ground" (34); "best of Books" to
"the Law" and "the Gospel" in the dusty room (30); "law of Truth" to the
bold man who storms the palace (33); "world was behind its back" to the
boy who "had his best things last" (31); "pleaded with Men" to Christ,
who pours the "Oyl of his Grace" upon the fires of devotion (32); the
"Crown of Gold" to the prophetic "Day of Judgement" (37). Interpreter
next tells Christian that this person is the only man authorized to be his
guide and admonishes him to "bear well in thy mind what thou hast seen"
lest he "meet with some that pretend to lead thee right, but their way goes
down to death" (29).

The Interpreter's House is plainly a mnemonic device, an instance of
the artificial memory professors like Christian would want to have about
them when engaging in verbal combat. Artificial memory correlates key
words or phrases with dramatic images disposed around an imaginary
room or building.[16] Interpreter, however, is not training Christian to mem-
orize texts but to reflect on who he is and how he should act. The catch
phrases – "eyes lift up to Heaven," "best of Books," and so on – are not,
as we might expect, keyed to Scripture. Bunyan turns the traditional memory system inside out, so that the architectural frame corresponds not to
the disposition of a text but to the disposition of a reader engaged in self-
reflection. The private room signifies Christian's mind, the candle his
inspiration, the portrait and attendant scenes his memories, experiences,
and anticipations. In a Baconian or Cartesian way, Bunyan substitutes an
epistemology of reflection for a text-centered logic. Rather than recalling
the authorities, Christian is taught, when confronted with dark places, to
meditate privily on what he is about. The professor, in this episode any-
way, is taught how to become an authority unto himself.

That is not to say that this is the only, or even the most common, use
to which meditation is put in *The Pilgrim's Progress;* Christian must know
his texts and when and how to deploy them. Two other allegories of interpretation illustrate Bunyan's more traditional reliance on authority. Confronting Apollyon, Christian is "wounded in his understanding, faith, and
conversation" (59). Nonetheless, the beast is sent packing by the word/

=

Forms of Reflection

sword when "*Christian* nimbly reached out his hand" for the proper passage (59). In the very next episode, however, we encounter "things that cared not for *Christian's* sword, as did Apollyon before" (63). The Valley of the Shadow of Death allegorizes dark places in Scripture (62): pilgrims there confront an "exceedingly narrow way" between a "very deep Ditch . . . into which the blind have led the blind in all Ages" (unthinking, orthodox interpretations) and "a very dangerous Quagg, into which, if even a good Man falls, he can find no bottom for his foot to stand on" (groundless, heterodox interpretations) (62). When Christian reflects inwardly (as per instruction), "one of the wicked ones . . . whisperingly suggested many grievous blasphemies to him, which he verily thought had proceeded from his own mind" (63). Bunyan's deluding demons, unlike Descartes's, do not dissolve upon the application of reason and reflection. Christian narrowly gets through this solitary passage by returning to an entirely traditional method of reading texts, the Analogy of Faith.

As these episodes indicate, Bunyan reproduces rather than resolves the seventeenth-century conflict between textual authority and the inner light. No one "way" works in all circumstances:

> He creeps, he goes, he stands; yea, who can tell
> Of all his postures? Yet there's none of these
> Will make him master of what Fowls he please.
> Yea, he must Pipe, and Whistle to catch this;
> Yet if he does so, that Bird he will miss. (3)

Bunyan's several postures are pretexts for a faith that ultimately denies all posturing. As Leopold Damrosch, Jr. expresses it: "One interprets correctly only by recognizing that all images are meretricious and are most reliable when least mimetic." Faith negates seemings, including those of the allegory itself.[17] Even the Flatterer transparently reveals himself to any "who have eyes to see" (133). In contrast to Bunyan's unmimetic images, Crusoe inhabits a more probable world of shifting appearances and complex characters: cannibals turn Christian, Christians turn pirate. The romance elements and the interpolated meditations persist, though transformed. These take on new appearances because the forms of reflection in *Crusoe* strive to combine textual authority and lived experience in a single way of interpretation that takes appearances seriously. Conceiving of both as concatenations of characters, types, and signs, the probable reasoner might reasonably hope for a common method of interpretation.

In "Of listening to the Voice of Providence," Defoe relates a series of

=

Providence or Prudence?

circumstantial narratives that take on the instructional role of the Interpreter's emblems. It is as though the sequence of episodes in which Bunyan locates interpretation were all to be contained within the House itself. As it turns out, Defoe's narratives do not fit very comfortably under a single roof. Denying himself a prior knowledge of God's moral purposes, Defoe is unsure how to organize his evidence: "It is in vain for me to run into a collection of stories; for example, where the variety is infinite, and things vary as every particular man's circumstances vary; but as every event in the world is managed by the superintendency of Providence, so every providence has in it something instructing, something that calls upon us to look up, or look out, or look in" (206). Defoe would like to offer readers a hermeneutic method that does not "vary as every particular man's circumstances vary." How can a mere "collection of stories" illustrate the great and unified design Crusoe refers to as Providence? In this essay, alone in the collection, Defoe attempts to impose order on his materials in the form a demonstrative argument. This deviation from probabilism fails miserably; it may be that Defoe intended it to fail all along.

"It is our unquestioned duty to inquire after everything in our journey to the eternal habitation which God has permitted us to know," reasons Crusoe; interpreters of Providence "make that straight path easy and pleasant to themselves, and make them useful to others by the way" (176). Defoe himself seems to sense something slightly satanic in this attempt to justify the ways of God to man: "I am making way here to one of the trees of sacred knowledge, which, though it may grow in the thickest of the wood, and be surrounded with some briars and thorns, so as to place it a little out of sight, yet I hope to prove that it is our duty to taste of it, and that the way to come at it is both practicable and plain" (177).[18] Crusoe begins his discourse with a *divisio* that distinguishes two kinds of providence:

> 1. that this eternal God guides by His providence the whole world, which He has created by His power.
> 2. that this Providence manifests a particular care over and in the governing and directing man, the best and last created creature on earth. (178)

The operative distinction is between "whole world" and "particular care," between government by regular causes or by special interventions. God exerted a predetermined design in creating the world but exercises

=

Forms of Reflection

free will in his management of human affairs. Crusoe's limitations as a theologian, already apparent from his conversations with Friday, appear again in his theodicy:

> Providence decrees that events shall attend upon causes in a direct chain, and by an evident necessity, and has doubtless left many powers of good and evil seemingly to ourselves, and, as it were, in our hands, as the natural product of such causes and consequences, which we are not to limit and cannot expressly determine about, but which we are accountable for the good or evil application of, otherwise we were in vain exhorted and commanded to do any good thing, or to avoid any wicked one. (182)

Milton had difficulties here, too. To argue the "evident necessity" of something we "cannot expressly determine about" raises theological difficulties with profound literary implications: how is God's will to be represented? To represent it as law, writers resort to demonstrative discourse; to represent it as freely offered grace, they turn to narrative. In a probable fiction that aspires to demonstration, Milton finesses this problem by putting his own demonstrations into the mouth of God (what God might have said on such an occasion), a probable fiction that aspires to demonstration. Defoe does something similar by assigning his arguments for design to Robinson Crusoe. But self-reflexive narrative strategies cannot help but undermine any claim to absolute historicity. Crusoe (like Milton and like Milton's God) has difficulties with representing providence as both design and contingency:

> It would be a very proper and useful observation here, and might take up much of this work, to illustrate the goodness of Providence, in that it is, as I say, particularly employed for the advantage of mankind. But as this is not the main design, and will come in naturally in every part of the work I am upon, I refer it to the common inferences, which are to be drawn from the particulars, as I go on. It is, indeed, the most rational foundation of the whole design before me. . . . But I return to the main subject—the voice of Providence, the language or the meaning of Providence. (180)

In fact, the "main design" must rest upon contingency—eventful structures of difference—for it is only by, in, and through historical circumstances that meditators apprehend the operations of providence. If Bunyan's pilgrim has access to truth through written authority or the inner light, Crusoe is left with only shadows of shadows: "By listening to the voice of Providence, I mean to study its meaning in every circumstance of life, in every event; to learn to understand the end and design of Providence in everything that happens, what is the design of Providence in it respecting ourselves, and what our duty to do upon the particular occasion that offers" (181–82).

We infer special providence when the outcome of an event differs from what general providence leads us to expect. Crusoe describes two kinds of special providence: concurrences and deliverances. As "strange surprizing adventures," concurrences and deliverances testify to providence by violating the regular process of cause and effect: "It is easy to know when that hand of Providence opens the door for, or shuts it against, our measures, if we will bring together, and compare former things with present, making our judgment by the ordinary rules of Heaven's dealing with men" (188). Defoe speaks of special providence as a cause ("The concurrence of events is a light to their causes," 187), yet by "concurrence" Crusoe means what we now call *coincidence*. Examples include the departure of the children of Israel from Egypt "even in the self-same day" of the year they had arrived 430 years before and the sentencing of King Charles on the very same day of the month he had signed the warrant for the Earl of Strafford's arrest (189–90). Concurrences depart from the "ordinary rules of Heaven's dealing with men" (188).[19] Deliverances testify to God's power by "the bringing of good events to pass by the most threatning causes" (201). Crusoe's unlikely deliverances are one example; in another, two condemned men are saved by three unlikely rolls of the dice (193).[20] Special providence is most probable when general providence is least probable—at those moments when historical narrative and rational demonstration refuse to coincide. "Of listening to the Voice of Providence" is one of those cases, as is *Robinson Crusoe* itself. Nowhere does Crusoe interpret the actions of providence in his life as a *whole* design; he reconstructs his life as his creator structures his romance, as a "collection of stories." In Crusoe's theology, as in picaresque narrative, episodes are the primary structural units.

Since the *divisio* between general and special providence covers all possible cases, there is no room for chance, which becomes the subject of the *confutatio* section of the demonstration. Crusoe illustrates this proposition with a fable of two travelers accosted by thieves. When one traveler attributes his fate to good fortune, the other to bad fortune, Crusoe reacts indignantly: "This is a sort of language I cannot understand; it seems to be a felonious thought in its very design, robbing Heaven of the honour due to it, and listing ourselves in the regiment of the ungrateful" (202). The travelers misread the signs, substituting their own "felonious" design for the intention of their creator. For Defoe, as for many modern historiographers, chance is unthinkable, a "mock-goddess," a sign without a referent:

> an empty idol of air, or rather an imaginary, nonsensical nothing, an image more inconsistent than those I mentioned among the Chinese; not a monster, indeed, of a frightful shape and ugly figure, loathsome and frightful, but a mere fantasm, an idea, a nonentity—a name without being, a miscalled, unborn, nothing, hap, luck, chance; that is to say, a name put upon the medium, which they set up in their imagination for want of a will to acknowledge their Maker. (202–3)

Chance is an awkward fiction, a narrative without an argument. Chance is the embarrassing inconsistencies Gildon found in *Crusoe* or the improbable relation of signifier to signified in traditional allegory. Chance is Milton's figure of Chaos, which Defoe is probably recalling in this passage.[21]

If "Of listening to the Voice of Providence" is unconvincing as theology, it remains a very canny piece of writing. It is Crusoe's theodicy, after all, and if it fails to stand on its own feet, we recall that it is an argument incorporated into an essay incorporated into a fiction. The choice of genre is strategic here, since the essay form stands between the uniformity of demonstrative logic and the multiplicity of collections of stories. As an essay, "Of listening to the Voice of Providence" can get by with the mere appearance of probability. Seventeenth- and eighteenth-century writers turned to essay, as they did to georgic, as a means of building consensus. If demonstrative arguments achieve certainty, they require a reader's assent to dogmatic first principles; probable arguments link causes to effects without certainty but require from readers only *common* sense. For some readers Crusoe's show of demonstrative reasoning would confirm previously held convictions; for others it would reinforce the conviction that demonstrative arguments are less convincing than merely circumstantial linkages of time and place. I suspect that Defoe was of the latter persuasion.

Like Donne in the *Essayes in Divinity*, Defoe turns to essay and prudential disposition to represent the prudence of "a wise disposer of things. . . . People that tie up all to events and causes, strip the provi-

=

Providence or Prudence?

dence of God which guides the world of all its superintendency, and leave it no room to act as a wise disposer of things" (198). Providence, like the essay genre, disposes its matter as the occasion warrants. Yet Defoe tries hard to give to Crusoe's merely probable arguments an appearance of demonstration:

> 'Tis sufficient to the honour of an immutable Deity, that, for the common incidents of life, they be left to the disposition of a daily agitator, namely, divine Providence, to order and direct them, as it shall see good, within the natural limits of cause and consequence. This seems to me a much more rational system than that of tying up the hands of the Supreme Power to a road of things [way or method], so that none can be acted or permitted but such as was appointed before to be acted and permitted. (199)

Crusoe seems to have forgotten his prior remark that "providence decrees that events shall attend upon causes in a direct chain."

Like the larger work of which it is a part, Defoe's essay is, in the last analysis, a collection of stories, a set of congruent or opposing narratives that together make a probable case for a providential design that interpreters must ultimately take on faith. In this respect it is like *The Pilgrim's Progress*. But unlike Bunyan, who changes his mode of interpretation as circumstances warrant, Defoe favors a single mode of interpretation that assumes variable circumstances while giving up the possibility of certainty offered by textual authorities or inward light. Defoe's slippage from demonstrative into probabilistic argument is typical of eighteenth-century writers who to avoid controversy assign to essay and fable the kinds of weighty critical tasks previously restricted to logical disputation and sacred history.[22] For them, as for us, truth was becoming a matter of adjudicating between competing representations.

For this reason, Defoe's attempts to wrestle with providence often have a familiar ring to them. The chief interest of *Robinson Crusoe* for Marxist criticism may now reside less in its economic themes than in its narrative strategies. Like post-Marxists today, Defoe had a troublesome relationship to "the good old cause": once the old prophecies failed to come to pass, dissenters needed to reformulate procedures for interpreting history. The ways in which Defoe cons providence often resemble those in which critics now construe History. Eroding distinctions between fact and fiction, post-Marxists assign to ideology something like the explanatory role Defoe assigns to fabulation. Geoffrey M. Sill argues that

=

Forms of Reflection
102

"rather than applying formal or generic definitions of 'fiction' to some of Defoe's work and not to the rest of it, we need to understand that, in Defoe's hands, ideology and fiction were related and interdependent forms of knowledge. Though neither ideology nor fiction is usually thought of as 'knowledge,' they were for Defoe a way of knowing and, finally, of changing the world."[23] McKeon, *The Origins of the English Novel*, reaches a similar conclusion: "*Robinson Crusoe* at times emits the aura of irony because, like all ideology, it is dedicated to the instrumental disclosure — in Defoe's case with unparalleled penetration and candor — of a complex of contradictions that it is simultaneously dedicated to mediating and rendering intelligible" (332). When all ideology is seen as dedicated to disclosing contradictions, Marxist criticism has indeed undergone a sea change.

Since providence and ideology serve equivalent explanatory functions (finding a concealed order in a complex of seemingly unrelated areas of experience, reducing apparent contingency to underlying prior causes, and providing a basis for moral judgments), do Defoe's hermeneutic procedures have a bearing on our own practices of writing history? I think so. If in traditional Marxist narratives History acts like general providence, according to regular laws, in revisionary Marxism History acts like special providence, appearing in contradictions and ruptures. As Tony Bennett writes, "There is no longer any political point to be served by the attempt to organize and validate continuist and unifying narratives of history through the constitution of literary texts as privileged representations through which the developmental course of the real might be deciphered."[24]

But if "the developmental course of the real" now seems thoroughly problematic, the desire for narrative closure is still strong. Historians still pursue the figure (or the disfigurement) in the carpet, now perceived as the design underlying a "complex of contradictions." Consider, for instance, the kind of history in which McKeon, *Origins*, locates *Robinson Crusoe*:

> At the beginning of the period of our concern, the reigning narrative epistemology involves a dependence on received authorities and a priori traditions; I will call this posture "romance idealism." In the seventeenth century it is challenged and refuted by an empirical epistemology that derives from many sources, and this I will call "naive empiricism." But this negation of romance, having embarked on a jour-

ney for which it has no maps, at certain points loses its way. And it becomes vulnerable, in turn, to a countercritique "extreme skepticism." . . . For questions of virtue, the terms alter, but the two-stage pattern of reversal is very much the same as for questions of truth. We begin with a relatively stratified social order supported by a reigning world view that I will call "aristocratic ideology." Spurred by social change, this ideology is attacked and subverted by its prime antagonist, "progressive ideology." But at a certain point, progressive ideology gives birth to its own critique, which is both more radical than itself, and harks back to the common, aristocratic enemy. I will call this countercritique, "conservative ideology." (21)

If the novel is still the privileged representation through which we are to perceive the "developmental course of the real," this account differs from traditional Marxist literary history in its bold recourse to allegory. Moreover, the allegory is plainly Defovian, since McKeon's history of fiction reproduces the younger-son narrative he discovers in *Robinson Crusoe*: a reigning world view "gives birth" to a rebellious ideology and epistemology "embarks on a journey." For Defoe, the "real story" is God's providence; for McKeon, it is the corruption and regeneration of a world view. But there are significant differences. As much as Defoe might like to believe in a general providence, his commitment to circumstantiality and probabilism leads him away from the kind of narrative McKeon uses to reduce multiplicity to an orderly design. Hence Crusoe's multiple narratives, his alternative explanations, his resistances to demonstrative argument and narrative closure.

If the idea of casting a history of eighteenth-century narratives as an eighteenth-century narrative is attractive, McKeon's design fails to pay due heed to the complexities of designs like Defoe's. *Robinson Crusoe* is not one story, but many stories—the Prodigal Son narrative is one narrative among others and not the whole story. The multiplicity of Defoe's storytelling, his deferrals of closure, and the variety of his narratives lend probability to his confrontations with providence. For all its impressive detail, McKeon's narrative lacks probability because it circumscribes the complexity and multiplicity of generic differences in seventeenth- and eighteenth-century literature. While competition between novel and romance is an important element, it is but one element among others. The major genres are too multiplicitous to be usefully cast as protagonists in an Oedipal narrative, nor do they correspond to social classes in any

=

Forms of Reflection
104

straightforward way; tinkers wrote romances, aristocrats sung ballads, and persons of all ranks penned meditations. The social significance of a genre is not intrinsic but depends on circumstances. If a generic history is to take these differences into account, a collection of stories might be preferred to more conventional kinds of narrative history.

In traditional Marxist historiography, the real story is material history, which literature is said to reflect. Since this distinction between the real and its representations now seems untenable, we may well ask whether the concept of ideology any longer serves a useful critical function. My own belief is that it does not. Rather than regarding genres as ideological constructs, I prefer to think of ideology as a literary construct, a way of combining particular kinds of material into a particular kind of history. As a literary construct, ideology is also a historical construct, a critical strategy used to impose closure on circumstantiality and, more recently, to reduce disciplinary differences to a comprehensive science of interpretation. Not all critics writing about ideology pursue such totalizing aims of course, but why then speak of ideology? Let us consider the differences that literature makes, the way writing as such operates within society. Bennett, *Outside Literature*, convincingly calls for "a sociology which, unlike classical Marxism or classical sociology, will not construe literary and other texts as the epiphenomenal manifestations of underlying social 'realities' but will rather insist on their status as directly active components in the organization of social relations themselves" (35). Since *Robinson Crusoe* is an instance of political, theological, and economic writing, we do not need a redundant term to explain how these matters function as parts of the work or how the work reflects an ideology or a culture. The real story, if we may still call it that, is in the writing, not above, below, or behind it. As we shall see, this is just the turn taken by Defoe's reflections on providence.

Traffic in Fictions

To bracket absolute claims to truth is not necessarily to do away with regulation; most often it implies shifting the work of regulation to social norms. This concluding section considers what Defoe has to say about the ethics of fabulation and the relation of honesty to commerce. Reflecting on "the happy concurrence of the causes which had brought the event of my prosperity to pass," Crusoe notices "how much of it all depended . . . upon the principle of honesty which I met with in almost all of the people whom it was my lot to be concerned with. . . . [I] could not but be something taken up with the miracles of honesty that I had met with among the several people I had met with" (16). Extraordinary as those providences were, Crusoe goes on to illustrate just how much of everyday life depends upon honesty, that "subtle and imperceptible thing" (22) which is the foundation of good criticism, religious faith, and commercial credit. Like everything else in *Crusoe*, honesty can only be known by inference, revealed through complexes of signs, characters, marks, notices, and testimonies. While issues of regulation and interpretation recur throughout *Serious Reflections*, they are the particular subjects of "The Trial of Honesty." The topic was close to home; in 1720, Defoe's reputation was in such disrepair that he may have had little choice but to enlist honest Crusoe in his defense.[25]

All he asks for is *justice,* the term probabilists use to describe the correspondence between circumstance and inference. As we have seen, "Robinson Crusoe's Preface" implies that Defoe's life is the "*just* subject of these volumes" and claims that "there is not a circumstance in the imaginary story but has its *just* allusion to a real story" (x, xii, my emphasis). Defoe's willingness to accept circumstantial evidence as "just" testimony contrasts sharply with hermeneutic procedures in *The Pilgrim's Progress*. In response to Christian's question, "*Will your Practice stand a trial at law?*" Formalist and Hypocrisy mount a probable argument:

> They told him, That Custom, it being of so long a standing, as above a thousand years, would doubtless now be admitted as a thing legal, by any Impartial Judge. And besides, said they, so be we get into the way, what's matter which way we get in? if we are in, we are in: thou art but in the way, who, as we perceive, came in at the Gate; and we are also in the way that came tumbling over the wall: Wherein now is thy condition any better than ours?

Drawing inferences from circumstances, the self-deceivers "perceive" that their case is no different from Christian's. But Bunyan's hero rejects the idea that truth can be gathered from custom and circumstances: "I walk by the Rule of my Master, you walk by the rude working of your fancies" (40).[26] Probability is also tried and found lacking in the Vanity Fair episode, where Faithful, hauled before Judge Hategood, is charged with "disloyal notions, which he in the general calls Principles of Faith and Holiness" (93). Envy, Superstition, and Pickthank charge Faithful with undermining the state, the church, and the social hierarchy, respectively.

≡

Forms of Reflection

The charges are just, and the evidence probable. But the law is shown to be "unjust" when the martyr "straightway was carried up through the clouds, with sound of Trumpet, the nearest way to the Coelestial Gate" (97). The trial of Ignorance likewise underscores the limits of perception: "*Indeed, the Word saith,* He hath blinded their eyes, lest they should see" (150).

The many trials discussed in *Serious Reflections* instruct readers to justify their faith by appearances and probable circumstances. Defoe's unhappy experiences in trade plainly inform Crusoe's understanding of divine justice. "No man can be just to his Maker" (23); neither can commerce thrive without the occasional forgiveness of debts:

> To pay every man their own is the common law of honesty, but to do good to all mankind, as far as you are able, is the chancery law of honesty; and though, in common law or justice, as I call it, mankind can have no claim upon us if we do but just pay our debts, yet in heaven's chancery they will have relief against us, for they have a demand in equity of all the good to be done them that it is in our power to do, and this chancery court, or court of equity, is held in every man's breast—'tis a true court of conscience, and every man's conscience is a lord chancellor to him. (17–18)

This distinction recalls that between general and special providence; common law measures the bare facts against a general rule, while chancery law takes circumstances into consideration by appealing to a particular defendant's general probity and probable intention. King David, while he committed the basest acts, remained in good credit with heaven; so too, a series of accidents can break a merchant without touching the principle of his honesty (40–41). To judge a person's *probity,* one reflects on circumstances and the marks of character. Crusoe declines to "examine whether honesty be a natural or an acquired virtue—whether a habit or a quality—whether inherent or accidental: all the philosophical part of it I choose to omit" (22–23). Instead of reasoning demonstratively, he discourses on honesty "as it looks from one man to another, in those necessary parts of man's life, his conversation and negotiation, trusts, friendships, and all the incidents of human affairs" (23). Honesty is not an inherent but a relative quality that is revealed in and through commerce. To bring this point home to his readers, Defoe claims his bookseller will accept returns from anyone who doubts Crusoe's veracity (24).

David Morris points out that, for Alexander Pope, character is where politics, property, and money necessarily intersect."[27] Like Pope, Defoe would regulate a moral economy by means of character, but, like Pope, he finds character a very slippery subject. Commerce requires propriety and integrity, but how are we to distinguish sincere honesty from apparent honesty? Cunning "is so like honesty, that many a man has been deceived with it, and has taken one for t'other in the market; nay, I have heard of some who have planted this wild honesty, as we may call it, in their own ground, have use of it in their friendships and dealings, and thought it had been the true plant, but they always lost credit by it" (29). To divine an intention, a circumstantial narrative is required.

Defoe asks us to imagine a rich gentleman who has lent money to his neighbor, a thriving merchant. When the merchant goes bankrupt, the lender rails at his dishonesty: He is a knave, a rogue, and don't pay people what he owes them" (34). But when the gentleman's title to his estates proves defective, "'Well,' says the merchant, 'and why don't you pay my cousin, your old neighbour, the money you borrowed him?'" To which the gentleman can only reply: "I really designed to be honest" (37). Thus far the story illustrates the difference between facts and intentions; Defoe next alters the circumstances to discriminate sincere honesty from its evil twin. After compounding with his creditors, the merchant becomes prosperous again and pays the debts for which he was no longer liable; the gentleman goes abroad and, making his fortune under a foreign prince, "sets up for the same honest man he did before"—leaving his debts unpaid (38). It is not particularly difficult to infer from circumstances who is the honest man; nor is it difficult to infer that the mercantile system of credit encourages virtue, while the legal system encourages chicanery. The merchants, who put a probable construction on events, look to the future and are rewarded accordingly.[28] The gentry, who concern themselves with titles rather than types, get only what they deserve.

Whether by accident or design, Defoe's remarks about honesty and credit engage another allegory, *The Fable of the Bees* (1714). "To make a great an honest hive," argues Bernard Mandeville, would certainly bring it low. At the heart of this sprawling menippean structure is *The Grumbling Hive* (1705), a verse fable describing how Jove, tired of civil brawling,

> At last in Anger swore, *He'd rid*
> *The bawling Hive of Fraud;*
> and did.[29]

Repentful of their sinful condition, the citizens retire into the shrubbery, reducing society to a situation not unlike Crusoe's island prior to improve-

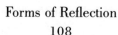

ment. The 1714 *Fable* appends a series of essays and reflections, beginning with an introductory "Enquiry into the Origin of Moral Virtue," which underscores the utility of fabling: "The Chief Thing, therefore, which Lawgivers and other wise Men, that have laboured for the Establishment of Society, have endeavour'd, has been to make the People they were to govern, *believe*, that it was more beneficial for every Body to conquer than indulge his Appetites, and much better to mind the Publick than what seem'd his private Interest" (1:42, my emphasis). The entire edifice of civilization rests upon this founding fiction; belief in disinterestedness divides society into a mass of "grov'ling Wretches" pursuing sensual gratification and a much smaller class of "lofty high-spirited Creatures" who seek to improve their minds (1:43–44). The system works to everyone's benefit: underlings praise virtue to conceal their vices, superiors to maintain their privileges. In addition to the "Enquiry," Mandeville points the moral of his fable in twenty-two (later twenty-four) appended essays. These explicate *The Grumbling Hive* in the same ways *Serious Reflections* explicates *Robinson Crusoe*, expounding the mysteries of providence through circumstantial evidence and inference.

Mandeville's history of civil society bears somewhat the same relation to the beast fable as the relation traditional Marxists draw between material history and eighteenth-century novels: the former is the real story that the latter allegorizes. But Mandeville, like Defoe, seems to have taken the post-Marxist turn, since *The Fable of the Bees* plainly understands the "real" as a relation between representations. If the "Enquiry" "reflects" the fable (inverted and transposed), this "real" story is itself offered as speculation: "This was (or at least might have been) the manner after which Savage Man was broke" (1:46).[30] Like most speculative histories, the "Enquiry" deduces its narrative from foundational philosophical principles: "It is impossible to judge of a Man's Performance, unless we are thoroughly acquainted with the Principle and Motive from which he acts" (56). Mandeville is quite aware that without Momus's glass, such a thorough acquaintance is fantasy. As in "Of listening to the Voice of Providence," we are confronted with a demonstration of principles that can only be known through probable inference, and, as before, narrative and demonstration pull in opposite directions. Why should Mandeville's speculations be any more credible than those of the misguided wights in his story:

> For it is highly probable, that some of them, convinced by the real
> Proofs of Fortitude and Self-Conquest they had seen, would admire in

Providence or Prudence?

others what they found wanting in themselves; others be afraid of the Resolution and Prowess of those of the second Class, and that all of them were kept in aw by the Power of their Rulers; wherefore it is reasonable to think, that none of them (whatever they thought in themselves) would dare openly contradict, what by everybody else was thought Criminal to doubt of. (1:45–46).

One of the chief props of disinterested virtue is, after all, "romance."

Since these citizens are misled by the same kinds of "proof" Mandeville offers himself (testimony, fable, and opinion), the argument appears to be at an impasse—one representation of human motivation squared off against another. Mandeville acknowledges the uncertainty of his conclusions when he confidently predicts that his fable will never demystify the idea of virtue: few persons will believe a story so contrary to received opinion. But this outcome only confirms the argument, since the beauty of providence (like that of history) is that it operates quite independently of anything we can know or say about it. Like modern exponents of some of the more radical critical theories, Mandeville regards critical reflection as useful only for consciousness raising; he exhorts readers "to look at home, and examining their own Consciences, be made asham'd of always railing at what they are more or less guilty of themselves" (1:8).

Unlike Mandeville, Defoe introduces a distinction between Providence and providence, inconsistently leaving the door open for irregularity. Because Defoe's notion of providence attributes consequences to human intentions, his moral economy requires regulations that Mandeville does not regard as necessary. The kind of interventions Defoe has in mind appear in his remarks on storytelling, for, unlike Mandeville, Defoe thinks that the kind of story one tells does make a difference. The principle of regulation upheld in *Serious Reflections* is honesty. Mandeville regards sharp dealing as necessary, even beneficial, to the great design of commerce. Defoe argues that since the whole system of credit turns on the honesty and good intentions of merchants, deception should not and cannot be tolerated. He compares trading upon bad credit to passing counterfeit coins:

> But if the fraud may be carried on, as you are manifestly willing, consenting, and instrumental in it that it should, behold the consequence: your first sin against honesty is multiplied in all the hands through whom this piece of bad money knowingly so passes, till at last it happens to go single to a poor man that can't put it off, and the wrong and injury may issue where it was wanted to buy bread for a starving family. (50)

=

Forms of Reflection

Private vices do not benefit the public when deceit undermines credit. Defoe is more confident than Mandeville that people will not be long deceived: those who practice cunning "always lost credit by it."

In "Of the Immorality of Conversation," Defoe returns to this issue in his attempt to differentiate between kinds of storytelling. There is "a spreading evil in telling a false story as true, namely, that you put it into the mouths of others, and it continues a brooding forgery to the end of time. . . . [But] parables and the inventions of men, published histori- cally, are once for all related, and, the moral being drawn, the history remains allusive only as it was intended" (99, 103). Speaking of this pas- sage, Lennard Davis writes: "Defoe apparently could not find a category to define the nature of his work. . . . The only preexisting category that defined a type of narrative both true and false was allegory." Judging that "Defoe's flight to the allegorical cannot be taken seriously," *Factual Fic- tions* describes Defoe's reasoning as "deranged."[31] Foucaultian premises lead Davis to discern an undifferentiated discourse, but surely the inven- tor of allusive allegorical history suffers, if anything, from an abundance of distinctions. In this instance, Defoe draws a circumstantial, rather than a categorical, distinction between fact and fiction: depending on how they are related, true stories become fictions, and fictions become true stories. As the counterfeit analogy suggests, the "honesty" of a representation is not a function merely of the referent (or "face value") but of where the rep- resentation comes from and where it is going. For this reason the essay on conversation discriminates four kinds of stories. Two are "forgeries": "Some tell formal stories forged in their own brain without any retrospect either on persons or things" while others, "out of the same forge of inven- tion, hammer out the very person, man or woman"; the first type of forg- eries begin, " 'There was a man,' or 'There was a woman,' " the second type begin, " 'I knew the man,' or 'I knew the woman' " (101).[32] Two other kinds are factual: parables like *Crusoe* and "stories which have a real exis- tence in fact, but which, by the barbarous way of relating, become as romantic and false as if they had no real original." There are four kinds because, to the traditional distinction between history and fiction, Defoe adds a second distinction between the honest or deceitful intention of the storyteller.

The issue is not just what the story says but how, when, and where it is told; unlike hopelessly mutable oral tales that are "vamped, doubled, and redoubled," vendable and published works like *Crusoe* bear the marks of probity: "The selling or writing a parable, or an allusive allegoric history, is quite a different case, and is always distinguished from this other jesting with truth, that it is designed and effectually turned for instructive and upright ends, and has its moral justly applied" (101).[33] Stories may be true in more than one way, even in the case of published works that remain "allusive only as intended" (103). Unlike a "chimney corner romance" (103), *Robinson Crusoe* supposedly alludes to real stories of God's providence but also self-reflexively to the design informing its several parts; by virtue of this literary design, *Crusoe* also testifies to the honest moral design of its human creator.[34] Any reader can infer honesty from its signs, signatures, and circumstances—but only the honest reader will take the trouble. *Just* representation requires honesty from both parties in the exchange; anyone misrepresenting an author's design is "a reading knave . . . and upon such an one all the labour is lost" (24). Such a reader is as much a rogue as the two travelers who misconstrue God's providence as mere chance.

Perhaps sensing that his argument is chasing its own tail, Crusoe announces that his trial of honesty is not finished yet: "If any man object here that the preceding volumes of this work seem to be hereby condemned, and the history which I have therein published of myself censured, I demand in justice such objector stay his censure till he sees the end of the scene, when all that mystery shall discover itself, and I doubt not but the work shall abundantly justify the design, and the design abundantly justify the work" (103). We are to wait for the concluding *Vision of the Angelic World*, Defoe's most daring juxtaposition of probabilistic narrative with devotional meditation. Readers who expect the crooked way to be made straight are in for further disappointment. Appearing with its own title page, *A Vision* is, on the one hand, just another "collection of stories" and, on the other hand, a key to *Serious Reflections* in the same way that *Serious Reflections* is a key to *Robinson Crusoe*. Defoe, in short, ups the ante without changing his game. As before, he juxtaposes several kinds of stories so that one kind of representation can comment on another. This time, however, the sequence of stories is more carefully plotted. Baine, *Daniel Defoe and the Supernatural*, is mistaken when he comments that "the vision framework itself is of little significance, and it was used for only a sixth of the entire work" (14). The relation between the visionary journey and its elaborate frames required a great deal of working out; to the probabilist, circumstances are all important.

The heart of *A Vision* is the two long yarns about spirits, but Crusoe precedes them with a complex and unusually skeptical discussion of the

=

Forms of Reflection
112

supernatural. The sequence of stories resembles that of *Pilgrim's Progress*, a series of false bottoms leading to the conclusion that doubt is the condition of faith ("if you are uncertain, that is a step to conviction," 304).[35] For example, the castaway describes how on the island "I saw, nay, I felt apparitions plainly and distinctly as ever I felt or saw any real substance in my life" (242); these vapors, the effects of solitude, dispersed when "I got my man Friday with me . . . and then, having company to talk to, the hypo wore off, and I did not see any more devils after that" (247). But neither can the matter be settled by merely appealing to probability or common sense; a skeptic argues that dreams cannot be considered significant because they fail to meet the probabilistic criteria of clarity, concurrence of causes, constancy, consistency, and uniformity. All five of these arguments are then answered by a believer: dreams may be from God even if we do not have the capacity to understand them. He too has probability on his side, in the testimony of sacred history and received opinion. In such difficult cases, Crusoe is willing to "let every one judge for himself" (255–58).

After this exchange (it is one of the "I knew the man" stories), Crusoe falls into a reverie or "waking dream," which, like Bunyan's allegory, leaves the dreamer in full possession of his faculties:

> Whether my imagination is more addicted to realizing the things I talk of, as if they were in view, I know not, or whether by the power of the converse of spirits I speak of I was at the time enabled to entertain clearer ideas of the invisible world, I really cannot tell, but I certainly made a journey to all those supposed habitable bodies in my imagination, and I know not but it may be very useful to tell you what I met with in my way, and what the wiser I am for the discovery; whether you will be the wiser for the relation at second hand, I cannot answer for that. (258–59)

Believe it if you will. Defoe probably intends an allusion to Lucian's skeptical *A True Story*, but the chief source for the vision is "Mr. Milton, whose imagination was carried up to a greater height than I am now" (273). Crusoe travels up to a vantage from which the springs and levers of providence are laid bare. There he enjoys a prospect of the "economy of Heaven" (274) by which spirits manage affairs below. Spirits, we learn, do not cause human actions but control them indirectly by manipulating human desires. Satan and his agents are dream merchants, traffickers in fiction. Literalizing Milton's epic similes (and parodying his georgic catalogues), Crusoe represents Satan as a trader colonizing distant parts of the globe:

> He has his peculiar agents for this work, which he makes detachments of, as his occasions require, some to one part of the world, and some to another, as to the North America, even as far as to the frozen province of Greenland; to the north of Europe, to the Laplanders, Samoiedes, and Mongol Tartars; also to the Gog and Magog of Asia, and to the devil-makers of China and Japan; again to the southern parts of Asia, to the isles of the Indian and South Seas, and to the south part of America and Africa. (268)

Arrayed against Satan and his minions are "good angels or good spirits which are employed by a superior authority, and from a place infinitely distant and high above the devil's bounds . . . not only equal, I say equal at least, in number, but infinitely superior in power" (269). The turn to Milton at this point is likely motivated by Gildon's hilarious parody of *Crusoe*; in a bit of Lucianic one-upmanship, Defoe rams *Paradise Lost* back down his literal-minded critic's throat.

As in Mandeville's speculative history of the origin of moral virtue, so in Crusoe's vision there is a self-reflexive relationship between the vision itself and the spirits the vision visualizes. Defoe ironically implies that historians of providence, like the agents of providence, are fabricators: "You will ask me how I came to know all this?" says Crusoe, "I say, ask me no questions till the elevation of your fancy carries you up to the outer edge of the atmosphere, as I tell you mine did" (270). He encourages readers to be skeptical, but not too skeptical:

> This thought, however laid down in a kind of jest, is very seriously intended, and would, if well digested [a Miltonic pun?], direct us very clearly in our judgement of dreams, viz., not to suggest them to be always things of mere chance; but that sometimes they are to be heeded as useful warnings of evil or good by the agency of good spirits, as at other times they are the artful insinuations of the devil to inject wicked thoughts and abhorred abominable ideas into the mind. (273–74)

Defoe gives us a peep behind the curtain to reveal that beneath appearances lie still further appearances. Once more, we are left with the problem of distinguishing between kinds of representation, and once more the criteria for judgment are circumstances and honesty. For circumstances we have the situation of the vision in a pious work, and for precedents,

=

Forms of Reflection

Scripture, *Scipio's Dream*, and *Paradise Lost*. Defoe's fabulation may also be distinguished from the Devil's by its "honest" intention—Crusoe represents his representation *as* a representation—and by its pious design. In sum, when they are not "things of mere chance," visions assume a form that enables us to judge where they come from and what they are worth.

The concluding tale of the Atheists' Club makes the same point in another way. This elaborate story about testimony falls into the "There was a man" type; since it is not attested, we are invited to regard it as fiction (296). Crusoe pits rational disputation against probable inference, dialectic against narrative hermeneutics. The atheists are divinity students who "ran up their superficial notions in divinity to such a height that, instead of reasoning themselves into good principles of religion, they really reasoned themselves out of all religion whatsoever" (296–97). Good dialecticians, they insist that only what can be "defined" counts as knowledge.

The story describes the conversion of two of these scholars, one by external, the other by internal, revelations. The first is taken aback when "a great flash of lightening more than ordinarily surprized him." He begins to reflect on circumstances: "'*Where* am I going? *What* am I going about? *Who* is it has stopped me thus? *Why* are these thunders, these rains, and this lightening thus terrible? and *whence* are they?' And with the rest came in this thought, warm and swift as the lightning which had terrified him before, 'What if there should be a God! what will become of me then?'" (298–99, my emphasis). Frightened half out of his wits, he still has enough presence of mind to work through the "places" and infer the will of Providence. He returns home rather than proceeding on to the club. The second scholar, also an atheist, knocks at his door but is turned away by a man who mimics the first scholar's voice: "O sir, beseech them all to repent; for, depend upon it, there is a God! tell them I said so" (300). This second scholar is then driven into a bookstall by the rain, where he meets a third scholar who is still a believer. This old acquaintance has just read some verses that put him in mind of his sodden friend, who naturally wants to see them. Drawing him to the back of the shop, he offers to let the atheist read the lines, but only if he can hold his hand and stare into his face. His friend consents reluctantly:

Ath. I'll warrant you I'll read them. [*He reads.*]
"But if it should fall out, as who can tell,

=

Providence or Prudence?

That there may be a God, a heaven, and hell,*
Had I not best consider well for fear
'T should be too late when my mistakes appear?"

[*He held him by the hand till that word, and then let it go, pressing gently one of his fingers.] (302, brackets in original)

The atheist betrays visible signs of emotion. He is even more moved when the third scholar unknowingly repeats the very words he had heard at the first scholar's house: "O sir, I beseech you, repent; for certainly there is a God, depend upon it; I say so" (305). Frightened by this concurrence, the second atheist returns to the first atheist, who of course knows nothing about the matter. Both are convinced that an invisible spirit has intervened, and they repent.

I've had to be somewhat circumstantial in relating this story, because the narrative stands upon circumstances. When the first scholar reflects probabilistically on the thunderbolt, he is convinced of what he had known all along but had been unable to explain dialectically. The third scholar infers, also on the basis of signs, that the second scholar was likewise a closet believer. The second scholar himself concludes from a concurrence of circumstances that he has heard a spirit. Like the journey to the upper atmosphere, this story permits us a peep behind the scenes: we know, as the characters do not, that the spirit was a human being—and in more ways than one. The verses in question first appear in Defoe's earlier providential history, *The Storm* (1703), which is presumably the book the third scholar was reading when the second scholar came in out of the rain.[36] Like one of the signature appearances of Alfred Hitchcock, Defoe dramatizes his instrumental role in fabricating providential history. But if this story encourages us to be skeptical, it also instructs us to credit an author's good intention:

Let me observe that this [fable] should not at all hinder us from making a very good use of such things; for many a voice may be directed from heaven that is not immediately spoken from thence. . . . So doubtless He that made all things and created all things, may appoint instruction to be given by fortuitous accidents, and may direct concurring circumstances to touch and affect the mind as much and as effectually as if they had been immediate and miraculous.   (313)

=

Forms of Reflection

If a providential history fails to be true in one sense, it may nonetheless be true in another. I doubt that Gildon would have accepted this apology for sacred fabulation, but he was not heard from again.

A Vision of the Angelic World attempts to set meditational writing on a different footing from that it occupied in the seventeenth century. The conventional opening lines recall the genres Defoe will subvert: "They must be much taken up with the satisfaction of what they are already, that never spare their thoughts upon the subject of what they shall be. The place, the company, the employment, must certainly be well worth our while to enquire after here" (237). Just so, Donne asks readers of his *Progres* to "Double on heaven, thy thoughts on earth emploid," and Bunyan's *Progress* also promises to make travelers of its readers. In his *Saint's Everlasting Rest*, Richard Baxter likewise endorses mental traveling:

> Suppose thou wert now beholding this City of God; and that thou hadst been companion with John in his Majesty, the Heavenly Hosts, the shining Splendor which he saw: Draw as strong suppositions as may be from thy sense for the helping of thy affections: It is lawful to suppose we did see for the present that which God hath in Prophecies revealed, and which we must really see in more unspeakable brightness before long. Suppose therefore with thy self thou hadst been that Apostles fellow traveller into the Celestial Kingdom, and that thou hadst seen all the Saints in their white Robes, with Palms in their-hands: Suppose thou hadst heard those Songs of Moses and of the Lamb: or didst even now hear them praising and glorifying the Living God; if thou hadst seen these things indeed, in what a Rapture wouldst thou have been? And the more seriously thou puttest this supposition to they self, the more will the Meditation elevate thy heart.[37]

In contrast to these seventeenth-century works, Crusoe returns from his progress a disillusioned traveler: "It is all romance . . . all visions, or propounded visions, either of heaven or hell, are mere delusions of the mind, and generally are fictions of a waking bewildered head; and you may see the folly of them in the meanest of the descriptions, which generally end in showing some glorious place, fine walks, noble illustrious palaces, gardens of gold, and people of shining forms and the like" (277). Such visions may be "lawful" extensions of scripture, but they violate all probability. They are not honest.

It is otherwise with writers who represent their fables as fables. Crusoe mentions a gypsy, "a little honester than her profession intimated, and [who] freely confessed it was all a cheat, and that they knew nothing of fortunes, but had a course or round of doubtful expressions, to amuse ignorant people and get a little money" (276). Like gypsies, authors exchange probable narratives for cash, but, unlike gypsies, they do not intend to deceive. Their design is not to inform readers of a fabulous future state but of what they are: "Yet let me give you this for a check to your imagination . . . you must not be surprised if I am come down again from the verge of the world of spirits the same short-sighted wretch as to futurity and things belonging to heaven and hell as I went up; for elevations of this kind are meant only to give us a clearer view of what we are, not of what we shall be, and 'tis an advantage worth travelling for too" (278). *A Vision* undermines earlier meditational procedures to underscore what Defoe regards as most valuable in contemplative writing—a just knowledge of who and what we are within the acknowledged limits of historical understanding, personal experience, and common sense. Providential histories teach prudence; prudence lends credit to providence: as "every event in the world is managed by the superintendency of Providence, so every providence has in it something instructing, something that calls upon us to look up, or look out, or look in."

Defoe combines meditational and narrative genres in order to address questions of authority left unresolved by appeals to sacred texts or the inner light. I have argued that (1) Defoe has Crusoe respond to Gildon's pamphlet in order to undermine ontological distinctions between history and fiction; that (2) he develops an innovative theory of types and probable inference that permits him to judge representations by using one narrative to comment on another; and that (3) he attempts to regulate interpretation by a commercial ethic of prudence, honesty, and credit. While there are precedents for Defoe's procedures, *Serious Reflections* innovates by establishing a common ground between literary criticism, theology, and commercial ethics. Rather than seeking a foundation for truth in texts, traditions, or the light of reason, Defoe looks to probable inference as a means for making judgments. Since inferences are made by reflecting on circumstance, Defoe's "allusive allegorical history" combines meditation with narrative genres. While many of his concerns are secular, Defoe's literary practices indicate that he is extending rather than diminishing the domain of providence and religious contemplation. Defoe's new conception of typology led to alterations in both meditational and narrative genres. He modifies sacred writing by introducing novelistic

≡

Forms of Reflection
118

standards of probability and Restoration fiction by correlating its themes of commerce and deception with providential history. If the *Serious Reflections* quickly dropped out of sight, Defoe's concept of allegorical history nonetheless became a staple of "serious" novels to follow, including *Tom Jones, Clarissa,* and *The Vicar of Wakefield* — all of which explore narrative territories first charted by Defoe's fugitive friend.

≡

Providence or Prudence?

4

Eighteenth-Century Georgic

Sexual Commerce
and the Hertford Circle

Eighteenth-century observers believed that commerce and refinement would femininize British literature and society, and so, by and large, they did. This chapter examines how meditational writings composed by, for, and about the countess of Hertford contributed to this civilizing process. Women obviously enjoy a high profile in this material: if earlier georgics catalogue a chaste wife as one among other domestic pleasures, in later poems the wife is likely to be the addressee, even the author. This shift in the place of women in poetry corresponds to a shift in the places where cultivation was pursued; with the decline of court and university patronage, private homes became centers for the production and consumption of polite literature; as taste challenged munificence as a criterion for social discrimination, women especially stood to benefit. Since genres concerned with civility and domestic life—fiction, essay, the familiar letter—were generally regarded as a feminine province, in this arena women could claim a status equal to or greater than that of their brothers and husbands.

But contemporary critics put the emphasis on commerce rather than competition; Addison, Pope, Johnson, and Richardson imitated feminine manners, and women writers returned the favor. In "Of Essay Writing," David Hume presents himself as an envoy between the academy and the tea table: "I am of the opinion, that women, that is women of sense and education (for to such alone I address myself) are much better judges of all polite writing than men of the same degree of understanding; and that 'tis a vain panic, if they be so far terrified with the common ridicule that is levell'd against learned ladies, as utterly to abandon every kind of books and study to our sex."[1] While some deplored feminization as evidence of luxury and corruption, eighteenth-century writers consistently measured the degree of refinement within a society by the respect it accorded to women. This chapter considers why sexual commerce was introduced into genres that reflect on manners and cultivation and how such writing acted as a force for social change.

Literary historians have always associated domesticity with the rise of prose fiction and of the middle class. This view needs strong qualification. As we have seen, celebrations of domestic felicity, supposedly a bourgeois innovation, were part of an aristocratic retirement tradition long before they became a constituent of eighteenth-century fiction. Moreover, the pursuit of domestic virtue implied choices available only to the few; only those with a place in the "World" were in a position to win merit by withdrawing from it. So it is that Margaret Cavendish—no middle-class writer she—advocates domesticity in her collection, *Sociable Letters* (1664): "But every one's delights are different, for the Lady S. P. delights her self with others, and I delight my self with my self; some delight in troubles, I delight in ease, and certainly much company and conversation cannot chuse but be troublesome; for in much company are many exceptions, much envy, much suspicion, much detraction, much faction, much noise, and much nonsense."[2] That a person so desirous of attention as the duchess of Newcastle advocates retirement indicates how fashionable domesticity was among the elite. It is notable that her published meditational essays are written in the form of familiar letters; she thus promotes the virtues of private life in a specifically feminine and private mode of address. Half a century later, Joseph Addison returns to her themes in *Spectator* 15, presenting retirement as an issue of special importance to women:

> True Happiness is of a retired Nature, and an Enemy to Pomp and Noise; it arises, in the first place, from the Enjoyment of ones self; and in the next, from the Friendship and Conversation of a few select Companions. It loves Shade and Solitude, and naturally haunts Groves and Fountains, Fields and Meadows: In short, it feels every thing it wants within it self, and receives not Addition from Multitudes of Witnesses and Spectators. On the contrary, false Happiness loves to be in a Crowd, and to draw the Eyes of the World upon her.[3]

≡

Forms of Reflection

Although Mr. Spectator advises women to withdraw from the public gaze, he trains his private eye squarely on their domestic lives, making their private lives a matter not only of public record but of public concern. The paradox is only apparent, however, since Addison is redefining the concept of what counts as public. As the pursuit of cultivation entered the domestic sphere, the ways in which women were expected to display themselves became a matter of public concern. The *Spectator* made discussions of manners a constituent of writing about domestic retirement and contributed to the growing public interest in the letters, memoirs, journals, and poetry in which polite women displayed their taste.

Commerce between the sexes redrew the boundaries between what was considered public and private and established new kinds of interaction between the citizens and the gentry and the aristocracy. As we have seen with Defoe, *commerce* was more than a financial concept, as Samuel Johnson emphasizes in his *Dictionary:* "Intercourse; exchange of one thing for another; interchange of anything; trade, traffick." As a form of commerce, "women's writing"—literature by, for, and about women, of which the *Spectator* is a prime example—undermined existing hierarchies by introducing new kinds of reciprocity. The resistance to this process and its ultimate triumph were the common themes of eighteenth-century fiction but also of the essays, letters, and journals that fiction imitated. Traffic between romance and nonfictional genres was one of the most important avenues of sexual commerce, a primary means by which new ideas were promoted and disseminated. This chapter considers how this and other forms of commerce operated within the community of writers associated with the countess of Hertford. The documentary evidence is extensive enough for us to observe different attitudes toward sexual commerce within the community and changes in concepts of domestic virtue over a period of decades. The discussion is organized around concepts of *place:* place as status in published works by and about the countess, place as domestic privacy in the notebooks in which the countess recorded discussions of retirement, and both senses together in four house poems describing the literal place where innovative relations between status and retirement were worked out.

Concepts of Status, Concepts of Place:
James Thomson, Isaac Watts, and Elizabeth Rowe

Frances Thynne Seymour, countess of Hertford (1699–1754), filled a niche roughly equivalent to that of Ralph Allen, Peter Walters, or Jonathan Wild: she was regarded as a touchstone character in writings on ethics and discussions of commerce.[4] She often pursued innovative kinds of commerce between sexes and social ranks in relationships with a group of writers that included Elizabeth Singer Rowe, James Thomson, Walter Harte, Isaac Watts, Elizabeth Carter, Moses Browne, Stephen Duck (who was saved from the gallows by her intercession with the queen), John Dalton, John Dyer, Richard West, James Hervey, and William Shenstone. Despite a sincere desire for privacy, the countess was always something of a public figure. Before the death of her father in 1708, she lived a retired life (in considerable splendor) at the Thynne estate of Longleat. In 1715 she married Algernon Seymour, heir to the vast Percy and Seymour fortunes; in 1723 she became lady of the bedchamber to Caroline, who was crowned in 1727. Lady Hertford used her place at court to secure her own financial position and to promote the interests of writers to whose progressive values she was sympathetic. At the death of the queen in 1737, the Seymours withdrew from public life to await their inheritance. It was a long wait: the old duke lived into his eighties; his son survived him by less than two years. After the deaths of her son and her husband, Lady Hertford lived as a virtual recluse at Percy Lodge, where she died in 1754.

Surviving correspondence indicates that letterwriting was regarded as a significant part of Frances Thynne's education, a measure of taste but also matter of political necessity.[5] Her grandmother thanks the child for a "pretty letter, which is so very well writ that I desire to lay it safe up" (*TGH*, 8). Verses in a letter from Elizabeth Rowe to the twelve-year-old girl encourage her writing as a means of attracting a suitable husband:

> Your growing wit shall gain immortal fame;
> And ev'ry muse shall learn Mirtilla's name;
> Nor less shall be the conquests of your eyes,
> When all your charms shall to perfection rise. (*TGH*, 12)

Such sexual frankness was common enough among persons of this class at this time. As matters turned out, Frances Thynne's beauty and skills were not required to attract a husband; she entered into a political match

≡

Forms of Reflection

with a man she had never seen. It was a marriage where the vows were spoken first and the courtship conducted afterward, at least partly in letters that have survived (*TGH*, 56). The ability to enter into sexual commerce now proved its usefulness—the marriage succeeded because both parties were willing to change to please the other. The letters record how Hertford, known for preferring his bottle to his book, was refined by his young but learned spouse. In a letter of 1719, the countess describes him reading to the family: "I have at last got Mr. Prior, which was kept in town by a mistake. We have only yet had time to read one book of his *Solomon* which I think extremely pretty. I have vast expectations of entertainment from *Robinson Crusoe*, which my Lord promises to read aloud to us as soon as we are got through *Solomon*, which is to be this evening's entertainment" (*TGH*, 49). The titles suggest a religious education. But if the husband had to become domesticated, the wife needed to adapt herself to courtly ways. However little to her taste, it was absolutely necessary that she appear in public and pursue the family interests.

This necessity resulted, strange to say, from straitened financial circumstances. The Seymours's income was originally two thousand pounds a year, of which seven hundred pounds went to the countess as pin money, an indication of just how much the family was spending on clothing and entertainment (*TGH*, 18). This amount was little enough to support two large houses, a stable and carriage, and a staff of perhaps forty or fifty servants. Maintaining status required displays of wealth: the Seymours were expected to throw lavish assemblies several times a season, to appear modishly dressed at court, and to give generous support to clients and charities (*TGH*, 147, 71). Lady Hertford's mother helped out with gifts of clothing and food (*TGH*, 48, 52), but the old duke, determined to keep his son on a close leash, allowed him but a thousand pounds a year, not always regularly paid (*TGH*, 33, 48, 52). Rumors that tradesmen were being turned away only soured relations with the family patriarch. Court connections were necessary to boost revenue: Hertford eventually secured a regiment and sinecures from the Walpole administration worth some four thousand pounds a year (*TGH*, 199). All the social skills Lady Hertford could muster were required to advance the family interests against keen competition from other claimants.[6] If the Seymours eventually became a model of retired elegance, their ability to work together in public was a precondition for success.

Maintaining a little place in the country was thus intimately bound up with maintaining a large place at court: to retire from the world it was necessary first to establish a position in the world, an enterprise requiring some patience and a sense of purpose. The rituals of hierarchy in the Seymour family had changed not at all since the old duke was a young man. A memoir describing Lady Hertford's entry into society records the minute scale on which the battle for place was waged:

> The day after the marriage, they dined at Northumberland House [the city residence of the old duke], and upon Mrs. Thynne's pointing out to Lady Hertford to go first out of the room, the Duchess of Somerset said: "Madam, that must not be; she is no less your daughter for being my son's wife." On another occasion, at the Drawing-Room, Lady Hertford was giving place to the Duchess of Beaufort, who was married to Lord Dundonald, when the Duchess of Somerset snatched her by her petticoat, and said she should be very sorry to see her son's wife give place to my Lord Dundonald's. (*TGH*, 18)

The manners of the elder Seymours led to more than one Richardsonian scenario. The duke once disinherited a daughter for sitting in his presence and rebuked a wife for daring to tap him on the shoulder.[7] The younger Seymours were equally insistent about adopting the easier manners advocated by Mr. Spectator. After relations with the duke were eventually broken off, Lady Hertford, with characteristic modesty, admitted her failure to please her father-in-law. The cadences of her prose, as much as the content of her letter, convey a new and more relaxed conception of civility:

> You, with the kindness of a person who was afraid it proceeded from melancholy and a timidity in my nature, would have been glad to see me oftener in company and with a greater air of freedom and cheerfulness when I was engaged in it, as you thought it the most likely cure for a sort of savage bashfulness which you observed in me upon those occasions, and which I cannot be quite blind to myself. Others, with less kindness and much more injustice, upbraided me with it as an effect of pride, and unpardonable misanthropy, that I thought few people worthy conversing with, and could not bear the foibles of others. Alas! alas! how do they mistake me! 'Tis not the failings of others but my own which banish me from the gay world. . . . Under the strongest ties of duty and gratitude to an husband whose unmerited indulgence to me made it my inclination as well interest to live well with his family, I had the misfortune (I think undeservedly) to fall under their displeasure

≡

Forms of Reflection
126

before I was nineteen years old, and how has his father till this time continued to load me with reproaches and injuries, in which my Lord has shared. (*TGH*, 34–35)

This letter expresses a dilemma familiar to more than one heroine of romance. Much as those fictional characters, the countess of Hertford played an exemplary role in introducing changes in manners. If Frances Seymour displeased her own family, she delighted Elizabeth Rowe, who comments, "How much must you merit, whose example has given such perfect patterns of virtue to the world. I never read *The Spectator* but I apply all his characters of a fine woman to you" (*TGH*, 26). Her character pleased others as well, as is apparent from her success at court and from the caliber of persons who cultivated her acquaintance. The countess ran her household like a finishing school:

> The establishment of the family in point of servants was large, and those of the second table, particularly the women, had good education, and had the behavior of real gentlewomen. Mrs. Rothery, Lady Hertford's first woman, who had lived with her from childhood, was a widow of genteel extraction; and her niece, Mrs. Nevinson, the second woman, was the daughter of a clergyman in the North; she was a woman of reading and parts, and though a servant, yet Lady Hertford treated her more like a companion than one of that capacity. (*TGH*, 96)

In a society where status is a matter of rank rather than class, face-to-face relationships within the hierarchy can diffuse manners and taste; at the time *Crusoe* was being piously read at Marlborough, Mrs. Arabella Marrow, one of the upper servants, wrote from Offchurch to her mistress, "Our entertainment is Robinson Crusoe, which Mr. Richard Knightly reads to us. I beg that your Ladyship would not fail to tell me yours and Lord Hertford's opinion of it, for I will not give mine till I hear yours" (*TGH*, 57).

Conversation and correspondence operated reciprocally: if ladies of the bedchamber introduced courtly tastes to those of lower status, the tastes of the countess's correspondents—Thomson, Watts, and Rowe— were making inroads at court. Such, at least, was the belief of her correspondents. The Seymours invited writers down to spend the summer, including James Thomson, which is how "Spring" came to be dedicated to the countess. Her character is thus the first to appear in the poem, appropriately enough, for she represents the new order Thomson celebrates in this greatest of georgic hymns to change:

O Hartford, fitted or to shine in courts
With unaffected grace, or walk the plain
With innocence and meditation joined
In soft assemblage, listen to my song,
Which thy own season paints—when nature all
Is blooming and benevolent, like thee.   ("Spring," 5–10)[8]

Thomson's handsome compliment points to the "unaffected grace" that marks the new manners, to the "benevolence" the countess bestows on her clients, and to the duality I have already marked: Lady Hertford excels both at display ("to shine in courts") and at retirement ("or walk the plain with innocence and meditation joined"). By establishing reciprocity between domestic virtue and public affairs, she became an agent of the progress Thomson and other Whig writers believed was transforming British society. In 1727 these praises were perhaps welcome enough, but as the years passed and her status became more secure, the countess made a habit of rejecting dedications—not because she was stingy but because she preferred to shine in private.

The countess's reputation for piety, politeness, and benevolence is also noted by Isaac Watts, who, like Thomson, recognized the value of having a friend at court:

I beg Leave, MADAM, to flatter my Self, that the same Condescension and Goodness which has admitted several of these Pieces into your Closet in Manuscript, will permit them all to make this publick Appearance before You. Your Ladyship's known Character and Taste for everything that is Pious and Polite, give an honourable Sanction to those Writings which stand Recommended by Your Name and Approbation; 'tis no Wonder then that these ESSAYS should seek the Favour of such a Patronage.[9]

This dedication appears in *Miscellaneous Thoughts* (1734), a work that illustrates the upward mobility of meditational writing. Modeled on Cowley's *Essays*, Watts's collection includes odes, psalms, epitaphs, epistles, meditations on the creatures, literary criticism, and a host of moral essays. The work wittily scans the manners of the great, while making patterns of politeness accessible to those who would never receive an invitation to Whitehall. Watts stresses the need for privacy even as he makes domestic matters public: "My particular Friends, to whom I have sent any of these pieces, will generally be pleased to read them in Print, and

≡

Forms of Reflection
128

address'd to a feigned Name, rather than their own: This I found the safest Way to avoid Offence on all Hands, and therefore I have not mentioned one proper Name here, but what was in Print before" (xv).[10] Watts documents his correspondences with important personages, albeit under cover of fiction. Combining devotional meditations with strictures on manners and taste, the work exemplifies the commerce the writer hoped to establish between pious persons and a libertine court. It adjusts boundaries between degrees of rank and privacy: if Watts's devotions find their way into Lady Hertford's closet, Lady Hertford's meditations, presumably penned in that very place, now appear before the world in essays published by Watts.

"Piety in a Court," a letter Watts addresses to Elizabeth Rowe, describes the court as a place where "a thousand Devils / In chrystal Forms sit tempting Innocence" (271). In a romance allusion Rowe would have enjoyed, he compares the court to Comus's rout and the countess to Milton's Lady. Watts describes how, after reading his poem to a group of Frances Seymour's "intimate friends," Alethina, a court insider, confirms its justice:

> I know Eusebia's modesty, said she, and a Blush will be easily raised
> in the Face of so much Virtue; yet I don't think the Writer hath mistook
> her Character; in my Opinion, 'tis just and sincere; her whole Conver-
> sation is of a Piece: Her publick and her private Hours are of the same
> Colour and Hue: She is much a Christian in the Family and the Closet,
> nor doth she put off any part of that glorious Profession at Court. I have
> been favour'd with some of the Fruits of her retir'd Meditations, and as
> I have long had the Happiness of her Acquaintance, I dare pronounce
> that she lives what she writes. (273)

Like Thomson, Alethina notes the public and private spheres occupied by the countess and asserts that her conversation in both is "of a piece." She then reciprocates by reading four devotional poems composed by the countess, works Watts presumably had permission to publish. "Piety in a Court" is a carefully crafted piece of negotiation, working up the scale of genres from memoir to sacred song, up the hierarchy of rank from Rowe to the women at court to Lady Hertford, and up the scale of privacy from familiar letter to private conversation to devotional soliloquy. At the center of this frame, however, Lady Hertford's "Dying Christian to his Soul" reveals that piety in a court is much the same as piety anywhere else. Watts's letter to Elizabeth Rowe thus both asserts and denies the value of rank and the privacy of its message. It makes the closeted voice public and harnesses the power of status—the essence of court "enchantment"—to a morality that undermines exclusiveness.

A similar strategy is at work in Elizabeth Rowe's *Letters Moral and Entertaining*, (3d ed., 1733).[11] If Watts inserts epistolary fiction into a collection of meditational essays, Rowe inserts devotional meditations into a collection of epistolary romances. She sets up reciprocal relations between two contrary genres, romance and devotion, both of which held special appeal for her women readers. It may be that David Hume has her very popular work in mind when he attempts to woo women away from these genres: "I mention Gallantry and Devotion as the same Subject, because, in Reality, they become the same when treated in this [affected] Manner; and we may observe, that they both depend upon the very same complexion."[12] Hume believed that sexual commerce required changes on either side: if the men needed to give up their pedantry, the women needed to give up their extravagances. Rowe clearly felt differently and attempted to harness romantic appeals to the passions to the work of reforming libertine values. While prose romance had little status among male writers, it enjoyed a higher standing with women. It was their genre, and it too could become a vehicle for cultivating civility.

Friendship in Death takes affinities between gallantry and devotion to their limits and beyond, juxtaposing pious with libertine values and imbuing both with a decidedly feminine complexion. Departed souls send messages to loved ones, describe their happiness, warn of impending dangers, and exhort mortals to tread the paths of righteousness. Such an extravagant conceit demands an equally extravagant style; Rowe's heaven is the stuff of romance:

> Whatever you have heard fabled of Fairy Scenes, of vocal Groves, and Palaces rising to Magick Sounds, is all real here, and performed by the easy and natural Operations of these active Spirits. . . . They have such a Command and Knowledge of the Powers of Nature, that in an instant they raise a variety of Sylvan Scenes, and carry the Perspective thro' verdant Avenues and flow'ry Walks to an unmeasurable Length; while living Fountains cast up their silver Spouts and form glittering Arches among the Trees, of Growth and Verdure not to be expressed. (17)

Rowe inserts devotional exhortations into the familiar romance scenarios; in the eighth of the little histories a husband, murdered defending his bride from pirates, writes from above to warn of the designs of an amorous Bassa: "Though he has courted you to increase the Number of his Wives, he seems to have such an absolute Command of himself, even in the Warmth of his youthful Desires, that you need fear no Violence from the generous Infidel: But should the worst you imagine arrive, Heaven has a thousand ways to protect your Innocence" (27). Only a cold heart indeed could resist such remarkable testimonies of an afterlife, particularly that of a dead infant who writes his grieving mother to tell of his new-found happiness. As in Defoe's *Serious Reflections*, religious devotion involves commerce with spirits, though in Rowe's more feminine fiction probability is not the issue.

The success of the work (ten editions, several French and German translations) made sequels obligatory. Wisely perhaps, Rowe confined herself, for the most part, to mortal correspondences. The *Letters Moral and Entertaining* mix prose and verse, essay and narrative, historical and contemporary characters. The majority of the eighty letters are brief novels in which the author runs wittily through the permutations of romance relationships. The fiction alternately affirms and denies its glittering objects of desire, as in one private history narrated by a statesman who has given up politics for piety. He writes, "You will tell me, this contempt of grandeur appears with an ill grace, in one that has the possession of a splendid post in the government: But this, my Lord, is what has given me a just opinion of the world, and of myself." In retirement, the great man finds solace in religion—or is it romance? "I have, indeed, heard from the men, who teach such holy fables, (as I then thought them,) that the soul was immortal, and capable of celestial joys: But I rather wished, than believ'd, these transporting truths, and put them on a level with the poet's rosy bowers, their myrtle shades, and soft Elysian fields; but now I am convinc'd of their evidence, and triumph in the privileges of my own being" (59). In converting to Christianity, the politician acquires a new and superior set of "privileges."

Like Watts, Rowe links the appeal of rank and place to what is finally a general morality: you too, reader, can enjoy the privileges of the great, if only in forgoing greatness. Rowe was never averse to merging romance with "holy fables." A later letter to the countess of Hertford boldly declares her faith in fiction: "If religion is a cheat, let me be still deceived; let me indulge the gay delusion, and recreate my soul with the transporting expectation. Stand forth ye glorious phantoms, and entertain my attention in all your visionary splendors! Let me be well deceived, and at ast be happy till death shall put an end to the pleasing dream."[13] Few Protestant writers have treated meditational themes with such license; the danger of scandal must have contributed mightily to her work's appeal.

Into her *Letters Moral and Entertaining* Rowe inserts eight "Letters to Cleora" and five "Letters to the Author by another Hand"—excerpts from her correspondence with the countess of Hertford. Mixing in these genuine letters gives an air of authenticity to her often highly improbable tales of high life. Gildon, Manley, and Haywood may claim to offer readers original letters from peers of the realm, but Rowe actually does so. Like Isaac Watts, she makes the private public; her readers are given the actual words of a noblewoman famous for piety and taste, words that also offer an insider's critique of aristocratic values. The real correspondence plays with romantic scenarios every bit as much as the fictional letters do. A counterpart to Rowe's retired statesman, the countess declares: "I am as busy in my garden, and as much surfeited with the Grand Monde, as ever Dioclesian was" (110–11). Now an emperor, now a hermit, Frances Seymour recalls roles familiar from romance. Elizabeth Rowe objects when her friend compares her own modest retirement to the extravagance of her fictions: "I must confess you have given me a sort of imaginary character, and I am a heroine of your own making" (104). The countess rallies Rowe's pretensions: "Whither shall I direct for you? are you still an inhabitant of the earth, or ascended to the aetherial regions? Am I addressing a mortal, or an immortal spirit?" (107). Such play obviously comments reflexively on the printed letters themselves. Rowe and her patroness appear in *Letters Moral and Entertaining* disguised as Philomela and Cleora, mingling with characters purely romantic: Celadon and Amasia, Bellamour and Almeda, the Earl of —— and my Lord ——. By setting up complex relations of exchange between real and fictional correspondences, Rowe both confirms the accuracy of her depictions of high life and undermines romancing as a fantasy world of self-delusion.

Writers in the Hertford circle promote feminine qualities in their meditational writings on retirement and domestic virtue; they redefine commerce by substituting for material relations a new emphasis on the passions and role of women in cultivating social virtue. In these works the countess of Hertford stands as a figure of commerce, mediating between court and country, private and public virtue, piety and politeness, material and spiritual values, and persons of higher and lower social status. The romance elements appearing in these works indicate the importance Thomson, Watts, and Rowe place on Frances Seymour's status as a peer

=

Forms of Reflection

and as a woman. They put the authority of rank behind a program of cultivation that undermines earlier hierarchies of class and gender. In associating cultivation with conversation and correspondence, they celebrate the countess as representative of the social process of refinement. The next two sections differentiate this eighteenth-century concept of cultivation from that in seventeenth-century georgic writing.

Lady Hertford's Commonplace Book:
Romancing the Aristocracy

Fiction and domesticity are, of course, the themes of Nancy Armstrong's *Desire and Domestic Fiction*.[14] To illustrate the distinction between cultivation and culture, it might be useful to contrast Armstrong's argument with what I take to be the social and literary implications of sexual commerce in the eighteenth century. My argument is that writing by and about women operated differentially within a field of genres, while Armstrong describes a contradiction between cultures:

> Eighteenth century conduct books and educational treatises for women forced open a contradiction within the existing cultural territory that had been marked out for representing the female. These authors portrayed aristocratic women along with those who harbored aristocratic pretensions as the very embodiments of corrupted desire, namely, desire that sought its gratification in economic and political terms. The books all took care to explain how this form of desire destroyed the very virtues essential to a wife and mother. Narratives of her ideal development would come later. The educational handbooks for women simply mapped out a new field of knowledge as specifically female. (59–60).

Armstrong's figure of a cultural territory contradicting a map of knowledge implies a high degree of consistency within manners and writings about manners. But both were in constant flux; moreover, each interacted with the other in ways that the map-and-territory figure obscures. Compare the emphasis on fluidity, change, and reciprocity in the prospect views Denham and other goergic writers used to express social and historical differences. Histories like *Desire and Domestic Fiction* resemble georgic writing in the way that figures and allegories carry the weight of argument, but metaphors for culture cancel the kinds of difference earlier writers described and enacted through their writing about sexual commerce. In the eighteenth century, women writers generally thought about class,

=

gender, and genre in terms of exchange, rather than opposition, and took pains to locate their writing within, as well as against, the heterogeneous social and literary structures they engaged.

Nancy Armstrong addresses this issue when she takes on Foucault over the issue of resistance: "If one could allow for such heterogeneity — the overlapping of competing versions of reality within the same moment of time — the past would elude the linear pattern of a developmental narrative. In the model I am proposing, culture appears as a struggle among various factions to possess its most valued signs and symbols" (23). But when versions of reality are understood as variations within a synchronic pattern, differences in the ways the signs and symbols articulate reality are less significant than they might seem. In the last analysis, the differences that matter to Armstrong are not within, but between, cultures: "The material composition of a particular text would have more to do with the forms of representation it overcame — in the case of domestic fiction, with its defiance of an aristocratic tradition of letters and, later on, with its repudiation of working-class culture — than with the internal composition of the text per se" (23). This formulation links a hierarchy of classes to a sequence of periods, so that only one form of representation would seem to count as real in a given century: aristocratic in the seventeenth century, bourgeois in the eighteenth century, and working class in the nineteenth century. In Armstrong's account, domestic novels do not resist a *contemporary* aristocratic tradition of letters (which would include works written by Lord Chesterfield, or Horace Walpole, Fanny Burney or Mary Shelley), but social norms Armstrong identifies with the Tudor and Stuart courts (70–71).

Conversely, works that do not correspond to a dominant culture are necessarily "fictional": "This book . . . shows as well that the domestic novel antedated — was necessarily antecedent to — the way of life it represented" (9). Given the mixture of real and fictional letters in the works discussed above and the commerce between peers and commoners one finds described and enacted in them, Armstrong's identification of genre, class, and culture begins to look problematic. The exclusion of romance and gothic resulting from this identification of domestic fiction with the novel and middle-class culture undercuts the claim that "competing versions of reality" are really being considered.

My point is not just that *Desire and Domestic Fiction* fails to be inclusive enough to sustain its argument but that its exclusions are characteristic of arguments that identify a class or genre with the kind of totality

=

Forms of Reflection

commonly referred to as a period, ideology, or culture. In this respect, Whiggish accounts of fiction like McKeon's or Armstrong's are much like Ian Watt's *Rise of the Novel*: pegging the fortunes of fiction to the middle class, they dismiss or ignore a highly innovative romance tradition that fails to correspond to the master narrative. This is more than a simple aesthetic prejudice. For literary historians in the Marxist tradition, a culture corresponds to one particular conjunction of epistemology and social history; *The Rise of the Novel* outlines such a structure in its famous opening chapters, "Realism and the Novel Form" (9–34) and "The Reading Public and the Rise of the Novel" (35–59). While their interpretations of novels give passing notice to the concept of heterogeneity, McKeon and Armstrong organize their books as Watt does: background chapters on epistemology and social history establish a paradigm that is then read into and out of a series of canonical masterpieces. This procedure is common to both old and new historicisms: in both, literary and social formations participate in an overarching culture that determines which fictions count as "real." In older literary histories this link to the real was often made through images or symbols; in *Desire and Domestic Fiction* it is described as a "figure, or turn of cultural logic" (24). Like Donne's *Anniversaries, Desire and Domestic Fiction* merges rhetoric ("figure") and logic ("cultural logic") to make its figural interpretation of history appear necessary; scientific claims are implied for a method that is not, strictly speaking, methodical. Relations between genres are seldom systematic, as Armstrong implies when she compares the relation between conduct books and novels to that between grammar and utterance:

> Under the sheer force of repetition, however, one does see a figure emerge from the categories that organize these manuals. A figure of female subjectivity, a grammar really, awaited the substance that the novel and its readers, as well as countless individuals educated according to the model of the new woman, would eventually provide. In such books one can see a culture in the process of rethinking at the most basic level the dominant (aristocratic) rules for sexual exchange. (60)

Armstrong suggests that by including conduct books in her history of the novel she is "dissolving the boundary between those texts that are considered literature and those that, like the conduct books, are not" (9). But once its figural logic has been abstracted, the conduct literature disappears; moreover, the "grammar" metaphor indicates the very different ways in which the genres are discussed: conduct books are treated synchronically, as though they did not significantly change between 1600 and 1800; novels are treated diachronically and seen as initiating social changes through their ability to manipulate reality and control desire. Conduct books are discussed in terms of their similarities ("sheer force of repetition"), while novels are discussed in terms of their differences ("substance"). If *Desire and Domestic Fiction* offers valuable discussions of the "rules for sexual exchange" in both conduct books and novels, it does not describe exchanges *between* conduct books and novels. The grammar metaphor cannot explain how or why conduct-book material was incorporated into fictions or fictions into conduct books. Nor does it go very far towards explaining the mutual antagonism between the novel and the conduct book. These inter- and intra-generic relations do not accord with the ways in which culture articulates relations between parts and wholes.

If, instead, we begin with the "internal construction of the text per se" (23), the focus shifts from cultural contradictions to generic relations. Both conduct books and novels of the era were internally various in ways that permitted and indeed encouraged reciprocal exchanges between various kinds of writing and between persons of different ranks and genders. A conduct book like *The Female Spectator* (1744–46), for instance, incorporates large quantities of narrative along with its advice to the lovelorn. Eliza Haywood, the "female spectator," published a conduct book that enters into sexual commerce with essayists like Addison and Steele, but also with novelists like Richardson, whose *Pamela, or Virtue Rewarded* (1740–41) is a conduct book manqué. All three authors employ spying and letterwriting to give readers insight into domains of feminine virtue and the social business being transacted there. Those readers included both men and women and persons of different social rank. Correspondences arose out of differences and, in turn, worked differences upon the correspondents. Spying and letterwriting lead the protagonists in *Pamela* to change their circumstances; something similar takes place in *The Female Spectator*, when, in the last number, we learn that the men have found out Elizabeth Haywood and her cabal of spies and that the augmented group is planning a new periodical as a joint venture.

While the social tensions are real enough, such epistolary reciprocity seems not to "force open a contradiction within the existing cultural territory" but to transform it amicably from within. The metaphor of cultural territory is too broad: the places in which conduct literature was produced and consumed were diverse, as was the literature itself. Changes

=

Forms of Reflection
136

occurred piecemeal, irregularly, and over relatively long periods of time. The ways in which writers address this diversity are instructive if we can resist the temptation to reduce these relations to a cultural logic. The transformations Armstrong describes certainly took place, and domestic fiction had everything to do with these transformations; but we do not need culture to explain them, nor do we need to argue that these changes began as a fiction. Letters and poems, conduct books and novels, not only represented social relations; they also enacted the innovative social relations they represent through generic procedures.

If we are to locate social changes in and through generic relations, however, a different kind of literary history is required. Rather than trying to read a paradigmatic structure into and out of a few exemplary works, this chapter emphasizes the diversity of structures within and among a set of diverse works, including letters, poems, biographies, and essays, as well as conduct books and novels. To say that sexual commerce is common to all of them is not necessarily to regard commerce as a paradigmatic structure in itself, for the transactions are of very different kinds. To make sense of such diversity, however, one needs to locate significant variation within significant continuity. The countess of Hertford is an excellent model for this purpose. Her long career illustrates how one intelligent and engaged observer reacted to both the courtly formalities of her youth and the unbuttoned romanticism of her later years. A single observer cannot be wholly representative of a sex, a class, or a period, though in her lifetime the countess was regarded as exemplary for all three. Contemporary observers of this privileged observer interpreted her exemplariness in different and opposing ways. The countess stood at the center of a diverse community that changed over time; since this community involved exchanges between aristocrats and commoners, court and country, women and men, its examination yields insight into how eighteenth-century communities operated more generally.

The volumes in which Frances Seymour recorded her literary transactions document a lifelong effort to translate romantic values into contemporary practice. Lady Hertford's ideas evolved as she grew older: as a young woman, she participated in exchanges of gallantry with wits and poets; in middle age, she pursued moral issues in correspondences with literary men and women; with the dissolution of her family in old age, she turned wholeheartedly to religious devotion. As her interests in romance and retirement were never merely speculative, the commonplace books played an active role in the development of her interests and influence.

=

Eighteenth-Century Georgic

137

The community defined itself through writing; the notebooks were made available to visitors to Marlborough and Percy Lodge; portions of them, as we have seen, were allowed to appear in print. Through such correspondence the countess investigated concepts of domestic virtue, while pursuing new forms of social interaction. The kinds of writing contained in these books respond to changes taking place in eighteenth-century literature, as georgic conceptions of literary and social cultivation became increasingly feminized. In keeping with the romantic tenor of the countess's values, these innovations often take the form of a return to older genres.

Among the recorded correspondences in the notebooks are a series of gallant lyrics James Thomson wrote to flatter his patroness. The poet appeals to their shared regard for romantic and devotional themes, as in "To Seraphina. Ode":

> To love thee, Seraphina, sure
> Is to be tender, happy, pure;
> 'Tis from low passions to escape,
> And woo bright virtue's fairest shape;
> 'Tis extasy with wisdom join'd;
> And heaven infus'd into the mind.   (ll. 17–22)

This is relatively chaste—but Thomson could also address his patroness in a more erotic Petrarchan vein:

> Oh tell Her what She cannot blame,
> Tho Fear my Tongue must ever bind,
> Oh tell Her that my heavenly Flame
> Is as her sacred Soul refin'd.[15]

Such poems present retirement as a private and somewhat dangerous place where patroness and client can indulge romantic fantasies under cover of equivocal fiction and shared pursuit of virtue. But the air of guilty secrecy is itself a fiction: by copying these poems into her commonplace book, the countess made them available to a variety of admiring friends. The social distance standing between the sender and the recipient of such courtly lyrics ensure their propriety; had the countess replied in kind, it would have been another matter.

There is also a series of ten verse epistles on platonic themes composed by Lady Hertford, Elizabeth Rowe, their friend Henrietta Knight, and the Reverend John Dalton. These take the form of a singing contest similar to those in Walton's *Angler* or Sidney's *Arcadia*. The topics are virtue, beauty, and friendship; each poem draws themes from its predecessor, while artfully notching up the level of compliment. The epistles insert the writers into a romantic topography, as when Dalton compliments the ladies by bemoaning their absence from Oxford:

> 'Would you but to our Groves resort,
> And in our Flow'ry Walks appear
> You'd fix both Wits and Beautys Court
> There Paphos, and Parnassus here. (*TGH*, 173)

If ladies were excluded from Oxford, and scholars from Whitehall, both enjoyed "gainful commerce" (*TGH*, 173) at the Seymour's romantic estate at Marlborough. The fairy fiction alludes to a very real situation in eighteenth-century literary production: the universities and the court were no longer patronizing literature. With a self-deprecating allusion to *Paradise Lost*, Dalton represents the country estate as Eden and the unpolished scholar as dancing bear:

> So when in Paradise the Fair
> Reclin'd beneath ye shade
> To please her was each creature's care
> And round ye brute Creation play'd. (*TGH*, 173)

Nor is this enchanted place without the "magic call" of sexual temptation, although the countess is no second Eve:

> Heav'n formed her fair as the first sacred Ground
> But wav'd the beamy Guard of Virtue round. (*TGH*, 177)

In a kind of poetical conversation piece, Mrs. Rowe pindarically summons Apollo to laud the group of figures assembled at the country house. The god declares that Urania, Clio, and Orpheus are eclipsed:

> 'Tis there the nymphs and swains I've taught
> With spirit, wit and Beauty fraught,
> Vie with the tuneful nine
> And make their concert more Divine. (*TGH*, 179)

The sylvan academy is bound together by harmonious ties of love and learning, ties equivocally expressed by Dalton in a little tailpiece to Mrs. Knight:

Give me the Friendship of my fair,

Give me that something still more Dear—.   (*TGH*, 181)

In these verse epistles, as in the Renaissance lyrics they imitate, religious devotion and erotic desire center on the courtly ideal of aristocratic womanhood.[16]

Retirement was thus a sexual as well as a political posture, as noted in a critical remark made in a letter from Elizabeth Rowe:

> Considering Tullia was design'd by Madame de Lambert for a perfect character, I think, she indulges a tender passion for Lentulus a little too far. However, that guilt is excus'd by the heroic virtue that appears in her retreat; and nothing can be more charming and natural than the effect of her retirement, when it sinks a tender passion into a generous and innocent friendship; and it delights the reader to find two persons of the greatest merit happy without a crime.   (*Works*, 2:173–74)

As eighteenth-century correspondences amply demonstrate, aristocratic women enjoyed flirtation as much in real life as in fictional representations. Gallantry afforded them the opportunity to engage in risks and to display "heroic virtue." In her youth, Lady Hertford was neither immune nor adverse to this kind of behavior.[17] If she did respond to Thomson's or Dalton's erotic advances, which seems most unlikely, the poets had discretion enough to destroy the evidence. It was necessary to control access to such writing; when the countess was caught out in another correspondence, the gossips at court were able to triumph gleefully over her folly. Years afterward, Lady Mary Wortley Montagu wrote to her daughter: "Some few months before Lord W. Hamilton married, there appeared a foolish song, said to be wrote by a poetical great lady, who I really think was the character of Lady Arabella, in the Female Quixote (without the beauty): you may imagine such a conduct, at court, made her superlatively ridiculous."[18] Lady Mary's use of *The Female Quixote* to besmirch a competitor at court is but another instance of the generic framing of romantic retirement: those who stood to gain by romantic airs also stood to lose by them.

When private writing became public, consequences could be serious. Mrs. Knight, when later accused of compromising herself with Reverend Dalton, was forced by her husband into unwilling retirement on a decrepit country estate. Forbidden to travel to London or to correspond with Lady Hertford, she experienced the life of a hermit in good earnest. Horace Walpole later used this episode to malign the pretensions of romantic

Forms of Reflection

retirement in a withering allusion to the sage and serious doctrine of virginity. Mrs. Knight, he relates, "had a mishap with Parson Dalton, the reviver of *Comus*, and retired to a hermitage on Parnassus, as she says herself. The seraphic Duchess, her friend, was suspected to have *chasse sur le meme terres*, and so it is no wonder they were intimate, as they agreed in *eodem tertio*."[19] Where the boundaries between fact and fiction are unclear, appearances count for all.

Members of the Hertford circle thus found themselves in danger of becoming characters in romances not of their own making. In 1736, Elizabeth Rowe expressed abject horror at the prospect of becoming the unwilling heroine of one of Edmund Curll's biographies:

> I am in pain till you know I am entirely ignorant of Curll's romance of
> my life and writings, only what I have seen is an advertisement. I was
> told of his design indeed, and wrote, and positively denied him the lib-
> erty of printing anything of mine. But they tell me he is a mere savage,
> and has no regard to truth or humanity; and as he has treated people
> of greater consequence in the same manner, I am advised to suffer no
> friend to take the least notice of his collection. (*TGH*, 137)

Curll's publications are graphic testimony of the keen public interest in the private lives of women of letters. Several of them collaborated with him, notably de la Rivière Manley. In the *Miscellanies in Prose and Verse* of 1718, genuine letters by Katherine Phillips appear alongside fictional letters by Aphra Behn; in the same year appeared *Letters, Poems, and Tales: Amorous, Satyrical, and Gallant. Which passed between Several Persons of Distinction. Now first Publish'd from their respective Originals, found in the Cabinet of that Celebrated Toast Mrs. Anne Long, since her Decease*—which offered readers a peep into the domestic affairs of Dean Swift. Such "romances" generated curiosity about the manners of the polite in a more direct if less elegant fashion than the periodical essays. Nor were Curll's representations of high life far off the mark, if we may compare the relationship of Henrietta Knight and John Dalton ("Venus" and "Adonis" in the countess's commonplace books) to Curll's *The Epistles of Clio and Strephon . . . who took an Affection to each other, by reading accidentally one another's Occasional Compositions both in Prose and Verse*.[20] Elizabeth Rowe, long a trafficker in sexual commerce, might easily have been made to look supremely ridiculous, but Curll's work eventually proved to be little more than a reprint of her 1696 collection of poems.

The best recourse against libel, as Pope had recently demonstrated, was to make one's private life public by publishing "authentic" documents. Rowe's posthumous *Works* (1739) contains an official biography, a corrected text of the poems, and a volume of letters documenting her private life as romantic spirit and religious devotee. Lady Hertford drew upon her commonplace books to assist the executors in representing the poet's retirement in the complex way she wished it to be perceived. The poems and letters explain why the author would desire to break off a successful commerce with an admiring public. Rowe's prose, like her poetry, often follows Cowley's lead, but she differs by describing retirement in greater detail and candor. Like other women writers, she relies less on classical authorities and more on her own experience, testing literary norms against the exigencies of life as it is lived.

Elizabeth Rowe's letters to Lady Hertford express a profoundly ambivalent attitude toward solitude. Though she receives the attentions of her neighbors at Frome very unwillingly, Rowe nonetheless seeks a larger community through epistolary commerce: "I begin to fancy I grow as humoursome as Moliere's Misanthrope. If I had as many visits from the good gentlewomen hereabouts, I should raise the price of hartshorn, to keep me from fainting fits; for oh! I sicken, I die — or sleep and dream, and am perfectly stupefied at their approach. . . . Your Ladyship's letters are my only entertainment, in a place where there is an absolute vacancy of common sense" (*Works*, 2:44). She despairs of having anything to report and is effusively grateful for news, or newspapers, or gossip. Yet very seldom can she be coaxed out of her "cave": "I am beyond expression oblig'd to your Ladyship for the offer of the pretty peaceful apartment, so suited to my taste, and your neighborhood is what I would prefer to all earthly enjoyments: But still — I want to be alone" (Works, 2:112). Rowe alludes to Thomson's *Sophonisba*, cited earlier in the correspondence:

> I want to be alone, to find some shade,
> Some solitary gloom, there to shake off,
> This weight of Life. . . .[21]

Both women tended to practice retirement as a form of literary criticism.

They also practiced letterwriting as a form of *social* criticism. A lady's correspondence was expected to be familiar in address, natural in style, and sincere in expression; yet Rowe writes from a position of social inferiority, in a highly artificial style, with an eye to publication. She addresses her correspondent deferentially while undercutting the value of deference; she criticizes herself in order to criticize her patroness:

=

Forms of Reflection

I . . . would fain have you believe this aversion to ceremony proceeds from greatness of mind, than from pride. . . . And yet I have too much sincerity to persuade you that 'tis rather my duty than my happiness that I should consult by this retreat from the public; and if I should confess that an absolute freedom from all the formalities and customs of the world is part of my felicity, you would think I have a very odd notion of happiness, and will certainly advise me to regulate such a licentious and irregular disposition; and not to fancy that to wake or sleep, to sit or stand, to laugh or cry at my own leisure, is a point of liberty worth struggling for.

I know not what orderly and governable inclinations some people have acquir'd; but to me it seems a vast privilege, to be rustic or polite, wise or impertinent, without being censur'd, or accountable to my fellow mortals. (*Works*, 2:115–16)

There is nothing rustic about this highly lacquered style. The passage vibrates with equivocation: rejecting formalities and customs in a studied compliment; asserting sincerity, while admitting that the writer changes from hour to hour; describing self-denial as the vast privilege of doing as one likes. Unlike Cowley's *Essays*, which strive mightily to present a consistent self, Rowe's letters are knowingly inconsistent, modulating character through modes of address that are rustic or polite, wise or impertinent.

If equivocation and role playing run contrary to the plain-speaking norms of stoic reflection, Rowe's writing does have its critical edge: "I begin to fancy . . . that my happiness has been all a romantic scene of my own forming: Perhaps I have only been entertain'd with some pleasing dream, and amusing myself with a glittering fallacy; or else, between sleeping and waking, fairy vision has smiled on me, and then forever vanished from my view" (*Works*, 2:66). By mixing romance with reflection, Rowe distances herself from the glittering objects of her desire. She turns to pastoral romance to represent social differences as a play of appearances: "If Mrs —— , instead of drawing the picture, could possibly be transformed into a real St. Genevieve; and would sit under a tree, with a good book in her lap, watching her sheep in a flowry picture that I could find for her, I should visit her at the rising morning and silent evening" (*Works*, 2:164). Such fictions also redraw social distinctions. But while she concedes "that people in low life take an innocent sort of pleasure in levelling their superiors," Rowe herself is no leveler. Her fictions imagine a society where distinctions are made according to taste rather than birth, where lesser gentry like herself could live on familiar terms with aristocrats like the countess of Hertford.

If the letters uphold commerce, they supplant the material history in earlier georgic with a turn toward romantic fantasy, as in this description of a drawing sent by the countess:

> You have brought back the sylvan scenes to their primitive grandeur, and a farm-house appears as polite as a palace. Instead of an air of low life, your cows and sheep give it the appearance of patriarchal wealth and plenty; and Lady ——, I presume, guards her fleecy charge, in as genteel a habit, as any poetical shepherdess that ever graced the stage. . . . I am glad you don't take a fancy to old hermits and philosophers; your devotees are young and handsome, and please with Coypel's airs. (*Works*, 2:150)

Rustics are metamorphosed into peers, a farmhouse is reconstructed as a palace, low life is invested with the grandeur of *opera seria*. As in the enchantments of romance (which often employs *ecphrasis* for similar ends), everything becomes that which it is not, or in this case, that which it is. The letter gently criticizes the countess's affectations (as Rowe well knew, the countess's closet was adorned with images of "hermits and philosophers"), reminding her of the social differences pastoral artifice tends to conceal. By such equivocations Rowe's epistolary reflections establish a new place for retirement: in the world, but not of it. From a romanticized retirement, Elizabeth Rowe pursued an active commerce with the polite world her letters deliberately undermine.

After the death of her mentor, Frances Seymour began corresponding with Henrietta Louisa Fermor, also a lady-in-waiting to Queen Caroline. These letters were published in 1805 as a handbook of polite taste and manners.[22] After the queen's death, the Seymours went into retirement, while the Fermors embarked on a continental tour. Horace Walpole, who visited the Fermors in Italy, found Lady Pomfret's vanity a constant source of amusement, recording a side of her character carefully omitted from her own letters: "She kept a correspondence with Lady Hertford and Lady Bell Finch, and continually employed her second daughter, to copy out the letters from and to herself, and made all the proper names be wrote in red ink" (14:248). The countess, of course, was also copying out a correspondence never meant to be wholly private. It ranges over a wide variety of topics—fashion, literary criticism, history, politics, affairs at court—in an almost equally wide variety of literary forms: char-

=

Forms of Reflection

acters, poetry, essays, fables, journals, and large amounts of description. It can be regarded as a kind of periodical paper written for circulation among members of the two households. Each writer adopts an eidolon (Lady Pomfret a pilgrim, Lady Hertford a hermit), and of course the letters are suffused with romantic reflections: inset tales of lovers and devotees, gossipy passages on courtship and gallantry, meditations on history and exotic places.

A recurring theme is feminine retirement, a subject on which the writers can be very pragmatic. Speaking of an aristocratic couple who married for love rather than money, Lady Hertford observes: "For people of their rank, this will require some prudence, as well as a great deal of passion; for, to live in a cottage on love, has a much better effect in a stanza of a ballad, than in real life" (*CHP,* 1:141). Lady Pomfret turns a discriminating eye on convents where nuns live in silence and in sackcloth and on convents where nuns, swathed in silk and finery, enjoy the company of poets and peers. Nothing could be more frightful than enforced retirement. She describes how the Medici electress recently suppressed an engagement between one of her maids with an impecunious younger brother. For three years the young woman had threatened to take the veil in protest; Lady Pomfret looks on in horror as she makes good her threat. The young woman

> entered the church with a cheerful and assured look, though so disordered within, as to tremble from head to foot. This she strove to hide, taking leave of every one with as much resolution and grace, as if she thought the electress was looking on; and surely she hoped it would be reported to her. When the mass was over, we all conducted her to the door of the cloister: where, turning round, she returned us thanks, and added "Adio, a rivederle in Paradiso;" then, entering the door, was encompassed by creatures all covered with black veils, each holding a lighted taper: the door then shut her in for ever.   (*CHP,* 1:128–30)

Lady Hertford confesses that "I have always entertained a notion that a monastic retirement is a very happy situation, under many circumstances," but adds, "I would not have it in the power of any parent, brother, guardian, or relation whatsoever, to shut up people against their inclinations" (*CHP,* 2:128). Returning home through Holland, Lady Pomfret discovers a Protestant woman who has successfully integrated privacy with social commerce: "Since the death of [her husband], and the disposal of her daughters, she is retired (with three or four servants) to prepare for the next world, and she calls herself the Solitaire. Her dress is plain, and she never goes into company; but if any persons come to her, she receives them with such vivacity and variety of wit, that you would imagine she was still in the midst of the beau monde" (*CHP*, 3:349). Retrospectively, one can see that the epistolary pilgrimage has all along been tending toward Mrs. Blount's little hermitage, a "small but convenient house, moated round" (*CHP*, 3:348).

Meanwhile, Lady Hertford had not been idle. With proceeds from their sinecures, the Seymours were able to purchase Riskings, a small estate whose romantic attractions Lady Hertford describes to her correspondent:

> We have now taken a house just by Colnbrook. It belongs to my lord
> Bathurst; and is what Mr. Pope, in his letters, calls his extravagante ber-
> gerie. The environs perfectly answer that title; and nearer to my idea of
> a scene in Arcadia, than any place I ever saw. The house is old, but con-
> venient; and when you are got within the little paddock it stands in, you
> would believe yourself an hundred miles from London, which I think
> a great addition to its beauty. (*CHP*, 1:172)

Lady Hertford is obviously delighted to find her house mentioned by such an authority on retirement and taste.[23] Humble as it was, Riskings was a house with a history; to a set of epigrams carved by distinguished authors on one of the benches, the countess adds verses of her own:

> By Bathurst planted, first these shades arose;
> Prior and Pope have sung beneath these boughs:
> Here Addison his moral theme pursu'd,
> And social Gay has cheer'd the solitude. (*CHP*, 2:3)

The couplets underscore the sense of community that is almost always a component of eighteenth-century concepts of retirement. The countess added them to underscore continuity with the past, even as she and her husband went about transforming the estate almost beyond recognition. To connect the house with their own romantic family history, the Seymours changed its name to Percy Lodge; they underscored this connection visually by cutting vistas looking out on Windsor Castle.

Her letters describe Percy Lodge as a monastic retreat, an indication of changing attitudes toward Gothicism and romance. If John Denham censured the "empty, airy contemplations" of the monks at Saint Anne's, and Andrew Marvell sneered at the romantic luxury of the nuns at Nunap-

=

Forms of Reflection
146

pleton House, Frances Seymour attempts to retrieve the contemplative life for modern manners and taste:

> There is one walk that I am extremely partial to; and which is rightly called the Abbey-walk, since it is composed of prodigiously high beech-trees, that form an arch through the whole length, exactly resembling a cloister. At the end is a statue; and about the middle a tolerably large circle, with Windsor chairs round it: and I think, for a person of contemplative disposition, one would scarcely find a more venerable shade in any poetical description. (*CHP* 2:3–4)

A grove of trees could substitute for a cloister because it produced the same aesthetic response in an observer versed in Milton and the romances.[24]

Lady Hertford did use her park as a kind of cloister, taking twice-daily contemplative walks around its two-mile circuit (*TGH*, 282) in a daily regimen that included historical retrospection and incidental meditation: "After my visit was over I retired to King Edward the Sixth's Bench (with my friend Tasso) from whence in less than ten minutes I saw six hares, one of them scarce bigger than a sucking rabbit" (*TGH*, 318).[25] The bench, the book, and the rabbits compose a little prospect in which they correspond to history, romance, and georgic, the genres that dominate the commonplace books of which this scene is a part. The volumes themselves offer a prospective view of the generic and social transformations being worked by feminine commerce. If they are dominated by women and feminine attitudes, the commonplace books nevertheless include writings by men and engage the larger world beyond the domestic circle. This circle was not closed but engaged, at a distance and with a difference, the kinds of writing and social thought being pursued in the clubs and coffeehouses of London. In both, private and public spaces were intimately bound together by links of literary, sexual, and economic commerce.

Percy Lodge and Domestic Virtue: House Poems by Frances Thynne Seymour, John Dalton, Moses Browne, and William Shenstone

English georgic was predicated on difference, reciprocity, and change; as Denham expresses it in *Coopers Hill*, commerce

Finds wealth where 'tis, and gives it where it wants,
Cities in Desarts, woods in Cities plants.

Writers of later georgics, however, began to disengage notions of cultivation and taste from such a materialist and historical understanding of the ways of commerce. As concepts of cultivation mutated into concepts of culture, poets began looking for alternatives to literary genres that encouraged reciprocity. These changes antedate the use of the word *culture* and begin in poems still recognizably georgic. This section examines this process as it appears in four house poems concerned with Percy Lodge, all written within a decade. If all of them are concerned with sexual commerce, generic differences indicate disagreements about the nature and function of retirement: Frances Seymour uses the verse epistle to define a quasi-monastic community of polite readers and conversationalists; John Dalton offers a prospect view of a society where men and women perform different but reciprocal political functions; Moses Browne writes a romance allegory opposing religious faith to worldly commerce; William Shenstone composes a lyric ode promoting a disinterested republic of taste. These formal and thematic differences point to substantial differences—within the Hertford circle—regarding gender, rank, and politics. While two of these poems are letters and three of them are parts of a larger correspondence, they introduce changes in notions of commerce that would eventually dissolve the social norms pursued in georgic writing.[26]

Frances Seymour's poem is part of the correspondence with Lady Pomfret. A reciprocal exchange between two writers of the same rank, it omits what for over a century had been a central component of the genre—the celebration of hospitality. In place of the rituals of deference, the countess describes what was, for her, the most important aspect of country living: a domestic routine modeled on the rule of a monastic order.[27] She is up at dawn, reads privately in her closet, joins the family for prayers and breakfast, and then, weather permitting, ventures out into the park:

We sometimes ride, and sometimes walk;
We play at chess, or laugh, or talk;
Sometimes, beside the crystal stream,
We meditate some serious theme;
Or in the grot, beside the spring,
We hear the feather'd warblers sing.
Shakespeare (perhaps) an hour diverts,
Or Scot directs to mend our hearts.

Forms of Reflection
148

With Clark, God's attributes we explore;
And, taught by him, admire them more.
Gay's Pastorals sometimes delight us,
Or Tasso's grisly specters fright us:
Sometimes we trace Armida's bowers,
And view Rinaldo chain'd with flowers.
Often, from thoughts sublime as these,
I sink at once—and make a cheese. (*CHP*, 2:38)

Cultivation being the common object of both gardening and literary criticism, the countess translates the usual catalogue of fruits and flowers into
a garland of authors. After dinner the family and servants assemble in
the hall for evening prayers, followed by supper and more entertainment:

Then tolls the bell, and all unite
In pray'r that God would bless the night.
From this (tho' I confess the change
From pray'r to cards is somewhat strange)
To cards we go, till ten has struck:
And then, however bad our luck,
Our stomachs ne'er refuse to eat
Eggs, cream, fresh butter, or calves' feet;
'Sparagus, peas, or kidney beans.
Our supper past, an hour we sit,
And talk of hist'ry, Spain, or wit:
But Scandal far is banish'd hence,
Nor dares intrude with false pretense
Of pitying looks, or holy rage
Against the vices of the age:
We know we all were born in sin,
And find enough to blame within. (*CHP*, 2:38–39)

The poem ends in this devotional *resolve* to be polite. The spare repast
recalls the board-bursting collations of earlier poems; in this household
material pleasures take a backseat to prayer and conversation. The "we"
of the poem is not defined through relationships of deference or charity
made manifest in a ritual feast but through relations of collegiality
expressed through polite exchange. Shared manners, rather than place at
table, define a conversable group that includes domestic servants, live-in
companions, and occasional callers, such as James Thomson, Elizabeth

Carter, or Lord Bathurst. The countess is at pains to underscore the promiscuity of a discourse including both sexes and covering a wide range of topics. The genres mentioned as staples of conversation — history, politics, and literary criticism — are the same genres that constitute the feminine correspondence of which the verse epistle is a part. Unlike the epigrams penned by Jonson and Marvell, which define a hierarchical community through public praises, this letter-in-verse defines a private circle through epistolary reciprocity. Lady Pomfret responded with a poetical epistle of her own.

The Reverend John Dalton (1709–63) originally joined the circle as tutor of the Seymour's son Beauchamp; his *Epistle to the Countess of Hertford at Percy Lodge* (1744, 1745) indicates the extent to which the concept of taste was leveling social differences between gentlemen and peers.[28] The servant addresses his mistress in the same familiar manner that she herself uses to salute Lady Pomfret; he describes a visit, reports a conversation, complains of the weather. He works these elements into a complex meditation on retirement, taste, and sexual commerce. Following the example of *Coopers Hill*, Dalton structures his poem by means of repetition and variation: a sequence of landscapes locates relations of authority within physical, social, and historical space. This structure underscores differences in the contemporary scene but also how the political landscape has changed in the intervening century: for Denham's castles and cathedrals, Dalton substitutes three landscape parks in the Thames Valley — Claremont, Esher, and Percy Lodge — indicating the displacement of cultivation into the private sector. As Denham alludes to Waller's poem in praise of the restoration of St. Paul's, Dalton alludes to Garth's poem praising Newcastle's Claremont, since landscaped by Kent.[29] In georgic poetics, repetitions within and between works signify the continuities that become grounds for measuring difference. Echoing Denham's comparison of Charles's liberality to the easy slopes of Windsor, Dalton modifies his source:

> In pleasure lost, I wish to gaze
> At once a thousand different ways,
> Awful or pleasing, every part
> Expands the soul, or glads the heart,
> Great, open, liberal, unconfin'd,
> Just emblem of its master's mind,

=

Forms of Reflection
150

Who knows unequall'd state to shew,

Yet, gracious, stoops to all below.   (1:113)

Dalton's *Epistle* defines its community through reciprocity, including its commerce with Denham's earlier georgic. Refinement here entails a literal revision: if this prospect view conveys the traditional virtues of detachment and superiority, the nature of commerce is changing: Newcastle differs from Charles by being liberal with his taste, rather than with his purse.[30]

When an approaching storm abruptly terminates the visit, the dampened traveler proceeds to Esher, seat of Newcastle's brother, Henry Pelham. The gates are closed; the prime minister is meditating war with France. In the tradition of georgic prophecy, foul weather signifies a coming war—a matter of immediate concern to Lady Hertford, since her son was abroad completing his education. Modulating into romance, Dalton describes how women contribute to the peace, comparing Pelham's recent visit to Percy Lodge to Numa's nocturnal visits to the nymph Egeria:

Nay, when the Atlas of our state

Throws off for You a nation's weight,

In courtly terms your ear to greet,

And casts himself beneath your feet,

You (like Egeria) in your grott

Or seek he must, or finds You not.

More cautious still, e'en when retir'd,

By wits nor censur'd, nor admir'd,

You say, (tho' every art your friend)

You dare to no one art pretend.

Your fear is just. Each state and nation

Assigns to woman reputation,

While man asserts his wider claim,

Jealous proprietor of fame.   (1:116)

In contrast to Claremont, where the artificial mount and sweeping prospect command admiration, Dalton characterizes Percy Lodge as a feminine place ruled by a nymph whose grot emblematizes retired virtue. His structure of repetition and variation calls attention to a reciprocal relation between the estates and their owners; the masculine prospect and the feminine grotto—"fame" and "reputation"—are equivalent, though different, parts of the same landscape. Using landscape to establish Frances Seymour's place in history, Dalton compares the countess's domestic virtues to the commanding prospect denied her by her sex: pretending to no one art, she stands in a superior position to them all. As a woman, she represents in the arena of feeling and emotion what someone like Pelham represents in the arena of reason and action: a "disinterestedness," different from, but equivalent to, that of her male counterparts.[31] At a time when masculine tempers run high, Egeria's conversations with the prime minister might temper the warlike and "jealous proprietor of fame."

Dalton describes two ways in which women act as exemplars of georgic refinement. From retirement, Lady Hertford, "without their leave," demonstrates to men how the world ought to be managed:

> Yet sure, without offence, You may
> On nature's open leaf display
> Your harmless unambitious skill,
> To sink a grott, or slope a hill,
> A dell with flowers adorn, or lead
> A winding rill along the mead,
> Or bid opposing trees be join'd
> In hospitable league intwin'd,
> Without their leave, whose madness dares
> Rouze human states to cruel wars.   (1:116)

Percy Lodge repeats Claremont and Esher with a difference: it is ruled by a woman who exerts power for innocent ends: she can form a league of elms, or defend her "feather'd folk" by making war on the "Bourbon of the air" (116). Lacking ambition and jealousy, and cultivating her estate in innocence and peace, the nymph can give laws to Numa. Lady Hertford is also an exemplar within the immediate family. Refined by such a mother, Beauchamp's part on the "civil stage" (117) will be to instill a taste for virtue in his peers. At a time when it was uncommon for a noblewoman to educate her own children, Lady Hertford supervised every aspect of her son's education: he *cultivated* a little garden at Percy Lodge and discussed painting, music, and literature in a lengthy correspondence with his mother.[32] Dalton regards education as an integral part of cultivating the estate; tutor and mother are "boastful builders" who together have "founded the structure of his mind" (112). A male version of Milton's Lady, Beauchamp will

> . . . th' enchanted cup put by,
> And every vain temptation fly,
> Of power, or pension, place, or name,
> If meant state-traps, that sink to shame. (1:117)

Through the genres of epistle, romance, and georgic, Dalton defines the reciprocal roles performed by men and women as actors in history. He refines *Coopers Hill* by substituting for material history a commerce founded on the passions and the education of the heart.

Dalton never delivered a promised sequel. Beauchamp died of smallpox at Bologna on the eve of his twentieth birthday, effectively terminating the political ambitions of the family. The Seymours commissioned Moses Browne (1704–1787) to memorialize a family estate doomed to dissolution. In contrast to Dalton's epistle, *Percy Lodge*, invokes a gothicized past in order to deride refinement and civility.[33] Browne announces that he will emulate Denham, Pope, and Dyer, but in fact his models for descriptive verse are Spenser, Milton, and Thomson.[34] Like *The Castle of Indolence* (1748), *Percy Lodge* is a sixteenth-century romance condensed into an eighteenth-century house poem discoursing on the mutability of pleasure. The different treatments of this Spenserian theme point to differences between the situations at Hagley Park and Percy Lodge: if Thomson attempts to discriminate between the kinds of changes wrought by progress and luxury, Browne casts mutability in a wholly negative light.

In *Percy Lodge*, georgic landscape mutates into an enchanted forest where a "Happy Libertine" (26) encounters adventures corresponding to the times of day and the ages of man. The allegory represents human life, appropriately enough, as a kind of labyrinth:

> Path after Path, from Change to Change:
> All free, I fetch a Compass large. (10)

Like the countess's park, Browne's labyrinthine poem packs maximal variety into minimal space, including, among other things, a rose garden, a shepherd's hut, a dusky grove, a grotto, a distant prospect, a hexagon, an amphitheater, a greenhouse, a canal, a "bongolo," a gothic seat, and a night piece. In Spenser's manner, Browne is ecphrastic rather than simply descriptive: he describes images rather than things, works of art rather than unadorned nature. The sunset is conceitedly described as

> a Picture to the Eye,
> Drawn on the Canvas of the Sky. (27)

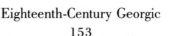

Eighteenth-Century Georgic

Lyric figures ("frequent Turns, of Fancy's chusing," 13) dramatize emotional responses to the "sweet Perplexity of Change" (14). Rather than observing operations of history in a landscape, the poem records how images operate on the passions. The rose garden, like Armida's bower, renders a "rural lover" helpless:

> I roam it's Walks, around, around,
> All where I go's enchanted Ground! (10)

In a parallel passage (a night piece complete with nightingale, beetle, bat, owl, weasel and toad), the overload of sensual pleasure leads to melancholy and despair. The wanderer is pulled up,

> When a black Horror spreads my Mind,
> Unusual, sudden Pang I find. (28)

At the bottom of the labyrinth, death awaits the traveler in an elegy for Beauchamp. In English georgic, allegories often appear as inset episodes, but in *Percy Lodge* this relation is reversed, as allegory becomes a containing genre for georgic episodes. The functions of landscape change: Dalton's poem discriminates between landscapes; in *Percy Lodge* the reader is asked to discriminate between natural appearances and supernatural truths. The empty garden is full of cryptic messages, marble creatures, and trompe l'oeil images; disembodied voices speak mysteriously from concealed locations. These evanescent, romantic fancies cut away at the material basis of georgic realism and the public values it sustains. A voice from the grot implies that the only way out of the labyrinth is to see it for what it is:

> Disclaim thy Hopes of earthly Good!
> False are those dazling Objects view'd
> As in the Mirrour of the Stream
> The Landscapes all inverted seem. (17)

The sybil's simile literalizes reflection *as* reflection, while rendering rural meditation groundless: to see the prospect right side up, one must see it upside down. Readers must displace the place described. There is no prospect view, as indeed there was no worldly prospect in view for the Seymour family.[35] The one historical retrospection documents corruption and discontinuity in the Protestant Reformation since the time of Edward VI (a Seymour ancestor). Like Beauchamp, Edward died tragically young. If *The Castle of Indolence* attempts to bring Spenser into the eigh-

=

Forms of Reflection

teenth century, *Percy Lodge*, undermining the eighteenth-century ideals of civility and progress, is unabashedly retrospective. No Knight of Industry appears or is desired.

Significantly perhaps, the poem addresses the master of the estate and not the mistress; no one is visited; no conversations are reported. Browne's poem articulates what the countess would be thinking in her twice-daily tours around her "cloister" (she may have dictated the program). To escape the labyrinth of mutability, his wanderer turns his back on the house and its sociable values:

> Far shall thy Soul nor need to roam,
> Look to the Skies and view thy Home. (18)

This ultimate displacement distinguishes *Percy Lodge* from earlier house poems; piety has become a private virtue:

> What tho' no Hill thy level Soil
> For Prospect yields, the Gazer's Toil,
> T[h]ere, like the OWNER's mind, is spy'd
> True Greatness, without swelling Pride. (31)

Praising the owner's piety, rather than his prospect, Browne succeeds in rendering the house poem homely. Compare Joseph Trapp's encomium, addressed to the previous generation of Somersets:

> Now for a nearer View, my Muse, prepare,
> But view with Rev'rence, and approach with Fear.[36]

At Percy Lodge no grand mount marks the place of the family in society; no stately frontispiece of poor calls attention to their wealth. The humility topos is reinterpreted: one need not "toil" to look up to virtue, as at Nunappleton House or Badminton. The message Browne finds inscribed in this fabulously ornate garden could be read from the most ordinary of human lives. As in the conduct books by Watts and Rowe, Christian values detach virtue from rank. But Browne's meditational poem strikes out in a different direction: in its lyric circumscription of conversation, its nostalgia for the past, its refusal to discriminate, and its resistance to cultivation, civility, and progress, *Percy Lodge* assembles much of the repertoire found in romantic concepts of culture.

In "Rural Elegance," William Shenstone substitutes a lyric poetics of harmonious identity for georgic discrimination. The poem emerged out of a complicated epistolary exchange between Shenstone, Frances Seymour (now duchess of Somerset), and Henrietta Knight, Lady Lux-borough—since retrieved from exile.[37] Lady Luxborough plotted with Shenstone in letters that read like epistolary romance and later appeared in something like that form in *Select Letters between the Late Duchess of Somerset, Lady Luxborough . . . William Shenstone, Esq. etc.* (1778), edited by Thomas Hull. The letters were intended for display; Marjorie Williams describes how

> Lady Luxborough probably took great pains over her letters to W.S. in her capacity of Egeria to a man of some merit. One very beautiful letter of hers to him is in the possession of a Warwickshire gentleman. On a double sheet of note-paper, she writes in French to the poet—A Shen-stone a la Ferme Ornee. The edge of the note-paper is pale blue, the figures of elegant eighteenth-century beaux and belles, beautifully painted by hand, the flower decoration likewise, the colour is delicate but bright, and the whole effect charming.[38]

Here is Shenstone romancing the two matrons:

> The Leasows, June ye 1st 1748
> Almost Night.
>
> Madam.
>
> I return my Lady Hartford's Letter by the very first opportunity I meet with; & herein I but discharge my conscience; as I am in Duty bound to obey your Ladyship's Commands; & also, to be no way instrumental in delaying your Answer to a Letter which has afforded me the highest satisfaction.
>
> As to the Choice or Preference of any Trifle of mine which may be thought most proper to send her Ladyship, it wou'd be most prudent in me to be guided by your own Opinion; as the Person best acquainted with Lady Hartford's Taste, & who, I am apt enough to flatter myself, wishes well to my Reputation. The Esteem I share at Percy-Lodge is entirely of your own creation; & as you have almost literally produc'd it out of nothing, I daresay you understand & will use the most proper means to keep it alive. Otherwise, it were much better for me it had never existed, as a Fall from the greatest Happiness compleats our Idea of the most consummate Misery. (63)

Lady Luxborough's idea was to make Shenstone a second Thomson by insinuating him into the duchess's good graces. While Shenstone was

Forms of Reflection
156

nothing averse, the plot failed, perhaps because Frances Seymour had doubts about her friend's character; more likely she was now unwilling to have her name appear in print, for whatever good cause.[39] Lady Luxborough, for whom retirement was perhaps more of a fashion statement than a religious commitment, failed to appreciate how reclusive her friend had become since the deaths of Rowe, Caroline, Beauchamp, and her husband. The duchess of Somerset subscribed to a set of prints of The Leasows and may have sent a gift, but Shenstone never met the great lady or saw the estate he celebrates.

This was less a material disadvantage than at first appears; "Rural Elegance" is a poem concerned with describing passions more than places. In that respect it is like *Percy Lodge*, but while Browne's poem turns its back on society and progress, Shenstone's purpose is to promote a new republic of taste founded upon contemplation and rural retirement. This project leads to dramatic modifications in georgic poetry. Shenstone abandons the familiar style in favor of a grand lyric utterance intended to be at once wholly personal and wholly public. As early as 1743 he was altering an earlier version of what was to become his manifesto on aesthetic commerce: "I do not like formal didactic poetry, and shall never be able to finish aught but the episodes, I doubt: unless I allow myself to treat the rest in *my own manner*, transiently" (*LWS*, 63; emphasis in original). In "Rural Elegance," common sense yields to personal genius; communal values, discrimination, and reciprocity to a visionary and holistic republicanism.

The ode unfolds in three sections, on nature, art, and their common basis in contemplation. The strophe excludes "Several Classes of Men from any Pretensions to comprehend the Beauties of Nature, [and fixes] upon ye Person of true Taste as ye only adequate Spectator" (*LWS*, 258). Shenstone disengages taste from membership in a particular class or community; if squires riding to the hounds and yeomen tilling the land participate in country pleasures, their "suspicious fearful care" (9) and "conceptions crude" (4) bind them to a narrow material vision that interferes with aesthetic or spiritual understanding:

> But though the various harvest gild your plains,
> Does the mere landscape feast your eye?
> Or the warm hope of distant gains
> Far other hope of glee supply?   (5)

Hunting and cultivation, the labors that produce the "various harvest" in conventional house poems, find no place here; Shenstone's repast is a "feast" for the eyes only. To persons of cultivated imagination, nature has different fruits to offer: disinterested pleasure in the mere landscape and a Christian hope of distant gains in a life hereafter. The glee in rural poetry springs from superior feelings for nature, a disposition nature disposes "where she pleases" (7). Unlike political disinterestedness, aesthetic disinterestedness is not a matter of owning property:

> Bonds, contracts, feoffments, names unmeet for prose,
> The towering Muse endures not to disclose;
> Alas! *her* unrevers'd decree,
> More comprehensive and more free,
> Her lavish charter, Taste, appropriates all we see. (9)

Coopers Hill is again the point of reference; in this revision, nature operates according to laws of taste, rather than to laws of material history; the new great "charter" underwrites genius, rather than property. Unlike Dalton, Shenstone sees no connection between disinterestedness and distinctions of rank and gender; but if his republic appears more inclusive than the other kinds of community we have considered, it is not, as they are, inclusive by virtue of heterogeneity. The universal standard upheld in nature's lavish charter is founded in human nature. Genius, the only adequate spectator, has everyone's interest at heart.

An episode adapted from Shaftesbury's *Characteristicks* modulates the argument from the economy of nature to the economy of art.[40] The nymph Adria scorns the doge's "bridal gold" (10) for life with a virtuous hermit. Poets, Shenstone implies, stand in a new relationship to their patrons; instead of exchanging praise for pelf, they exchange passion for passion:

> Not that the poet's boasted fire
> Should Fame's wide-echoing trumpet swell;
> Or, on the music of his lyre
> Each future age with rapture dwell;
> The vaunted sweets of praise remove,
> Yet shall such bosoms claim a part
> In all that glads the human heart;
> Yet these the spirits, form'd to judge and prove
> All Nature's charms immense, and Heav'n's unbounded love. (13)

=

Forms of Reflection

Surrounded by courtiers who "slight her merit, but adore her place" (12) the duchess of Somerset, like the nymph Adria, pursues in solitude the "sweets" of retired contemplation (11). If Fame's trumpet leads some to admire her place, the muse's lyre enables "sweetly pensive" (13) readers to "claim a part" in her greatness through aesthetic contemplation. Unlike the other addresses made to Frances Seymour, "Rural Elegance" does not imply a community based on difference or reciprocity: Shenstone appeals to universal passions, striving to form a lyric bond that renders the private public and the great common.

But Shenstone is still close enough to georgic that he feels obligated to consider the material implications of this aesthetic program; with these three stanzas on the social function of poetry he pairs three on gardening and political economy:

> Why brand these pleasures with the name
> Of soft, unsocial toils, of indolence and shame?   (16)

Improving the private estate will contribute to the public weal because this "bounteous work" supplies income for the laborer and his "train of helpless infants dear" (15). Charity (making a belated appearance in these poems) looks on approvingly as householders rechannel wealth back into the countryside. Aesthetic production contributes to the larger economy; even estate owners participate in the labor:

> And sure there seem, of human kind,
> Some born to shun the solemn strife;
> Some for amusive tasks design'd,
> To soothe the certain ills of life.   (17)

For gardeners, leisure is labor; their amusive task is to produce useful pleasure for others. Just what kinds of ills or what kinds of life Shenstone does not say; differences within "human kind" tend to be generalized away into a holistic and psychologized view of society as it appears to aesthetic contemplation. The problem of the division of labor, which will preoccupy generations of writers on culture, is recognized by Shenstone, but only just.

A second digression, encouraging citizens and poets to resist "splendour's irksome beams" (20, 21), leads into an epode arguing that aesthetic contemplation will foster virtue within the state. Shenstone responds to an obvious objection: "How must faithless Art prevail," should virtuous persons (like the duchess?) pursue the good in solitude? (24).

≡

The answer is that aesthetic commerce transforms retired privacy into a form of public engagement:

> Ah no, from these [sons of fancy] the public sphere requires
> Example for its giddy bands;
> From these impartial Heav'n demands
> To spread the flame itself inspires;
> To sift Opinion's mingled mass,
> Impress a nation's taste, and bid the sterling pass. (24)

The belief that taste can circulate underwrites Shenstone's argument that persons of genius are (or should be) the unacknowledged legislators of mankind. Under the new charter, meditation becomes both the object and the means of cultivation. Shenstone de-materializes the social progress celebrated in English georgic in an allegory for mental cultivation:

> Yet all embody'd to the mental sight,
> A train of smiling Virtues bright
> Shall there the wise retreat allow,
> Shall twine triumphant palms to deck the wanderer's brow. (11)

Traditional concepts of civic virtue are obviously under stress when the victor's palm is granted to those who retreat. But perhaps it is only in retreat from a social life that imposes difference and change that wanderers can realize a common humanity, the impartiality that identifies individuals with the whole in which they participate.

As the generic structures defining cultivation mutate into those defining culture, the georgic poet stands in a new relation to the landscape; if Marvell's narrator goes into the wood when he loses sight of the house and its objective social values, Shenstone's poets of nature become "dazzled maniacs" (19) when, smitten by the glare of "art's rival seat" (18), they are beguiled by commerce and material cares. Rather than making discriminations, Shenstone's lyric metaphors link persons and things through relations of mediated identity: echo, reflection, radiance, charm. These metaphors, often reified into concepts, are the stuff and substance of most writing about culture. Shenstone resorts to them in order to engage his reader in an innovative way; instead of using georgic figures to mediate differences through conversation and reciprocity, he employs lyric figures to substitute aesthetic union for epistolary commerce. The poet concludes his ode with a craftily equivocal address to Frances Sey-

=

Forms of Reflection
160

mour that notes differences of gender and rank only to erase them in a lyrical appeal to identity:

> her candour will not exclude
> The lowly shepherd's votive strain,
> Who tunes his reed amidst his rural chear,
> Fearful, yet not averse, that SOMERSET should hear. (27)

Shenstone asks the duchess to *correspond*, although in a different sense from that heretofore seen: if she emotes sincerely—passions glowing candidly, imagination resonating in harmony—the ode will have established its bond of social identity.

This failed to happen. The poem was graciously accepted at Percy Lodge, but the duchess, Whig though she was, proved unwilling to identify herself or her estate with Shenstone's republican ideas:

> Will it not appear strange if I confess to you, that the Honour you have done me by the inscription of [the ode], and a Stanza or two in the Poem itself, has given me some pain? And I shall look upon it as a very great Addition to the Favour, if whenever my Name, or that of Percy-Lodge occurs, you will have the Goodness to fill the Blanks (which leaving out those Words must occasion) with Stars, Dashes, or any other Mark you please, without suspecting me of an affected or false modesty.[41]

The poet regarded this as failure; but Lady Luxborough, comically misjudging both the poem and the response, chose to interpret the duchess's reply as a feminine ploy: "She is, I am sure, proud of its being inscribed to her, though too bashful, in her retirement, to choose her name to be at the head of it; yet well knowing with inward satisfaction, that every body will know she is the heroine of the piece, as much as one knows who was Waller's Sacharissa, without her real name at the top" (1123). Lady Luxborough failed to perceive the new directions romance was taking in the duchess's Gothicism and Shenstone's republicanism. "Rural Elegance" remained unpublished until after the death of the duchess; in 1758 it appeared as the first poem in the fifth volume of Dodsley's *Collection*.

Shenstone's innovative house poem describes how aesthetic meditation might function within a new kind of society. The poem attempts to call this society into being through lyric figures and to show how this new society would sustain and reproduce itself through the circulation of aesthetic productions. Not the least striking thing about Shenstone's poem is the ways in which it challenges older forms of social discrimination in the process of defining society as an imaginative whole. Critics still use the devices Shenstone was inventing to define social relationships as aesthetic relationships, as when Armstrong (*Desire and Domestic Fiction*) speaks of the "figure, or turn of cultural logic, that both differentiates the sexes and links them together by sexual desire" (24). This is sexual commerce as Shenstone understood it. There are differences; what Shenstone describes as human nature Armstrong identifies as eighteenth-century ways of thinking about gender. She distinguishes one kind of culture from another. But none of the critics discussed here identify the concept of culture itself with changes taking place in eighteenth-century writing. This is the connection I attempt to make, not by ascribing a particular kind of culture to the figures found in eighteenth-century writing but by identifying such concepts of culture with the generic procedures found in particular kinds of eighteenth-century writing. By thinking of these as generic procedures, rather than cultural norms, we can make better sense of the differences we encounter in eighteenth-century writing and the historical continuities that make eighteenth-century writing a factor in our own critical practices.

Generic distinctions made a difference then, and they still do. Taking georgic procedures for discriminating differences as my point of departure from cultural critique, I have discriminated between the kinds of changes taking place in the house poem and the community it describes and enacts: the exclusion of significant features, such as deference and charity; the addition of new material, such as discussions of taste and catalogues of authors; the reevaluation of topics such as monasticism and progress; shifts in the status of senders and receivers so that householders (who write poems themselves) are addressed familiarly; a shift from materialism to aesthetic psychology; and generic shifts from epigram to romance allegory and lyric ode. These changes are not uniform within contemporary instances of the genre; generic differences articulate differences with regard to religion, gender, rank, and political outlook.

These are significant variations, yet there are continuities with earlier instances of the genre: country-house poems continue to be concerned with labor and luxury, piety and patriotism. Their meanings and social functions are altered when these topics are worked into different kinds of generic structure. A country-house ideology is difficult to discern in these

=

Forms of Reflection
162

poems: the authors are alike in upholding domestic virtue, yet they use Percy Lodge as the model for very different kinds of community. Lady Hertford's letter defines a quasi-monastic enclave where pious and polite conversation supplants courtly gossip. Dalton's georgic prospect view describes how corruption might be resisted by disinterested peers acting in and through history. Browne's Christian allegory undermines commerce and material values. Shenstone's lyric pursues a republican form of aesthetic commerce. If variation was itself a georgic procedure, in these poems we see georgic writing in the act of mutating itself out of existence, a process completed when nineteenth-century concepts of culture supplanted seventeenth- and eighteenth-century concepts of cultivation predicated on material history and social difference.

5

Cultivation into Culture

Shaftesbury, Coleridge, and the
Social Functions of
Aesthetic Contemplation

T he discussion of the Hertford circle considered literary commerce at close range; this final chapter offers a longer view of
the shift in forms of reflection. By juxtaposing two works written
a century apart I can underscore the significance of the incre-
mental changes observed in the last chapter and consider in
more detail why and how georgic conceptions of difference were
rejected by later critics. Forms of reflection pioneered by Coleridge are still used to represent the history of aesthetics from
Shaftesbury to Coleridge as a development, rather than a social
or literary change. R. L. Brett, for instance, uses the notion of
"guiding ideas" to demonstrate that "Coleridge was attempting
the same task as Shaftesbury." Ernest Tuveson identifies a "kind
of thinking" or "complex of thought" pioneered by Shaftesbury
that influenced later writers and ultimately Coleridge. Robert
Marsh finds "intellectual continuity" between Shaftesbury and
Coleridge in a basic kind of theory.[1] Like Coleridge, these critics
abstract ideas or complexes of ideas from kinds of writing,
thereby circumscribing the historicity of philosophical writing
and the social functions performed by concepts such as introspection or disinterestedness.

These and related "ideas" are treated here as generic constituents that address a changing set of literary and social issues.
Shaftesbury's *Soliloquy, or Advice to an Author* (1710, 1711) and
Coleridge's *The Friend* (1809–10, 1818) both pursue cultivation
through forms of reflection, but their contrary uses of contempla-

tive genres imply very different literary and social programs. Shaftesbury meditates to establish critical distance, Coleridge, to erase distances imposed by critics. Shaftesbury presents the mind as a little society that governs itself through dialectical self-scrutiny; Coleridge presents society as a mind writ large, regulating itself by subordinating the passions of uneducated persons to the reason of an intellectual elite. Their forms of reflection differ accordingly: in *Soliloquy* the gentleman critic, as polite speaker, discriminates social and historical differences, while in *The Friend*, the man of letters, as inspired reader, divines the foundations of human nature and the social order in works of universal genius.

Both writers explore literary and social formations within the parameters of republican theories of government. Upholding the Revolution Settlement against Tory politicians and Louis XIV, Shaftesbury makes a Whig case for cultivation through commerce: "Hence it is that those *Arts* [of civilization] have been deliver'd to us in such perfection by *free Nations* who, from the Nature of their Government, as from a proper Soil, produc'd the generous Plants: whilst the mightiest bodies and vastest Empires, govern'd by *Force* and *a Despotick Power*, could, after Ages of Peace and Leisure, produce no other than what was deform'd and barbarous of the kind."[2] Opposing the republican principles upheld by Napoleon and the French Revolution, Coleridge was less enthusiastic about prospects of boundless liberty: "The notion of our measureless superiority in Good Sense to our Ancestors, is somewhat less fashionable, than at the commencement of the French Revolution: we hear less of the jargon of *this enlightened Age*."[3] Coleridge opposes to French republicanism what can be described as a country or "old Whig" form of republican politics; he will "uphold those Truths and those Merits, which are founded in the noble and permanent Parts of our Nature, against the Caprices of Fashion, and such Pleasures, as either depend on transitory and accidental Causes, or are pursued from less worthy impulses" (2:18).[4]

Since both writers are concerned with republican politics, both make commerce a focus of their reflections on how authority is best exercised in a complex society. If both seek to cultivate an elite, Shaftesbury promotes commerce as a means of diffusing liberty and refinement, while Coleridge, associating commerce with leveling, rejects trafficking in social differences in favor of an organic unity founded upon powers of genius. The grounds of continuity and difference between *Soliloquy* and *The Friend* might be expressed this way: Shaftesbury seeks to render philosophy polite, while Coleridge seeks to render the polite philosophical.[5]

=

Forms of Reflection

Neither author claims to offer original ideas; instead, they emphasize their literary innovations, which use forms of aesthetic reflection to alter the relation of critical writing to history, politics, literature, and philosophy. Since their critical practices, by and large, became normative in eighteenth- and nineteenth-century discussions about what we now call culture, their arguments for changing critical practices are of the first importance for understanding subsequent literary history. They can be considered under three interrelated heads: authority, history, and method.

Critical Reading versus the Well-Read Critic: *Soliloquy* and *The Friend*

Shaftesbury's belief that politeness should mediate between knowledge and action leads him to begin even his discourse on interior colloquy with a comment on manners: "However able or willing a Man may be *to advise*, 'tis no easy matter to make ADVICE a free Gift. For to make a Gift free indeed, there must be nothing in it which takes from Another to add to Our-self. In all other respects, *to give*, and *to dispense*, is generosity, and good-will; but to bestow Wisdom, is to gain a Mastery which can't so easily be allow'd us" (1:103). How can one give advice without assuming a position of authority? Disclaiming any pretension to instruct his readers in what to think, Shaftesbury insists that his purpose in *Soliloquy, or Advice to an Author* is "not so much to give Advice, as to consider of *the Way and Manner of advising*" (1:104). He prefers the "mannerly" way of conversation to methodical argument by definition and division not merely because it is more polite but because it is less authoritarian. Describing his dialogical method as "self-dissection" (1:105), he notes the relation of his work to the anatomy genre employed by Donne and Burton, while underscoring a difference: his *Art or Science* (1:105) is founded upon commerce, rather than formal definition and division.

As we have seen, presenting a work as a revision of earlier instances of the genre was central to the idea of cultivation. Shaftesbury criticizes the advice genres against which he innovates—essay, tract, and memoir—as part of the program of refinement undertaken in *Characteristicks*. Writers of "Meditations, Occasional Reflections, Solitary Thoughts or other such Exercizes as come under the notion of this *self-discoursing Practice* . . . conceive suddenly" and accordingly produce conceited "Miscarriages and Abortions." Combining the least desirable parts of urban frivolity and country rusticity, essayists "exhibit on the Stage of the World

=

Cultivation into Culture

167

that Practice which they shou'd have kept to themselves." The essayists have perverted meditation into a theater for wit: "Though they are often retir'd, they are never *by themselves*. The World is ever of the Party" (1:109).[6] He heaps particular scorn on the pious effusions of "Pseudo-ascetics": "A *Saint*-Author of all Men least values Politeness. He scorns to confine that Spirit, in which he writes, to the Rules of Criticism and profane Learning. Nor is he inclin'd in any respect to play the Critic on himself, or regulate his Style or Language by the Standard of good Company, and People of the better sort" (1:110). Whether chopping logic or speaking in tongues, dissenters brook no dissent: "Instead of Controul, Debate, or Argument, the chief Exercise of the Wit consists in uncontroulable Harangues and Reasonings, which must neither be question'd nor contradicted" (1:111). At the other social extreme, court wits, "common *great Talkers*," produce scandal chronicles equally impolite: "Their Page can carry none of the Advantages of their Person. They can no-way bring into Paper those Airs they give themselves in Discourse" (1:111). The several genres of advice giving—essays, devotional tracts, and memoirs—prove unfit vehicles of counsel because authors who mistake self-regard for self-knowledge only inhibit the critical self-reflection they purport to offer.

If the first essay in *Soliloquy* is a psychological critique of literature, the second is a literary critique of psychology. The mind is no transparent medium: "One would think, there was nothing easier for us, than to know our own minds. . . . But our Thoughts have generally such an obscure implicit Language, that 'tis the hardest thing in the world to make 'em speak distinctly. For this reason, the right method is to give 'em Voice and Accent" (1:113). Shaftesbury imagines a kind of talking cure: meditators should "give voice and accent" to the internal factions comprising the self. Called to the bar, the unruly elements of character will speak their own condemnation:

> By this means it will soon happen that Two form'd *Partys* will erect themselves *within*. For the Imaginations or Fancies being thus roundly treated, are forc'd to declare themselves, and take party. Those on the side of the elder Brother APPETITE, are strangely subtle and insinuating. They have always the Faculty to speak by Nods and Winks. By this practice they conceal half their meaning, and, like modern Politicians, pass for deeply wise, and adorn themselves with the finest Pretext and most specious Glosses imaginable; till being confronted with their Fellows of

=

Forms of Reflection

a plainer Language and Expression, they are forc'd to quit their myste-
rious Manner, and discover themselves mere Sophisters and Impos-
tors, who have not the least to do with the Party of REASON and *good
sense.* (1:123–24)[7]

As Shaftesbury argues in *A Letter Concerning Enthusiasm*, suppressing a
faction only renders it more insistent (1:20–21). Giving voice to the passions is sound epistemology, since only by attending to the less articulate
parts of our character can we comprehend ourselves in our very complexity. However opaque they may appear at first, the "Imaginations or Fancies" nonetheless speak with an art familiar to literary critics—the
language of gesture and rhetoric. An educated person can read the mind
like a book.

In Shaftesbury's view, character consists of multiple elements standing in a dialogical relationship to one another. A philosophy of characters, if it is to take the measure of such complexity, must be likewise
complex. By way of analogy, Shaftesbury compares his method of addressing the characters of mind to the generic procedures poets use to
address the characters of men in society. He considers the uses of dialogue in writings by Homer and Plato, the "Prince of Poets and the divine
Philosopher" (1:130):

> Besides their force of Style and hidden Numbers, [Plato's writings]
> carry'd a sort of *Action and Imitation,* the same as the *Epick* and *Dram-
> atick* kinds. They were either real *Dialogues,* or Recitals of such *person-
> ated Discourses:* where the Persons themselves had their Characters
> preserved thro'out, their Manners, Humours, and distinct Turns of
> Temper and Understanding maintain'd, according to the most exact
> *poetical Truth.* 'Twas not enough that these Pieces treated fundamen-
> tally of *Morals,* and in consequence pointed out *real Characters* and
> *Manners:* They exhibited 'em *alive,* and set the Countenances and Com-
> plexions of Men plainly in view. (1:127–28)

By distinguishing characters, dialogical philosophy teaches us "to know
ourselves." Plato discriminates between kinds of character by combining
different kinds of writing: Socrates is "the philosophical hero" of a brief
epic in which appear "both *the heroick* and *the simple, the tragick,* and
the comick, Vein." In the generic complexity of Platonic dialogue, Shaftesbury discovers a model for interior colloquy, "a sort of *Pocket-mirrour,*
always ready and in use" (1:128). What is true of Plato is equally true of

Homer, "great *Mimographer*" (1:129), whose epic consists of "an artful Series or Chain of Dialogues, which turn upon one remarkable Catastrophe or Event. He describes no Qualities or Virtues; censures no Manners; makes no encomiums, nor gives Characters himself; but brings his Actors still in view. 'Tis they who shew themselves. . . . [The poet-painter] makes hardly any Figure at all, and is scarce discoverable in his Poem. This is being truly *a Master*" (1:129–30). Refraining from censure, Homer lets vicious or foolish characters speak their own condemnation. Shaftesbury's attention to manners departs from Renaissance norms of euhemerizing Homer. Noting a "conceal'd sort of Raillery intermix'd with the Sublime [A dangerous Stroke of Art!]," he discovers philosophy in Homer's comedy and satire. Attention to the minutiae of language and expression makes the writings of Plato or Homer "a kind of Mirrour or looking-glass to *the Age*" (1:131). To comprehend the operations of passions within his own place and time, the philosophic spectator has only to turn this mirror about.

In the third essay, Shaftesbury offers additional reasons for recovering dialogical writing. Neglecting the critical method favored by the Greeks, modern essayists and memoir writers fail to display the disinterestedness that was the aim of classical philosophy. Authors interested in dramatizing their wit allow their own characters to be stamped by those whom they mean to impress: "AN AUTHOR who writes in his own Person has the advantage of being who or what he pleases. He is no certain Man, nor has any certain or genuine Character: but sutes himself, on every occasion, to the Fancy of his Reader, whom, as the fashion is now-a-days, he constantly caresses and cajoles" (1:131). In dialogue, however, "*the Author* is annihilated; and *the Reader*, being no way apply'd to, stands for No-body. The self-interesting partys both vanish at once" (1:132). His relation to his subject is disinterested. Stolnitz argues that for Shaftesbury the opposite of interest is not a mode of action (benevolence), but a mode of perception: "A man is 'disinterested' now, when he takes no thought for any consequences whatever. When, furthermore, Shaftesbury goes on to describe the virtuous man as a spectator, devoted to 'the very survey and contemplation' of beauty in manners and morals, the initial 'practical' significance of 'disinterested' is supplanted altogether by the perceptual." Disinterested is, then, "a mode of attention and concern."[8] This description accords better with Shenstone's "adequate spectator" than Shaftesbury's own notions of disinterested virtue. While there are strictly lyrical and contemplative passages in the *Characteristicks*, other passages

=

Forms of Reflection
170

dramatize disinterested thought by locating it within dialogues and narratives. Shaftesbury describes contemplation as a "practice" (1:104), and he offers pragmatic social reasons for altering earlier forms of reflection. The function of a generic procedure like colloquy, or a philosophical concept like disinterestedness, turns on its place within a complex of literary constituents.

In Shaftesbury's philosophy, disinterestedness is plainly a moral and political concept linked to critical dialogue. But its functions remain problematic, even for the exceptional critic, like Robert Markley, who attends to Shaftesbury's writing as writing: "For our purposes, a study of the relationships between Shaftesbury's style and his thought becomes an examination of the interests—historical, social, literary, and critical—that the author uses to promote philosophical disinterest."[9] In each instance, Markley discovers that the posture of disinterestedness conceals a hidden interest: "The literary dimensions of Shaftesbury's work are ultimately defined by the goals of his 'performance' as an author—to demonstrate the values of an *aristocratic culture* that, in itself, remains essentially unchanged by the stylistic forms in which it is described" (153, emphasis added). The differences that Shaftesbury belabors so much—stylistic differences—fail to make a real difference because all of them may be seen as instances of a single cultural totality. Shaftesbury's disinterestedness is a form of ideological concealment, a "rhetoric of aristocratic exclusion" (149), an attempt "to create an authoritative discourse, to redefine the traditional 'authority' of language itself" (151).

Conceding that the third earl of Shaftesbury was a spokesman for aristocratic values and that disinterestedness was a politically engaged argument does not negate the objection that this criticism underestimates the subtlety of Shaftesbury's writing and ultimately misses the point. If stylistic differences in Shaftesbury's writing do not make a difference (a debatable point), it can still be argued that literary differences in *Characteristicks* are not limited to matters of style in the sense Markley implies: as we have seen, Shaftesbury's arguments turn on *generic* differences that set his writing in opposition to that of other polite authors. In fact, he makes a sophisticated version of Markley's own argument when he describes how Greek writers challenged obscure, implicit language by employing a multiplicitous philosophical discourse (Plato's philosophy is both comic and tragic; Homer's poetry is both sublime and satirical). Shaftesbury seeks to recover this dialogical method from Plato and Homer because he resists the idea that philosophical enquiry should be

=

unified, self-validating, or exclusive. In ways that we have seen before, *Characteristicks* is a very inclusive and heterogeneous piece of writing.

As Lawrence Klein notes, the object of writing like Shaftesbury's was to engage, rather than suppress, literary and social difference: "Discourse became deeply figured with models of social interaction. It is in keeping with eighteenth-century idiom to refer to this process as one of commercialization. 'Commerce' in the eighteenth century, like 'conversation' as well, related to a wide range of interactional situations."[10] Commerce and conversation imply differences. Shaftesbury composed the several parts of *Characteristicks* in different and opposing genres; even in *Soliloquy* itself the "grand *Arcanum*" (1:122) is dialogical opposition. Robert Markley takes up Shaftesbury's use of dialogue in another essay, arguing that "truth, for Shaftesbury, is always class-specific and ideologically delimited; his dialogues and images of the theater, in this regard, operate in what Bakhtin terms single-voiced or monological fashion."[11] The implication seems to be that real dialogue is only possible between members of different classes and that differences between Whigs and Tories, theists and skeptics, humanists and rationalists, can be comfortably accommodated within a monological "aristocratic culture."[12] But whatever they may signify to a twentieth-century Marxist, the different voices heard in Shaftesbury's dialogues plainly mark oppositions that were politically significant to eighteenth-century readers. Shaftesbury's dialogues may not be democratic, but they are dialogical in the ways their author describes as disinterested. Is it Shaftesbury's philosophy or the concept of aristocratic ideology that is delimiting?

Shaftesbury's philosophy of commerce and manners does uphold elite values, but they are the values of an elite that promoted tolerance and a limited pluralism. The extent to which this elite was open was and remains a debatable point, but that it was more open than the society it succeeded seems beyond dispute.[13] To understand the historical, literary, and political importance of the *Characteristicks* we need to discriminate: Shaftesbury's writings are better described as whiggish or republican than as aristocratic. To the extent that republicanism implies membership in a commonwealth of virtue, Shaftesbury's values, as much as Milton's or Coleridge's, may be considered hierarchical and elitist.[14] Nonetheless, Shaftesbury did not undertake a philosophy of disinterestedness in order to exclude the uncultivated but to diversify relations of authority among the ruling class. The lower ranks were not much of a political consideration; Tories and nonjurors were another matter.

≡

Forms of Reflection

In time, of course, this situation changed. A century later Coleridge directed his periodical against the republican intellectuals he held responsible for the disaster in France and for inciting dissent in Britain. Attempting to establish ethical principles to regulate the "communication of truth," *The Friend* defends censorship in cases where "the style, price, mode of circulation, and so forth" indicates the intention of a publication "to render the lower classes turbulent and apt to be alienated from the government of their country."[15] Unlike Shaftesbury, Coleridge is very much concerned with issues of class conflict. Toleration, even among the elite, he barely tolerates; in contrast to Shaftesbury's pluralism, Coleridge asserts that "as far as opinions, and not motives; principles, and not men, are concerned; I neither am tolerant, nor wish to be regarded as such. . . . That which doth not *withstand,* hath *itself* no standing place. To *fill* a station is to exclude or repel others – and this is not less the definition of moral, than of material *solidity*" (1:96–97). This is indeed a rhetoric of exclusion. If the political landscape changed dramatically between 1710 and 1810, echoes of Tory and old Whig politics still reverberate in Coleridge's charges against commerce, fashion, and modernity.

Perhaps the fullest and most successful realization of Shaftesbury's program of giving advice by reflecting on the characters of men and writing was Addison and Steele's *Spectator*. The author is "annihilated" (1:132): silent, invisible, and anonymous, Mr. Spectator observes the manners of his time with polite detachment. The *Spectator* shares with *Characteristicks* a range of topics – manners, art, Whig politics, and literary criticism – and a battery of genres – dialogue, allegory, epistle, satire, and the character genre. The editors share Shaftesbury's confidence that norms of taste and behavior can be implemented through "exquisite and refined raillery" (1:128). Coleridge singles out the *Spectator* as the work against which his own periodical will innovate. *The Friend* will share some objectives with earlier periodicals, but "in journeying to the same end I have chosen a different road" (2:28). Since the days of Queen Anne the "diffusion of uniform opinions, of Behaviour and Appearance, of Fashions in things external and internal, have combined to diminish, and often to render evanescent, the distinctions between the enlightened Inhabitants of the great city, and the scattered Hamlet" (2:27–28). Coleridge believes that the Enlightenment project of diffusing cultivation through commerce had largely succeeded, at least in a geographical sense. But in making learning fashionable, the periodical essay also reduced learning to mere fashion. Addison promises to bring "Philosophy out of Closets and Libraries, Schools and Colleges, to dwell in Clubs and Assemblies, at Tea-Tables, and in Coffee-Houses"; Coleridge proposes a *translatio studii* from the assembly and the tea table to "Closets and Libraries" (2:287). Relations between writers and readers were to be governed by philosophical principles, rather than social norms.[16]

On no issue are the two philosophers farther apart than on that of "seriousness," which Shaftesbury regards as "the very essence of Imposture" (1:10). For Coleridge, seriousness implies sincerity toward self and others: "Only by means of Seriousness and Meditation and the free infliction of Censure in the spirit of Love, can the true Philanthropist of the present Time, curb in himself and his Contemporaries; only by these can he aid in preventing the Evils which threaten us, not from the terrors of an Enemy so much as from our fears of our own Thoughts, and our aversion to all the toils of Reflection" (2:86). Above all else, nineteenth-century readers need to be *serious*. Periodicals have erred by assuming a "character" of levity that lowers intellectual inquiry to the status of popular entertainment:

> All must now be taught in sport—Science, Morality, yea, Religion itself.
> . . . Of the most influencive Class, at least, of our literary Guides, (the anonymous Authors of our periodical Publications) the most part assume this Character from Cowardice, or Malice, till having begun with studied ignorance and a premeditated levity, they at length realize the Lie, and end indeed in a pitiable destitution of all intellectual power. (2:86)

The titles of earlier periodicals wore their levity like a badge: the *Entertainer* (1717), the *Agreeable Companion* (1744), the *Prater* (1756), the *Idler* (1758), the *Lounger* (1785), the *Trifler* (1795). Sincerity was out of the question when names like Caleb D'Anvers, Adam FitzAdam, or Mr. Town were used to represent an anonymous committee of writers. Coleridge places himself and his sincere feelings at the center of his experiment in new means of communicating truth:

> Were but a hundred men to combine a deep conviction that virtuous Habits may be formed by the very means by which knowledge is communicated, that men may be made better, not only in consequence, but *by* the mode and *in* the process, of instruction: were but a hundred men to combine that clear conviction of this, which I myself at this moment feel, even as I feel the certainty of my being . . . the promises of ancient prophecy would disclose themselves to our Faith. (2:69–70)

≡

Forms of Reflection

To insist on seriousness and sincerity was to redirect the locus of authority from anonymous social norms to the genius of a particular writer.

The posture of sincerity is not, of course, a romantic invention; since the time of Ben Jonson, retirement writers have adopted modes of plain speaking to differentiate their writings from courtly wit and the fashions of the town.[17] But if Coleridge's ridicule of fashions and manners had a long pedigree in country politics, he was breaking new ground with his retirement periodical. This amounted almost to a contradiction in terms. Earlier papers required an urban setting, in part, because they were produced by multiple authors working in close collaboration with book-sellers. Periodicals distributed to coffeehouses or households were intended to be perused in a social setting, read aloud, and criticized by groups of friends. Mr. Spectator haunted these sites and sometimes made these very conversations the subjects of his essays. Readers became authors, either by having their conversations reported by one of the spies or by having their letters reprinted by the editor.[18] Such dialogical relationships are not fit material for *The Friend*, a periodical written in solitude and delivered by post to a widely scattered readership. Living with the Wordsworths, miles from the nearest town and fearful of the cost of stamps, Coleridge is obviously on very distant terms with his subscribers. Very few letters are printed in *The Friend*, and conversational writing is virtually absent. Apart from the managerial problems, Coleridge regarded his isolation as advantageous.[19] As a serious writer, he converses not with the town but with his library, not about the manners of the times but about the wisdom of the ages.

In taking a conversational genre into retirement, Coleridge shifts the locus of periodical authority from manners to written texts. To counter "many prejudices of many of my readers," Coleridge will uphold "some principles both of Taste and Philosophy, adopted by the great Men of Europe from the Middle of the fifteenth til toward the Close of the seventeenth Century."[20] *The Friend* will imitate "the stately march and difficult evolutions, which characterize the eloquence of Hooker, Bacon, Milton, and Jeremy Taylor" (2:150). Simplicity may be a moral virtue, but it is a literary vice. If Coleridge concedes that habits of "silent and solitary meditation" have "injured my style with respect to its' facility and popularity," he proudly asserts an "aversion to the epigrammatic unconnected periods of the fashionable *Anglo-gallican* Taste" (2:150). Coleridge's Spenserian eidolon, Satyrane, connotes both British nationalism and a lack of refinement. A reviewer of the 1818 edition praised *The Friend* for

=

reviving "the genuine old English style of our Taylors, and Miltons, and Hookers, and which were so lamentably frittered away into the cautious and nerveless neatness and timid simplicity of the Popes and Addisons of an after generation."[21] In a complete reversal of Enlightenment norms, difficulty becomes a standard of value: "Short and unconnected sentences are easily and instantly understood: but it is equally true, that wanting all the cement of thought as well as of style, all the connections . . . are as easily forgotten. . . . Nor is it less true, that those who confine their reading to such books dwarf their own faculties, and finally reduce their Understandings to a deplorable imbecility" (2:150). The editor's extensive reading in obscure tomes and his powerful mental faculties were intended to be the chief selling points for *The Friend*.

If Shaftesbury cultivates a conversational manner, Coleridge's neo-Gothic prose is self-consciously bookish and literary. Long sentences and twisted syntax require "attention" from a reader and encourage mental reflection. Coleridge makes this point mimetically in an allegory that literally and metaphorically departs from the earlier, tea-table standard of conversibility: "Like idle morning Visitors, the brisk and breathing Periods hurry in and hurry off in quick and profitless succession; each indeed for the moments of its' stay prevents the pain of vacancy, while it indulges the love of sloth; but all together they leave the Mistress of the house (the soul I mean) flat and exhausted, incapable of attending to her own concerns, and unfitted for the conversation of more rational Guests" (2:151). *The Friend*, it goes without saying, is all but incomprehensible when read aloud. Coleridge insists on difficulty because his principles "require the attention of my Reader to become my fellow-labourer; all the primary facts essential to the intelligibility of my principles, the existence of which facts I can prove to others only as far as I can prevail on them to retire *into themselves* and make their own minds the objects of their steadfast attention" (2:151). Readers are not asked to enter into critical commerce but to attend carefully, reproducing the experience upon which universal principles are founded. But if the message is intended to be universal, the manner in which it is expressed is clearly exclusive: Coleridge's exchange of ideas excludes Cobbett's readership as much as Addison's.

Looking for alternatives to commerce led Coleridge to reorder the parts within his work as a whole; indeed, the process of publishing by numbers led him to rethink the nature of composition itself. The eighteenth-century periodical was both an open and a closed form. In its orig-

=

Forms of Reflection

inal appearance it would add topics and change direction in response to give-and-take with the readership; after a sufficient number of essays had appeared they would be gathered into a completed volume, to be sold and read as a piece.[22] Rather than accumulating closed forms within an open-ended whole, *The Friend* subsumes a series of open-ended essays (often breaking off in midtopic, sometimes in midsentence) into a single, methodically developed argument. The prospectus to *The Friend* stresses that the periodical will differ from "the *Spectator* &c . . . chiefly by the greater Length of the separate Essays, by their closer Connection with each other, and by the Predominance of one Object, and the common Bearing of all to one End" (2:19).

As taste, morality, and politics are "no mechanical compost, no chemical combination" (2:8) of heterogeneous elements, neither can a work that purports to establish the underlying unity of these elements consist of a miscellaneous accretion of essays. Closer connections and common bearing require a single hand, rather than the loose-knit collaborations producing earlier periodicals. In place of accretion and mixture, *The Friend* unfolds as a metaphorical tree of syllogisms, the "Branches and Boughs" of one extended argument "deduced" from a "hidden root" (2:5–6). The labyrinthine plan of the whole accords with the labyrinthine prose of its parts: instead of attending to a "profitless succession" of short periods, subscribers would attend to a complex argument long drawn out—over months and years. Reflecting on the organic structures of Coleridge's unfolding trains of thought, readers will cultivate their intellectual powers "*by* the mode and *in* the process, of instruction" (2:69). Contemplative readers will reproduce not only the editor's processes of thought but the very organic structures that sustain the social order.

If the emphasis on contemplation marks the most significant continuity between Shaftesbury and Coleridge, it also enables us to measure their differences. In *Characteristicks*, commerce is understood as the basis of contemplation, as it is of the social order; in *The Friend*, these functions are taken over by cognition. Stolnitz's description is surely applicable here: "the initial 'practical' significance of 'disinterested' is supplanted altogether by the perceptual." Like Shaftesbury, Coleridge sometimes argues that his intent is to shift the locus of authority from the writer to readers themselves: "In short, I wished to convey not instruction merely, but fundamental instruction; not so much to shew my Reader this or that Fact, as to kindle his own Torch for him, and leave it to himself to chuse the particular Objects, which he might wish to examine by it's light"

=

(2:276). But Coleridge appropriates Enlightenment rhetoric in order to undermine Enlightenment objectives; it is perfectly clear that readers are to follow their instructor in contemplating only the most "serious" works, those from which "fundamental" instruction may be drawn.

Though Coleridge follows Addison and Steele in promising to combine pleasure with instruction, the range of material included in his periodical narrows considerably. *The Friend* largely excludes humorous reflections on manners because "serious readers" will take greater pleasure "in the distinct perception of a fundamental Truth" (2:276). "Cultivation" is severed from the practical concerns of everyday life. The editor, "compelled by the general Taste of my Readers to interrupt the systematic progress of the Plan by Essays of a lighter kind, or which at least require a less effort of Attention" (2:282), reluctantly includes the literary devices employed by the *Spectator* as vehicles of instruction. The topics of the "amusements" included in *The Friend* — rape, murder, defeat, madness, and death — make metaphysical ruminations a relief by comparison. If cultivated minds are to adopt a disinterested attitude toward manners and ephemera, they ought to take a lively *interest* in fundamentals. But only a few can be expected to rise to the challenge; might there be four or five hundred readers throughout the kingdom who are "desirous to derive pleasure from the consciousness of being instructed or ameliorated, and who [feel] a sufficient *interest* as to the foundations of their own Opinions in Literature, Politics, Morals, and Religion, to afford [the necessary] degree of Attention"? (2:277).

Apparently there were not. As the periodical began to fail, the editor blamed his subscribers for their lack of seriousness: "THE FRIEND never attempted to disguise from his Readers that both Attention and Thought were Efforts, and that the latter a most difficult and laborious Effort . . . nor from himself, that to require it often or for any continuance of time was incompatible with the nature of a periodical Publication, even were it less incongruous than it unfortunately is with the present habits and pursuits of Englishmen." Defending himself from the "unwarrantable assumption of superiority" (2:277), Coleridge dismisses with contempt the remarks of one subscriber, who concluded that all was "learned nonsence and unintelligible Jargin" (2:275). Some torches are harder to light than others, but it is also possibile that readers rejected the subordinate role assigned to them, proving the truth of Shaftesbury's maxim that "to bestow wisdom, is to gain a mastery which cannot so easily be allowed us" (1:103).

≡

Forms of Reflection

Reflecting on Difference:
Change as Progress, Change as Corruption

Both Shaftesbury and Coleridge validate their opposing conceptions of cultivation by appealing to literary history. Not surprisingly, they construe history in different ways. Shaftesbury upholds processes of differentiation and refinement; Coleridge, the progressive unfolding of a single grand design. Shaftesbury describes literature as the changing expression of social values; Coleridge, as the repository of unchanging truths about human nature. If one contemplates history in order to establish a sense of critical detachment and the other to identify himself with the sources of universal knowledge, both make meditations on literary history central to their programs for reforming society through mental cultivation.

As we have seen, for Shaftesbury the practice of soliloquy is dialogical and therefore intrinsically social and political. Before revealing the "grand *Arcanum*" of his method of interior reflection, he devotes the second part of his discourse to an illustration of how the dialogical method has operated with respect to society at large. Shaftesbury devotes a second triplet of essays to literary history, examining how literary commerce takes place between writers and their patrons, critics, and public. Each essay underscores parallels between the *characters* of genre, genius, and government. Not all genres flourish under all forms of government. The tragic muse of Shakespeare and the epic muse of Milton reflect the "ancient *Poetick Liberty*" enjoyed in Britain: "The Genius of this [tragic] Poetry consists in the lively Representation of the disorders and misery of *the Great*" (1:142); it teaches "*the People* and those of *a lower Condition*" to value equality and justice. Such republican values cannot flourish in despotic France, where the "long Series of Degrees" teaches each subject to "idolize the next in Power among 'em" (1:143). The less contestatory "genius" of French literature fosters politeness, correctness, and grace of style. Such a society might produce a noble satirist like Boileau, but epic is less successful, and tragedy fares ill, where the spirit of criticism is wanting (1:142).

The first essay, on patronage, considers Augustus as a cautionary example. Virgil and Horace "taught him how to charm Mankind. They were more to him than his Arms or military Virtue; and, more than *Fortune* her-self, assisted him in his Greatness, and made his usurp'd Dominion so inchanting to the World, that it cou'd see without regret its Chains of Bondage firmly riveted." As poetry lost its critical edge, a comfortable

=

Cultivation into Culture
179

lyricism promoted the "corrupting Sweets of . . . a poisonous Government"; literature and liberty could not survive an "Inchantment which wrought so powerfully upon Mankind, when first this Universal Monarchy was establish'd" (1:144). Without a properly critical relationship between poets and patrons, absolute government held sway.[23] But taking a hint from Horace, Shaftesbury argues optimistically that monarchs "must remember that their Fame is in the hands of *Penmen;* and that the greatest Actions lose their Force and perish in the custody of unable and mean Writers" (1:146). Since memorable writing will only flourish under conditions of freedom, "our Potentates and GRANDEES . . . appear to have only this Choice left 'em: either wholly, if possible, to suppress *Letters;* or give a helping hand towards their Support. Wherever the *Author*-practice [soliloquy] and *Liberty of the Pen* has in the least prevail'd, the Governors of the State must be either considerable Gainers or Sufferers by its means" (1:147–48). Ideally, patronage should operate as a kind of fruitful commerce: "princes and great men" bestow honor and advantages, poets bestow praises and criticism; in either case "the ill placing of Rewards is a double Injury to Merit" (1:149). Rightly maintained, patronage promotes liberty and refinement; abused, it leads to luxury, corruption, and absolutism.

The second essay extends this argument to literary critics, the "*Props and Pillars*" who uphold the "Commonwealth of Wit and Letters" (1:153). Progress in liberty and refinement requires an active commerce between writers and critics. Those who regard critics as parasites on literature ("Pests, and Incendiarys") mistake the purpose and consequences of critical dialogue. As in the body politic, so in the commonwealth of letters nature "provides for the Cure of what has happen'd amiss in the Growth and Progress of a Constitution" (1:161–62). Healthy growth is ensured by a progressive differentiation of functions within the commonwealth.

Taking Greek literature as his text, Shaftesbury illustrates how an undifferentiated discourse evolved into the several genres of criticism, poetry, and philosophy. As Greek society became more specialized, a class of critics appeared alongside the original vatic poets and legislators: "These were honor'd with the name of *Sophists:* A Character which in early times was highly respected. . . . When such a Race as this was once risen, 'twas no longer possible to impose on Mankind by what was specious and pretending. The Publick would be paid in no false Wit or jingling Eloquence" (1:156). As critics became authors, the original unitary

≡

Forms of Reflection

discourse divided into the self-regulating dyad of poetry and philosophy. Poetry itself was refined into separate and competing genres: "The Manner of this Father-Poet [Homer] was afterwards variously imitated and divided into several Shares" (1:158), notably tragic and comic drama. Comic writers refined poetry by debunking the excesses of the tragedians, only to have their own excesses refined by later and more polite genres of comedy: "Thus the florid and over-sanguine Humour of the *high Style* was allayed by something of a contrary nature" (1:162). Contrary genres assured "gradual Reform in the Commonwealth of wit, beside the real Reform of *Taste* and *Humour* in the Commonwealth or Government it-self" (1:163). The other half of the original dyad was undergoing parallel changes: "In Philosophy it-self there happen'd, almost at the very same time, a like *Succession* of Wit and Humour; when in opposition to the sublime Philosopher, and afterwards to his grave Disciple and Successor in the Academy, there arose a *comick* Philosophy in the Person of another Master and other Disciples" (1:165). Like Homer's epic, Plato's writings supplied the raw material that later writers would refine. Imitation itself was practiced as a form of commerce and a critical act.

Here again, Robert Markley misses the point: "The 'several Manners' of poetic and philosophical discourse are similarly original. They are not redefined or invented by subsequent generations of writers but exist embryonically within the works of Homer and Aristotle. For Shaftesbury, then, the role of the poet or philosopher is to develop, explicate, or (as Pope said of poets who must follow in the footsteps of Homer) paraphrase an authoritative discourse which already exists."[24] This is not at all Shaftesbury's understanding of succession, though it is very close to how Coleridge understands cultural transmission. In Shaftesbury's literary history, predicated on commerce and refinement, differences are as significant as continuities. Susan Staves's discussion of Pope's "refinement" is useful here: "The volumes which are Pope's Homer thus attempt both to appropriate what is valuable in Homer for English Literature and to assert that they are the product of a more humane civilization than Homer's, one superior in some ways to his, a civilization entitled to judge Homer and to find him, on occasion, wanting" (154). There is nothing in classical literature resembling *Characteristicks*; Shaftesbury's commerce with Homer and Plato results in a very different kind of dialogical writing.

The series concludes with a third essay on the "people," as Shaftesbury refers to citizens (as opposed to "those of a lower Condition," 1:143). Ancient writers and readers refined each other through mutual criticism; poets "formed their Audience, polish'd the Age, refined the publick Ear and fram'd it right; that in return they might be rightly and lastingly applauded" (1:172). Living in more corrupt times, his contemporaries fail to exercise critical detachment; they "regulate themselves by the irregular Fancy of the World; and frankly own they are preposterous and absurd, in order to accommodate themselves to the Genius of the Age. In our Days *the Audience* makes *the Poet* and *the Bookseller the Author*, with what Profit to the Publick, or what Prospect of lasting Fame and Honour to the Writer, let any one who has Judgment imagine" (1:172–73). Panegyrics have devolved into unwitting satires (1:173); satire has degenerated into gladiatorial spectacle (1:175–76); drama and literary criticism have declined into gallantry and Gothicism (1:177). As with patronage, the misplaced desire to flatter dampens the critical faculty in writers and readers, with a resulting loss of discrimination and refinement. Commerce has taken a wrong turn, declining into luxury and corruption; a further fall into barbarism is not unlikely. To get commercial relations back onto a critical footing, authors and their public must learn to practice disinterested contemplation, beginning with "our old Article of ADVICE; that main Preliminary of Self-study and *inward Converse* which we have found so much wanting in the Authors of our Time" (1:180).

The three essays—a long historical digression, really—describe how literary commerce engages and sustains the larger commonwealth. Shaftesbury describes cultivation as a process of social refinement acted out over the span of generations but also as a more limited process of improving one's faculties by means of critical self-reflection. This begins to take *cultivation* in the direction of *culture*, as does Shaftesbury's use of *genius* to define homologies between kinds of writing and kinds of society: we hear of the "genius" of Homer, the "genius" of tragedy, the "genius" of Britain. But unlike many later theorists, Shaftesbury employs this concept to make discriminations; in this respect it is analogous to *character*, the master term in this philosophy of aesthetic forms. Authors display their characters through the genres in which they write; establishing relationships with readers—critical or corrupt—that further characterize the genius of a particular class, nation, or age. Shaftesbury, like romantic aestheticians, uses *genius* to underwrite a politics of cultivation, but, unlike them, he uses *genius* (and *genre*) to differentiate opposing values within a self, a literature, or a society. In Coleridge's philosophy the term *genius* serves very different critical functions.

In *The Friend*, genius is what remains after a critic has siphoned off

=

Forms of Reflection

all that is specifically historical about a great writer's compositions. If Shaftesbury is interested in the "Greekness" of Plato, Coleridge is interested in his universality. The 1818 *Friend*'s account of Greek history invites comparison with Shaftesbury's in *Soliloquy*; it is much the same history, really, but the values are inverted. Coleridge describes sophists as "wholesale and retail *dealer*[s] in wisdom" (1:436) "who offered to the vanity of youth and the ambition of wealth a substitute for that authority, which by the institutions of Solon ha[s] been attached to high birth and property" (1:438). Reducing philosophy "exclusively to things of quantity and relation" (1:439), their "superstition of the senses" undermines "the superior science, metaphysics" (1:440). Shaftesbury praises those "honor'd with the name of *Sophists*" for undermining priestly utterances; for this reason Coleridge singles them out for special censure: "If the Invisible be denied . . . the component parts can never be reduced into an harmonious whole, but must owe their systematic arrangements to accidents of an ever-shifting perspective" (1:441). The literary commerce Shaftesbury describes as "the Cure of what has happened amiss in the Growth and Progress of a Constitution" (1:161–2) Coleridge casts as the corruption of Truth.

Coleridge's remarks about materialism and commerce imply a parallel between democratic Athens and republican France. Like sophists, Physiocrats overturn natural, social, and intellectual hierarchies: "Statesmen should know that a learned class is an essential element of a state — at least of a Christian state. But *you* [Jacobins] wish for general illumination! You begin with the attempt to *popularize* learning and philosophy; but you will end in the *plebification* of knowledge. A true philosophy in the learned class is essential to a true religious feeling in all classes" (1:447). Coleridge's historical illustration reinforces his general position that social harmony requires a restricted class of secular hierophants: "As long as the spirit of philosophy reigns in the learned and highest class, and that of religion in all classes, a tendency to blend and unite will be found in all objects of pursuit, and the whole discipline of mind and manners will be calculated in relation to the worth of the agents" (1:444). If the French were deceived by Enlightenment sophistry, *The Friend* supplies "the preparatory steps" for an antimaterialist illumination in Britain (1:446).[25]

The case for a British counter-Enlightenment is argued in the long letter from Mathetes, one of the few pieces of correspondence appearing in *The Friend*.[26] Mathetes offers a "history of a pure and noble mind"

(2:223) seduced by Enlightenment sophistry into a misguided belief in "the perpetual progression of human nature towards perfection" (2:225). The correspondent calls for a "superior Mind" to "assume the protection of others" (2:227). William Wordsworth, Mathetes suggests, is the man of genius who might best assume "this complete control over the minds of others" (2:229). Coleridge turns to his friend for a response. Wordsworth denies that such a protector is necessary, but he does so with an argument that seems to grant to genius the very authority that Mathetes craves. Because human nature does not change, Wordsworth argues, there is nothing exceptional about the dangers faced by modern youth. Even if the present times are worse than most, progress is not necessarily hindered: "For in proportion as we imagine obstacles to exist out of our-selves to retard our progress, will, in fact, our progress be retarded" (2:232). Opposing what is "out of ourselves" to the life of the mind, Wordsworth shifts the locus of progress from material and social history to the spiritual development of individuals. Even in bad times, "it is enough for complacency and hope, that scattered and solitary minds are always labouring somewhere in the service of truth and virtue; and that by the sleep of the multitude, the energy of the multitude may be pre-pared" (2:260). Wordsworth denies the Enlightenment premise that material progress is a prerequisite for cultivation, driving a firm wedge between "the separate life of an Individual" and the "Species . . . as an aggregate."

If Wordsworth denies the need for a "Teacher . . . conspicuous above the multitude in superior power" (2:228), he describes the powers of contemplative genius in terms that imply just such a superiority. Like Shaftesbury and Coleridge, Wordsworth expects citizens to pursue virtue by "steady dependence upon voluntary and self-originating effort, and upon the practice of self-examination, sincerely aimed at and rigorously enforced" (2:261). He recalls Prodicus's "Choice of Hercules." In Shaftesbury's redaction (in *Tablature*), the contemplative hero chooses between pleasure and virtue, but in *The Friend* a choice is made between "THE WORLD" and "INTELLECTUAL PROWESS."[27] For Shaftesbury, as for most republican theorists, to pursue the life of the mind apart from polit-ical engagement is to fail to exercise virtue at all. But in accordance with the emerging epistemological sense of disinterestedness, Wordsworth's youth makes an aesthetic rather than a political choice: the "disinter-ested and free condition of the youthful mind" is ascertained by an affirmative answer to the question, "to what degree do I value my faculties and my attainments for their own sakes?" (2:261).[28] Wordsworth goes so far as to *oppose* virtue to political engagement: self-contemplators will produce "works of pure science . . . works which, both from their independence in their origin upon accident, their nature, their duration, and the wide spread of their influence, are entitled rightly to take place of the noblest and most beneficent deeds of Heroes, Statesmen, Legislators, or Warriors" (2:265).[29] Practiced as a pure science, contemplation has, properly speaking, no history at all. Yet Wordsworth implies at least a mediated relation to practical affairs, since the "influence" wielded by disinterested men of genius parallels the virtuous actions to which it is opposed. Like the poetic "senators" in Shenstone's "Rural Elegance," men of genius exercise authority through imagination.

Like Wordsworth, Coleridge believes that disinterested virtue springs from the pure science of philosophical contemplation, but like Mathetes he also believes that the cultivation of science requires a heroic philosopher to banish the sophists from the temple of truth. Such tasks fall "to the successive Few in every age (more indeed in one generation than in another, but relatively to the mass of Mankind always few) who by the intensity and permanence of their action have compensated for the limited sphere, within which it is at any one time intelligible" (2:52). The belief that cultivation is the work of Wordsworth's "scattered and solitary minds" leads Coleridge to reconceive Enlightenment notions of cultivation, and with them, the scheme of his periodical. In contrast to Shaftesbury's account of cultivation as historical change generated through critical commerce, Coleridge represents cultivation as the preservation of "permanent" truths in the face of historical difference:

> From the great æras of national illumination we date the commencement of our main national Advantages. The Tangle of Delusions, which stifled and distorted the growing Tree, have been torn away; the parasite Weeds, that fed on its' very roots, have been plucked up with a salutary violence. To us there remain only quiet duties, the constant care, the gradual improvement, the cautious unhazardous labors of the industrious though contented Gardener—to prune, to engraft, and one by one to remove from its' leaves and fresh shoots, the Slug and the Caterpillar. (2:56)

Both Shaftesbury and Coleridge recognize that writing and society change, and both try to distinguish change as progress from change as corruption. But because they conceive processes of change very differ-

≡

Cultivation into Culture
185

ently, they formulate relations between history and literature very differently. Where progress is measured by refinement, diversification and self-difference are positive achievements; where progress is measured by organic growth, diversity and self-difference signify corruption, a literal falling apart.

It follows that the uncritical relations Shaftesbury describes as corrupt Coleridge regards as necessary to "gradual improvement": "If by the *reception* of truth in the spirit of Truth, we *become* what we are; only by the retention of it in the same spirit, can we *remain* what we are" (2:56). Since all writings of genius exhibit permanent truths about human nature, literature can hardly be said to "progress"; what improves is not literature but critical apprehension of literature. The changes that matter take place in the growth of an individual's powers of perception, powers developed by assimilating the unchanging truths manifested in great writing. Readers will accept Coleridge as the guardian of the one truth if they will "recollect, that I have been giving [in *The Friend* as a whole] the History of my own mind. . . . To a sincere and sensible mind, it cannot but be disgusting to find an Author writing on Subjects, to the investigation of which he professes to have devoted the greater portion of his Life, and yet appealing to all his Readers promiscuously, as his full and completed judges, and thus soliciting their favour by a mock modesty, which either convicts him of gross hypocrisy or the most absurd presumption" (2:277– 78). Only facile critics prostrate themselves "before the superiority of their Readers, as supreme judges, [and] will yet in their works pass judgements on Plato, Milton, Shakespeare, Spenser, and their Compeers" (2:278). If the growing tree is to be freed from the tangle of delusions, critics should subordinate themselves to authority, and readers to critics.

Coleridge presents *The Friend* as both a digest of authoritative writing and as a history of his own labors to comprehend them. His attempts to assimilate one with the other lead to practices that Shaftesbury would regard as not only tangled, but corrupt. It becomes very difficult to separate the testimony of history from the progress of the argument: Coleridge suppresses the contexts of the passages he cites, doctors quotations, and weaves sources imperceptibly into his own writing. In the epigraphs that preface the essays, Coleridge tacitly patches and alters his authorities at will, even inventing imaginary citations when no authority is at hand (e.g. 1:25, 245, 298). Unlike eighteenth-century imitators who encouraged discrimination by printing originals on the facing page, Coleridge erases historical difference by ventriloquizing earlier writers, pro-

=

Forms of Reflection

jecting his arguments onto sources and the authority of his sources onto his own arguments.

This overriding concern for historical continuity leads Coleridge to deploy *character* in new ways: the virtuous character is sincere rather than polite and serious rather than ironic. He does not adopt a disinterested attitude toward historical works. For Shaftesbury, character is what is most peculiar to "men, manners, opinions, times"; Coleridge, on the other hand, opposes character to difference: "I have . . . derived the deepest interest from the comparison of Men, whose Characters at the first view appear widely dissimilar, who yet have produced similar effects on their different Ages, and this by the exertion of powers which on examination will be found far more alike, than the altered drapery and costume would have led us to suspect" (2:111). A character is authoritative insofar as it transcends its age; from manners, by contrast, critics can only derive "superficial knowledge," useful only as the ground against which the character of genius stands out.

If Shaftesbury's meditations on genius discriminate characters by drawing up catalogues and sequences (familiar georgic devices), Coleridge's meditations on genius isolate character by epitome and revealing anecdote. The parallel between sophists and Jacobins, collapsing historical difference into a common character, is a good example of Coleridge's way of reflecting on history: "Ample room is afforded for the exercise of both the Judgement and the Fancy, in distinguishing cases of real resemblance from those of intentional imitation, the analogies of Nature revolving upon herself, from the masquerade Figures of Cunning and Vanity" (1:111). To distinguish "Nature" from "masquerade figures"—the verities of culture from the vanities of civilization—a new method is required. Rather than trafficking in mutability and difference, critics will learn to recognize in works of genius the fixed principles underlying their own powers of perception. They will echo these principles, fall under their enchantment. The cultivated mind will reflect them rather than reflect upon them.

Reprise: Critical Method and the Varieties of Discourse

Both Shaftesbury and Coleridge explore the longstanding relation between meditation and method, turning to Descartes's "rules for the direction of the mind" genre to establish regulative principles for aesthetics. Differing attitudes toward regulation and authority, of course, lead to very different concepts of method. Shaftesbury concludes *Soliloquy* by opposing rules as norms to rules as principles. It is ridiculous, he argues, to expect the fruit of wisdom to sprout from a tree of syllogisms: "There can be nothing more ridiculous than to expect that *Manners* or *Understanding* should sprout from such a Stock" (1:186). "I shall willingly allow [metaphysics and logic] to pass for *Philosophy* when by any real effects it is prov'd capable to refine our Spirits, improve our Understandings, or mend our Manners" (1:188). So little are logical formalists masters of their subject that none are "found more impotent in themselves, of less command over their Passions, less free from Superstition and vain Fears, or less safe from the common Imposture and Delusion, than the noted Head-pieces of this stamp" (1:190); metaphysicians are not necessarily wrong, but their writing is barbaric and their character ridiculous: "The most ingenious way of becoming foolish is *by a System*" (1:189). A critical philosophy must begin elsewhere:

> Come on then. Let me philosophize in this manner; if this be indeed the way I am to grow wise. Let me examine my *Ideas* of *Space* and *Substance.* Let me look well into *Matter* and its *Modes;* if this be looking into MY-SELF; if this be to improve my *Understanding,* and enlarge my MIND. . . . If this remains unsolv'd; if I am still the same Mystery to myself as ever: to what purpose is all this reasoning and acuteness? Wherefore do I admire my Philosopher, or study to become such a one, myself? (1:194–95)

Reviewing Descartes and Locke on substance, Shaftesbury concludes, "My Mind, I am satisfy'd, will proceed either way alike: for it is concern'd on neither side—'Philosopher! Let me hear concerning what is of moment to me'" (1:196). The ad hominem argument indicates that he will seek this new basis for philosophizing in common sense and in social norms.

Setting aside formal reasoning by definition and division, Shaftesbury attempts to ground his judgments on *characters,* qualities apprehended by and through experience. But how is experience itself to be apprehended? Returning to his mental theater, Shaftesbury stages a masque that presents experience in the guise of allegorical figures representing the passions. No syllogistic monstrosities here: such a "Method of examining our *Ideas* is no pedantick Practice. Nor is there anything ungallante in the manner of thus questioning the Lady-Fancys, which present themselves as charmingly dress'd as possible to solicit their Cause and

=

Forms of Reflection

obtain a Judgement, by favour of that worse Part and corrupt SELF to which they make their application" (1:202).

The nine muses appear before the disinterested spectator, each a different character, each making a different appeal to the affections. The masque begins as an enchantress enters, dressed "in a sort of dismal Weed, with the most mournful Countenance imaginable" (1:202). This is Melpomene, the tragic muse representing fear of death; "Her Art is to render her-self as forbidding as possible; that her Sisters may by her means be the more alluring" (1:203). The fear of death encourages mortals to pursue "luxurious Fancies, and give their ERATOS and other playsome *Muses* a fuller Scope in the support of Riot and Debauch" (1:203). The antimasquers are put to rout by Calliope, muse of epic poetry, who ushers in history and philosophy in the persons of Clio and Urania, followed by Thalia (comedy), Polyhymnia (oratory), Terpsichore (dance), and Euterpe (music). The relative worth of each character is judged by the affections she inspires—a problematic argument, since it implies that no prior experience is needed to judge experience. Beginning with tragedy, the earliest and most comprehensive genre, the sequence recalls the progress of differentiation and refinement in Greek literature described by Shaftesbury in the previous section. As characters or genres, the figures embody collective social experience as it might be encountered in a traditional humanist education. The student cultivates his mind by contemplating the arts, not by chopping syllogisms: "To be a *Virtuoso* (so far as befits a Gentleman) is a higher step towards the becoming a Man of Virtue and good Sense than the being what in this age we call a *Scholar*" (2:214).

Shaftesbury's scheme parallels the progress of education with the progress of literary history, but in so doing it presupposes a false homology between psychology and sociology and between passions and genres: if the passions are universal, the genres, we have been led to believe, are specific to particular times and places. Moreover, tragedy and comedy are keyed to a single passion, and lyric poetry treats one or another, while a comprehensive genre like epic embraces all the passions and most other literary kinds. At this point, the argument abandons historical thinking; Shaftesbury wants to assert that taste, founded on the affections, is natural: "In the very nature of Things there must of necessity be the Foundation of a right and wrong TASTE, as well in respect of inward Characters and Features as of outward Person, Behavior, and Action" (1:216–17). Shaftesbury's appeal to common sense might have carried weight among the community of humanist scholars, but the inconsistency of the argument is obvious. It crops up even more acutely in *Sensus Communis, An Essay on the Freedom of Wit and Humour*, the second part of *Characteristicks*, where *common* sense is sometimes the refinement that permits educated persons to disagree amicably and sometimes the innate human ability to apprehend beauty and truth. As the century wore on and literary commerce brought disjunct communities into contestatory relationships, the limitations of Shaftesbury's inconsistent position on "sense" became more and more apparent. The new science of aesthetics was founded on the propositions that taste is grounded in the affections and that the affections are universal; it was this ahistorical aspect of *Characteristicks* that later writers chose to pursue. By the time Coleridge was writing *The Friend* the search for fixed principles had been under way for two generations.

To accuse Shaftesbury of inconsistency, however, is in one respect beside the point. Perhaps the most interesting aspect of the method in *Characteristicks* is Shaftesbury's attempt to play the critic on himself by introducing contrary arguments into his dialogues and by maintaining a kind of conversation between the different parts of *Characteristicks*. It may be that this is what he intended by describing *Soliloquy* as the "Inlet or Introduction" (2:240) to the other treatises while also asking readers to "consider the present Method and Order of my Author's [Shaftesbury's] Treatises, as in this *joint*-Edition they are ranged" (2:238).

If *Soliloquy* is indeed the key to *Characteristicks*, we should expect multiple and contrary principles of order in the work as a whole—it could hardly be "disinterested" otherwise.[30] On the one hand, the order of the treatises suggests a Baconian organon or monumental discourse of discourses. *A Letter Concerning Enthusiasm* and *An Essay on the Freedom of Wit and Humour*, as *exordio* and *narratio*, raise the question of characters: they make the case that intellectual exchanges should be regulated by manners and common sense. As *divisio*, *Soliloquy* outlines a method of proceeding. *An Inquiry Concerning Virtue or Merit*, the most regular and substantial treatise, acts as *confirmatio*. *The Moralists*, where objections are put to Theocles, becomes a *confutatio*; and the *Miscellanies* are summary, *conclusio*, and envoy. *Characteristicks* is thus methodical by the standards of humanist rhetoric. On the other hand, each treatise is a whole unto itself, and each is composed in a different genre: epistle, essay, soliloquy, treatise, dialogue, miscellany. Shaftesbury quite deliberately confronts readers with multiple and contrary kinds of order, fulfilling the program described in *Soliloquy*. In accordance with the maxim "Recognize yourself; which was as much as to say, divide yourself, or be two" (1:113), the author presents himself under different and opposing characters. The *Miscellanies*, for instance, refers disinterestedly to the preceding works as "some late pieces of a British author" (2:160).

Shaftesbury keys the miscellaneous essays to the five preceding treatises, which they paraphrase, amplify, qualify, or undermine. Describing himself as an "airy Assistant and humorous *Paraphrast*" (2:244), he concludes in a farcical genre that has "properly no top nor bottom, beginning or end":

> According to this Method, whilst I serve as *Critick* or *Interpreter* to this
> new Writer [of *Characteristicks*], I may the better correct his Flegm,
> and give him more of the fashionable Air and Manner of the World:
> especially in what relates to the Subject and Manner of his two *last*
> Pieces [the *Inquiry* and *Moralists*], which are contain'd in his second
> Volume. For these being of the more regular and formal kind, may eas-
> ily be oppressive to the airy Reader; and may therefore with the same
> assurance as *Tragedy* claim the necessary Relief of the *little Piece* or
> *Farce* above mentioned.   (2:161)

The time is now past when "*Regularity* and *Order* were thought essential in a Treatise. . . . In effect, the invidious Distinctions of *Bastardy* and *Legitimacy* being at length remov'd; the natural and lawful Issue of the Brain comes with like advantage into the World, and Wit (mere WIT) is well receiv'd without examination of the Kind, or censure of *the Form*" (2:157–58).

If Shaftesbury deliberately undermines authority (including his own), he also upholds a notion of historical kinds that allows him to discriminate between legitimate mixtures and "Bastardy." Readers are to distinguish his miscellanies from those of writers who mix genres indiscriminately. Pursuing originality for its own sake (2:159), such writers produce monstrous olios that in the last analysis prove to be curiously similar: "This is the Manner of Writing so much admir'd and imitated in our Age, that we have scarce the Idea of any other Model. We know little, indeed, of the difference between one Model or *Character* of writing and another. All runs to the same Tune, and beats exactly one and the same Measure" (2:171). Shaftesbury, who expects his readers to distinguish between "*Letter, Essay, Miscellany,* or ought else" (2:172), writes in mixed and contrary genres, not to level generic differences, but to differentiate the several characters of writing. The innovations achieved by this more sophisticated commerce should not be confused with the meaningless variations produced by fashionable authors who, like "Manufacturers in Stuff or Silk" (2:159), pursue meaningless variety as an end in itself.

The third miscellany "yokes" with the author of *Soliloquy*, "comprehending *Him*, the said Author, as one of the Number of the Advised, and My-self too (if occasion be) after his own example of *Self-admonition* and *private Address*" (2:240). Reflecting conversationally on the earlier treatise, Shaftesbury turns to a contrary genre to initiate an exchange between the opposing characters of philosopher and wit: "He (the author of *Soliloquy*) begins, it's true, as near *home* as possible, and sends us to the narrowest of all Conversations, that of SOLILOQUY or *Self-discourse*. But this Correspondence, according to his Computation, is wholly impracticable, without a previous Commerce with the World: and the larger this Commerce is, the more practicable and improving the other, he thinks, is likely to prove" (2:252). Miscellanies are by their mixed nature already commercial ventures; writing in this vein, Shaftesbury can flesh out the method of *Soliloquy* by situating it within a broader range of concerns. If *Characteristicks* begins a dialogue between ancient and modern writing, *Soliloquy* repeats the performance by initiating commerce between popular genres and philosophical writing. No one can understand his philosophy, Shaftesbury writes, except "those who delight in the open and *free* Commerce of the World, and are rejoic'd to gather Views and receive Light from every Quarter; in order to judg *the best of what is perfect, and according to a just Standard and true TASTE in every kind*" (2:252).

The method requires both inclusiveness and discrimination; Shaftesbury does not identify philosophy with manners, although he does set them in a close reciprocal relation: "To *philosophize*, in a just Signification, is but to carry *Good-breeding* a step higher. For the Accomplishment of Breeding is, to learn whatever is *decent* in Company or *beautiful* in *Arts;* and the Sum of Philosophy is, to learn what is *just* in Society and *beautiful* in Nature, and the Order of the World" (2:255). The philosopher justly bears a higher character than the wit, yet each is required to play the critic on the other. The libertine miscellanies ballast and correct the more authoritative philosophical utterances made elsewhere. Likewise, the humanist program outlined in the allegorical masque needs to be supplemented by the experience of engaging with contemporary society, frivolous though that may be. Self-difference, the method in and of

≡

Forms of Reflection
192

Characteristicks, is thus the high road to refinement, in self-colloquy and in the commonwealth at large: "All Politeness is owing to Liberty. We polish one another, and rub off our Corners and rough sides by a sort of *amicable Collision*. To restrain this, is inevitably to bring a rust upon Mens Understandings" (1:46).

The Friend, of course, undertakes a very different kind of meditational discipline. Coleridge's remark that "to think at all is to theorize" (2:124) suggests both the extent to which he was committed to method and how broadly his conception of method might be extended. In the first number he declares: "It is my object to refer men to PRINCIPLES in all things; in Literature, in the Fine Arts, in Morals, in Legislation, in Religion" (2:13). *The Friend* is not only a work about method, it was intended to be a methodical work as well, with free will "the foundation of my future Superstructure with all its ornaments, the hidden Root of the Tree, I am attempting to rear, with all its Branches and Boughs" (2:6). In practice, the shapely tree became a twisted thicket. Few works making such strong claims to order have proven so disorderly in execution: digressions become difficult to distinguish from the thread of argument, topics are abruptly begun, dropped, and resumed. The overall plan was several times foreshortened and redirected in response to personal difficulties and straitened financial circumstances.

Realizing that *The Friend* was insufficiently "methodical," in 1818 Coleridge published the *refacciamento* in an "arrangement altogether new" (1:3).[31] In the course of making over his periodical as a three-volume treatise, he excised many of the inset poems, letters, and narratives, segregating others into three interludes or "landing places." The discursive essays were arranged into sequences on ethics, practical morality, and principles of method. Comparing his work to a winding stair (1:149), Coleridge describes how three progressive sections circle around a single axis, ascending toward the union of mind with God that concludes the final sequence. Yet his firm conviction that everything is somehow analogous to everything else and his willingness to demonstrate this at fulsome length renders the *refacciamento* almost as labyrinthine as the periodical. Rather than completing the original plan, Coleridge added a new third section, on method, consisting of material adapted from his contributions to the *Encyclopedia Metropolitana*.[32] Like Shaftesbury, Coleridge places the discourse on method at the end, rather than at the beginning, of the treatise; for these reflexive philosophers, method is both the means to and the end of the contemplative process.

Coleridge argues that "all Method supposes A PRINCIPLE OF UNITY WITH PROGRESSION; in other words, progressive transition without breach of continuity" (1:476). The essays illustrate this principle in their meandering progress through discussions of literature, natural science, philosophy, history, and religion. While these are domains of knowledge rather than literary genres, Coleridge's sequence resembles Shaftesbury's allegory of the muses insofar as it presents a series of kinds. In *Soliloquy*, a disinterested spectator discriminates between kinds of writing by attending to the moral value of the passions they provoke; in *The Friend* an interested spectator reduces different realms of experience to unity by methodically applying a set of foundational principles. For Shaftesbury, progress is measured by degrees of particularity and differentiation, for Coleridge by degrees of abstraction and universality. If Shaftesbury rejects the anatomy conception of method as insufficiently dialogical, Coleridge rejects it for obscuring fundamental relations of identity. Linnaeus's "scheme of classific and distinctive marks," for instance, confuses a mere "alphabet" with "the central idea of vegetation itself" (1:466–67). Rather than distinguishing mere "characters," the truly methodical mind reflects on its own constitutive role in forming the concept of what it means to be a plant. Meditation becomes a constituent element of scientific writing, just as scientific writing becomes a constitutive element of meditations on culture.

As the connotations of cultivation veer from refinement and discrimination to principles of unity and progression, Coleridge reconceives the relation of character and method. The supplementary discourse on method begins by distinguishing between the characters of learned and ignorant speech. "What is that which first strikes, and strikes us at once, in a man of education?" asks Coleridge: "It is the unpremeditated and evidently habitual *arrangement* of his words, grounded on the habit of foreseeing, in each integral part, or (more plainly) in every sentence, the whole that he then intends to communicate. However irregular and desultory his talk, there is *method* in the fragments" (1:448–49). Speech is methodical to the extent that it approximates written utterance; meaning resides in a whole foreseen, rather than emerging out of dialogical exchange with another speaker. By contrast, the "leading feature" of uneducated speech is a reliance on the here and now of the oral situation, "an habitual submission of the understanding to mere events and images as such, and independent of any power in the mind to classify or appropriate them. The general accompaniments of time and place are the only

≡

Forms of Reflection
194

relations which persons of this class appear to regard in their statements" (1:451). The cultivated mind, led by habitual meditation to attend not only to things but to relations of things (and eventually to relations of relations), reveals its depths by detaching itself from local difference and mere contingency. Its character is marked less by the ability to discern differences of kind than by the ability to discern universals in particulars, reflexively grasping its constitutive power in the unity of phenomena.

A disinterested detachment from particularities is the particular character of genius. Coleridge illustrates his distinction between ignorant and cultivated intellect by comparing Mrs. Quickley to Hamlet, whom Coleridge takes as the very type of the reflective mind and methodical intellect. But the point of the exercise is less to discriminate the characters of Shakespeare's characters than to use these differences to establish the depth of the powerful intellect that comprehends and transcends their very contingency. Shakespeare is the font of method:

> It is Shakespeare's peculiar excellence, that throughout the whole of his splendid picture gallery . . . we find individuality every where, mere portrait no where. In all his various characters, we still feel ourselves communing with the same human nature, which is every where present. . . . Speaking of the effect, i.e. his works themselves, we may define the excellence of *their* method as consisting in that just proportion, that union and interpenetration of the universal and the particular, which must ever pervade all works of decided genius and true science. (1:457)

Shakespeare's poetry illustrates Coleridge's belief that all methods are ultimately one. Insofar as the poet and scientist both meditate upon nature, their method is the same: "If in SHAKESPEARE we find nature idealized into poetry, through the creative power of a profound yet observant meditation, so through the meditative observation of a DAVY, a WOLLASTON, or a HATCHETT . . . we find poetry, as it were, substantiated and realized in nature" (1:471). There is, of course, a reflexive relation implied between Coleridge's meditations and those of the meditators he meditates upon: just as the poet discovers "the same human nature" in the multiplicity of human actions, and the scientist the unity of law in the multiplicity of natural phenomena, so Coleridge discovers the identity of method underlying these different domains of knowledge. Indeed, insofar as he is reflecting on relations of relations rather than on relations of things, he displays even greater depth than the poet or scientist. What Coleridge does not do is distinguish literary kinds. Generic differences between

=

Cultivation into Culture

195

drama and scientific writing are not considered, nor is the fact that comic characters speak differently from tragic characters, or even that characters in a dramatic poem speak differently from characters encountered on the street.

Progressing from poetry and natural science to philosophy, Coleridge observes that "from Shakespeare to Plato, from the philosophic poet to the poetic philosopher, the transition is easy, and the road is crowded with illustrations of our larger subject" (1:472). Just as Shakespeare's dramas can be reduced to the paradigm of displaying unity in a manifold, so "the larger and more valuable portion [of Plato's writings] have all one common end, which comprehends and shines throughout the particular purpose of each several dialogue; and this is to establish the sources, to evolve the principles, and exemplify the art of METHOD" (1:472). Shaftesbury illustrates the common character of Greek poetry and philosophy by noting the parallel functions of dialogue in Homer's epic and fiction in Plato's dialogues. But Coleridge is not interested in the characters of kinds of writing or the manners these display — mere "classific marks" (1:466). The issue is not genre but genius:

> If, in collating the philosophical works of Lord Bacon with those of Plato, we, in both cases alike, separate the *grounds* and essential *principles* of their philosophic systems from the inductions themselves . . . and if we moreover separate the principles from their practical application . . . we shall not only extract that from each, which is for all ages, and which constitutes their true systems of philosophy, but shall convince ourselves that they are radically one and the same system.   (1:487)

No matter that one composed dialogues and the other an organon: having stripped away all that pertains to their historical or literary specificity, the meditator can contemplate the character of genius as one: "Thus the difference, or rather distinction between Plato and Lord Bacon is simply this: that philosophy being necessarily bi-polar, Plato treats . . . the *ideal* pole . . . while Bacon confines himself, for the most part, to the same truth as manifested at the other, or material pole" (1:492). Both Plato and Bacon, it appears, were attempting to produce a philosophical work very much like *The Friend*. What differences there are are differences of degree, rather than of kind (a "distinction," rather than a "difference").

If the principles of knowledge are always the same in kind, knowledge nonetheless progresses by degrees; Coleridge proves "deeper" than Plato and Bacon by attending to the unity underlying their partial truths. The

=

Forms of Reflection
196

essays on method make a similar progress, becoming more general still as Coleridge moves from progressive philosophy to progressive history:

> We can now, as men furnished with fit and respectable credentials, proceed to the historic importance and practical application of METHOD, under the deep and solemn conviction, that without this guiding Light, neither can the sciences attain to their full evolution, as the organs of one vital and harmonious body, nor that most weighty and concerning of all sciences, the science of EDUCATION, be understood in its first elements, much less display its powers, as the nisus formativus of social man, as the appointed PROTOPLAST of true humanity. (1:493–94)

Method, that is, radiates not only through the writings of philosophers and men of genius but through human history itself. The historic importance of method seems to lie in the fact that history unfolds methodically. Reflecting on universal history, Coleridge discovers his "guiding Light" is both progressive in the evolution of science and continuous in the unchanging nature of "true humanity." The fixed and moving poles come together in the concept of cultivation, the "protoplast" by which the organism progresses and reproduces itself. If Shaftesbury's method of contemplating history underscores the value of historical differences, Coleridge emphasizes the continuity, indeed, the identity of human experience. The guiding light is the same for all; all science progresses in one direction; all methods are finally one.

Thinking of human history as mind writ large, Coleridge discovers in it the two poles he described earlier—a mutable, objective pole, which is "civilization," and an unchanging subjective pole, which is "cultivation." History illustrates "the permanent distinction, and the occasional contrast, between cultivation and civilization" (distinguished when kept in balance, contrasted when one dominates the other) (1:494). Coleridge and his contemporaries used such formulations to transform the old debate between "ancients and moderns," into the modern conception of timeless arts and progressive sciences.[33] Like most champions of culture, Coleridge pursues a historical method that would reduce the flux and mutability of history to a set of principles—in this instance, principles of mind. Meditating from a vantage high enough "to neutralize or render insignificant the disturbing factors of accident" (1:504), Coleridge reduces Hebrew, Greek, and Roman civilizations to three characters of mind, points on a "living line" which converges in a Christian synthesis (1:506). (The line is hardly a straight one, since the earlier Hebrews

=

Cultivation into Culture
197

occupy the "fixed mid-point" between Greek idealism and Roman empiricism.) Universalizing these generalizations, Coleridge finds that while the two poles are "connatural," the character of a nation or age will vary as it pursues the wants of the body or the wants of the mind, trade or literature respectively (1:507). These "two forms of method, inseparably coexistent" produce

> very different effects according as one or the other obtains the primacy.
> . . . In tracing the epochs, and alternations of their relative sovereignty
> or subjection, consists the PHILOSOPHY of History. In the power of distinguishing and appreciating the several results consists the historic
> SENSE. And under the ascendancy of the mental and moral character
> the *commercial* relations may thrive to the utmost *desirable* point, while
> the reverse is ruinous to both.   (1:507–08)

Cultivation is both one pole of the opposition and the protoplast which holds both poles in balance. Thinking of history as a principle of unity with progression, contemplative historians seek "some ground common to the world and to man, therein to find the one principle of permanence and identity" (1:508).[34] Contemplating the rise and fall of civilizations, they discover this principle in the constitutive act of reflection, in the unfolding progress of their own mental faculties.

The sequence of essays concludes with a theological rhapsody describing the union of this contemplative mind with "the indemonstrable [from which] flows the sap, that circulates through every branch and spray of the demonstration" (1:523). Coleridge's invocation to the unutterable resembles, in style, Theocles' in *Characteristicks;* in substance, Plotinus's *Enneads:*

> This elevation of the spirit above the semblances of custom and the
> senses to a world of spirit, this life in the idea, even in the supreme and
> godlike, which alone merits the name of life, and without which our organic life is but a state of somnambulism, this it is which affords the sole
> sure anchorage in the storm, and at the same time the substantiating
> principle of all true wisdom, the satisfactory solution of all the contradictions of human nature, of the whole riddle of the world.   (1:524)

While *The Friend* asserts that "this alone belongs to and speaks intelligibly to all alike, the learned and the ignorant, if but the heart listens" (1:524), Coleridge's theology, like his understanding of cultivation, implies that priests are necessary to light the torches of the unlearned.

≡

Forms of Reflection

The rhapsody begins by asking us to "imagine the unlettered African, or rude yet musing Indian, poring over an illumined manuscript of the inspired volume, with the vague yet deep impression that his fates and fortunes are in some unknown manner connected with its contents" (1:512). The uncultivated savage ponders "cyphers, letters, marks, and points," arranging the characters into classificatory schemes of separate elements, "mere orderliness without METHOD," until a "friendly missionary" arrives to teach him to read characters "as though he saw them not" (1:513). It is not difficult to see in this episode an analogy to the social mission of *The Friend* itself.

If aesthetic meditations pervade eighteenth-century literature, procedures for writing about cultivation were both diverse and changing in the years that separate *Soliloquy* from *The Friend*. In the intervening century, concepts of character shifted from a concern with distinctions of kind to a concern with distinctions of depth. Shaftesbury instructs readers to refine themselves by contemplating differences of character and discriminating their relative merits. On the other hand, Coleridge would have his unlettered savage regard characters as though he "saw them not," disregarding differences of kind in order to perceive the unity in a manifold, the genus in the species, the universal in particulars. Critics, like poets, are men speaking to men: they differ from others not in kind or character, but by their greater degree of mental cultivation.

The previous section, on history, shows how Shaftesbury emphasizes the timeliness of writing, instructing readers to contemplate how the characters of writing reflect the characters of society and how both these characters change as writers engage in commerce with patrons, critics, and readers. While Coleridge recognizes that writing and society change, he distinguishes the accidents of custom from the regularity of principle. The permanent distinction between civilization and cultivation underwrites a set of meditational procedures for extracting historical difference from literary interpretation. Properly cultivated, even unlettered savages can acquire the method necessary to commune "with the spirit of the volume as a living oracle" (1:513). The first section shows how Shaftesbury instructs readers to discriminate between the different voices appearing within works (including his own), that they might exercise their own authority as disinterested spectators and judges. Coleridge instructs readers to form their minds by contemplating authoritative works, and, like a friendly missionary, presents his own contemplations as authoritative insofar as they repeat and assimilate the wisdom of the West.

=

Cultivation into Culture

A passage from Goldsmith indicates something of the social significance of the title of Coleridge's paper. Speaking of an earlier periodical, the *Connoisseur* (edited by "Mr. Town, Critic and Censor General"), Goldsmith censures the authority claimed by "men of letters": "This Writer may be stiled the *Friend* of Society, in the most agreeable acceptation of the that term: For he rather converses with all the ease of a chearful companion, than dictates, as other Writers in this class have done, with the affected superiority of an Author."[35] Coleridge pursued such relationships with his intimates; indeed, he was a legendary conversationalist. But with subscribers it was otherwise. Lacking a face-to-face relationship with readers, the "friend" makes little pretense of discoursing as an agreeable companion; nor does he shy away from asserting his own superiority: "To attempt to make a Man wiser is of necessity to remind him of his ignorance" (2:282)—not for this friend to propose things unknown as things forgot. The diffusion of literacy and its potential political consequences seemed to Coleridge to require new principles for educating an elite and regulating the "communication of truth" (2:38) between writers and a readership that was no longer a community.

If earlier critics, including Shaftesbury, ridiculed the book trade and commercial literature, they nonetheless regarded cultivation as a form of commerce, a joint venture undertaken by writers and readers. Commerce, however, served the interests of innovation; to establish an alternative set of permanent principles, Coleridge found it necessary to rethink the ways in which literature is contemplated and criticism written. He took on the Enlightenment by appropriating the genre that, perhaps better than any other, defined its program of reforming society through commerce and reflection—the periodical essay. In extracting its dialogical constituents and substituting the authority of method, he laid the groundwork for many modern critical practices. Coleridge could regard the very failure of *The Friend* as evidence of the need to methodize cultivation under the supervision of professional critics. He was more successful elsewhere; recasting the history of his mind in the less inscrutable form of the *Biographia Literaria*, he found his cadre of elite readers and shaped the course of literary criticism for generations to come.

Despite obvious differences, Coleridge's project has much in common with current attempts to define a discipline or method of cultural studies. Several strains of contemporary Marxism have given a kind of second wind to nineteenth-century ideas about culture. Terry Eagleton, for

≡

Forms of Reflection

instance, calls upon critics to reject fashion and the babel of theory; in place of divisive "commodification" — read commerce — he suggests critics "weld" symbolic and political discourses into "a collective political force."[36] Coleridge would approve. David Kaufmann underscores the Arnoldian (Coleridgean, I would argue) impetus behind demands for a unified science that would be at once specifically literary and holistically cultural: "The various attempts to use theories of textuality to redefine all areas of human knowledge reflect a drive to place the study of the text — the traditional function of literary criticism — at the center of human knowledge."[37] It is only on the basis of some such holistic notion that literary and social differences can be defined as contradictions. To be sure, critics now discourse on rupture and aporia rather than permanence and purity, on historicism and materialism rather than universality and spirituality. But discussions of culture are still carried on within the framework of nineteenth-century understandings of identity and history, be they derived from Coleridge or Hegel, Arnold or Marx. Consider the Coleridgean echo in Nigel Leask's proposal to demystify Coleridge: "Only by *an act of historical self-reflection* can we be aware of that persuasive cultural mystification, in the inauguration of which Coleridge played such an important part."[38]

If we are to demystify criticism, I suggest, we ought to reflect not on culture itself but on the literary procedures that generate the belief in culture, to reflect on them in ways that do not reduce differences to functions or disfunctions within an implicit totality. I have tried to show how concepts of culture lead even sophisticated readers to see through structures of difference as though they saw them not. I have tried to resist such procedures by presenting culture as a function of writing, rather than writing as a function of culture. I have used generic analysis to underscore the differences that literature and history make, differences that have too often been obscured by a criticism that resolves relations between writing and society into world views, ideologies, or discursive formations.

If our business as literary historians is to account for literary and social change, we would do well to begin with a nuanced means for describing how works differ from antecedents, from contemporary works, and from themselves. To this end, I have used generic analysis to discriminate between kinds of mixture and kinds of change, calling attention to the ways both early modern and postmodern critics have used forms of reflection to mediate between literary and social structures. If academic writers stand in a different relation to those structures of difference from

≡

that of Donne's courtiers, Shaftesbury's gentlemen, or Coleridge's men of letters, we, as much as they, are confronted with the problem of making sense of a past that continues to inform the present. A better understanding of how writers have employed literary genres in the past will greatly facilitate our attempts to define new roles for criticism in the present.

=

Forms of Reflection

Notes

Chapter One. Donne in Meditation

1. Louis A. Montrose, "Renaissance Literary Studies and the Subject of History," *English Literary Renaissance* 16:1 (Winter 1986): 5–12, 6.

2. See H. Aram Veeser, editor, *The New Historicism* (New York: Routledge, 1989), especially the essays by John Klancher, Elizabeth Fox-Genovese, Frank Lentricchia, and Vincent P. Pecora.

3. Carolyn Porter, "Are We Being Historical Yet?" *South Atlantic Quarterly* 87:4 (Fall 1988): 743–86, 764–65.

4. Jonathan Goldberg, *James I and the Politics of Literature: Jonson, Shakespeare, Donne, and Their Contemporaries* (Baltimore: Johns Hopkins University Press, 1983), xiii, xi.

5. For a useful discussion of the contributions of Hegel and Burkhardt to this process, see E. H. Gombrich, *In Search of Cultural History* (Oxford: Clarendon, 1969).

6. George Savile, Marquess of Halifax, *Complete Works*, edited by J. P. Kenyon (Baltimore: Penguin, 1969), 193. These meditations were first published in 1750; the date of composition is not known.

7. Louis L. Martz, *The Poetry of Meditation: A Study in English Religious Literature of the Seventeenth Century* (New Haven: Yale University Press, 1954), 3.

8. Barbara Keifer Lewalski, *Donne's "Anniversaries" and the Poetry of Praise* (Princeton: Princeton University Press, 1973), 142.

9. Barbara Keifer Lewalski, *Protestant Poetics and the Seventeenth-Century Religious Lyric* (Princeton: Princeton University Press, 1979), ix.

10. Cited in Leonard D. Tourney, "Joseph Hall and the *Anniversaries*," *Papers on Language and Literature* 13:1 (Winter 1977): 25–34, 30. Hall's more recent biographer is more sympathetic: Frank Livingstone Huntley, *Bishop Joseph Hall,*

1574–1656 (Cambridge: D. S. Brewer, 1979). See also Leonard D. Tourney, *Joseph Hall* (Boston: Twayne, 1979); Richard A. McCabe, *Joseph Hall: A Study in Satire and Meditation* (Oxford: Clarendon, 1982); Ronald J. Corthell, "Joseph Hall and Seventeenth-Century Literature," *John Donne Journal* 3:2 (1984): 249–68; Thomas Kranidas, "Style and Rectitude in Seventeenth-Century Prose: Hall, Smectymnuus, and Milton," *Huntington Library Quarterly* 46 (Summer 1983): 237–69.

11. U. Milo Kaufmann, *The Pilgrim's Progress and Traditions in Puritan Meditation* (New Haven: Yale University Press, 1966), 120–33; on Hall's influence, see also Martz, *The Poetry of Meditation*, 331–32, and Lewalski, *Protestant Poetics*, 150ff.

12. For general discussions of devotional meditation in England, see, in addition to those mentioned in n. 11, Helen C. White, *English Devotional Literature (Prose) 1600–1640* (Madison: University of Wisconsin Press, 1931); and C. J. Stranks, *Anglican Devotion: Studies in the Spiritual Life of the Church of England between the Reformation and the Oxford Movement* (London: SCM Press, 1961).

13. Robert Persons, *Christian Directory* (Rouen, 1585), sec. 24.

14. Joseph Hall, *The Arte of Divine Meditation* (London, 1606); reprinted in Frank Livingstone Huntley, *Bishop Joseph Hall and Protestant Meditation in Seventeenth-Century England* (Binghampton: Medieval and Renaissance Texts and Studies, 1981), 67, 88. Citations are from *The Works of Joseph Hall, b. of Exeter* (London, 1634). Page numbers are also given for Huntley's modernized text.

15. Cited in Martz, *The Poetry of Meditation*, 14.

16. Hall, *The Arte of Divine Meditation*, 72. On Hall's Anglicanism, see John Booty, "Joseph Hall, *The Arte of Divine Meditation*, and Anglican Spirituality," in *The Roots of the Modern Christian Tradition*, edited by E. Rozanne Elder (Kalamazoo: Cistercian Publications, 1984), 200–28.

17. Lisa Jardine, *Francis Bacon, Discovery and the Art of Discourse* (Cambridge: Cambridge University Press, 1974), 5.

18. Cited in ibid., 30, 41.

19. O. B. Hardison, *The Enduring Monument: A Study of the Idea of Praise in Renaissance Literary Theory and Practice* (Chapel Hill: University of North Carolina Press, 1962), 171.

20. Lewalski, *Donne's "Anniversaries,"* 73–74.

21. Rosalie L. Colie, *The Resources of Kind: Genre Theory in the Renaissance* (Berkeley and Los Angeles: University of California Press, 1973), 193; Lewalski, *Donne's "Anniversaries,"* 74.

22. Lewalski, *Donne's "Anniversaries,"* 11, 134.

23. Thomas Willard, "Donne's Anatomy Lesson: Vesalian or Paracelsian?" *John Donne Journal* 3:1 (1984): 34–64.

24. Lewalski, Donne's "Anniversaries," 83; Tourney, "Joseph Hall and the *Anniversaries*," 34, 26; Huntley, *Bishop Joseph Hall and Protestant Meditation*, 24.

25. A conflation of art and science that has provoked disciplinary contentions not unlike those of the sixteenth century; see Stanley Fish, "Being Interdisciplinary Is So Very Hard to Do," in *Profession 89* (New York: Modern Language Association of America, 1989), 15–22; David Kaufmann, "The Profession of Theory," *PMLA* 105:3 (May 1990): 519–30.

26. Michael McCanles, "The Authentic Discourse of the Renaissance," *Diacritics* 10 (Spring 1980): 77–87, 81. Jean E. Howard offers a summary treatment of how New Historicists have engaged this issue in "The New Historicism in Renaissance Studies," *ELR* 70 (Spring 1986): 13–43.

27. Stephen Greenblatt, "Invisible Bullets: Renaissance Authority and Its Subversions," *Glyph* 8 (1981): 40–61.

28. Michael McKeon, "Historicizing Absalom and Achitophel," in *The New Eighteenth Century: Theory, Politics, English Literature*, edited by Felicity Nussbaum and Laura Brown (New York: Methuen, 1987), 23–40, 23, 39.

29. See Carolyn Porter's discussion of "a formalist legacy" in New Historicism in "History and Literature: 'After the New Historicism,'" *New Literary History* 21:2 (1990):253–72.

30. McKeon, "Historicizing Absalom and Achitophel," 39.

31. Herbert J. C. Grierson, editor, *The Poems of John Donne*, 2 vols. (London: Oxford University Press, 1912), 1:229–66. Citations are from this edition.

32. On the relation of Galen to diagnosis, prophecy, and rhetorical structures, see Douglas Lane Patey, *Probability and Literary Form: Philosophic Theory and Practice in the Augustan Age* (Cambridge: Cambridge University Press, 1984), 36–42.

33. From a handbook on method by Robert MacIlmane, cited in Wilbur S. Howell, *Logic and Rhetoric in England, 1500–1700* (Princeton: Princeton University Press, 1956), 184.

34. On this compendious subject, see Howell, *Logic and Rhetoric*; Walter J. Ong, *Ramus, Method, and the Decay of Dialogue* (Cambridge: Harvard University Press, 1958: reprint, 1983); Neal W. Gilbert, *Renaissance Concepts of Method* (New York: Columbia University Press, 1960); and Patrick Grant, *Literature and the Discovery of Method in the English Renaissance* (Athens: University of Georgia Press, 1985).

35. George Puttenham, *The Arte of English Poetry* (London, 1589), edited by Gladys Doige Wilcox and Alice Walker (Cambridge: Cambridge University Press, 1936), 9.

36. On poetry and prophecy in the English Renaissance, see William Kerrigan, *The Prophetic Milton* (Charlottesville: University of Virginia Press, 1974): 17–82.

37. Lewalski, Donne's "Anniversaries," 160–62.

38. Hans W. Frei, The Eclipse of Biblical Narrative: A Study in Eighteenth and Nineteenth Century Hermeneutics (New Haven: Yale University Press, 1974), 28.

39. Donne represents the dispensations in five emblematical conceits: the heart (ll. 173–74), the compass (ll. 220–22), the ark (ll. 317–20), the ring (ll. 341–44), and Moses's rod (ll. 389–90). The emblems would seem to be a mnemonic device, in keeping with the theme of the poem. The new world of the inset meditations and eulogies consists of five "elements": extension, substance, proportion, color, and power, and is known by five senses: taste (section 1), smell (section 2), sound (section 3), sight (section 4), and touch (section 5). This "application of the senses" obviously accords with Ignatian procedures.

40. See Lewalski, Donne's "Anniversaries," 16.

41. On Donne's flirtations with idolatry, see Ernest B. Gilman, Iconoclasm and Poetry in the English Reformation (Chicago: University of Chicago Press, 1985), 117–48.

42. Ben Jonson, "Conversations with Drummond of Hawthornden," in Ben Jonson, edited by C. H. Herford, Percy Simpson, and Evelyn Simpson, 11 vols. (Oxford: Clarendon, 1925–52), 1:133.

43. McKeon, "Historicizing Absalom and Achitophel," 23.

44. Jonathan Dollimore and Alan Sinfield, Political Shakespeare: New Essays in Cultural Materialism (Ithaca: Cornell University Press, 1985), vii.

45. John Dryden, "Discourse Concerning Satire," in The Poems of John Dryden, edited by James Kinsley, 4 vols. (Oxford: Clarendon, 1958), 2:620.

46. See Michel Foucault, "Nietzsche, Genealogy, History," in Language, Countermemory, Practice, translated by Donald F. Bouchard and Sherry Simon (Ithaca: Cornell University Press, 1977); and Jonathan Arac, Critical Genealogies: Historical Situations for Postmodern Literary Studies (New York: Columbia University Press, 1989).

47. On imitations of Donne's poems, see Lewalski, Donne's "Anniversaries," 307–70.

48. Arthur F. Marotti, John Donne, Coterie Poet (Madison: University of Wisconsin Press, 1986), 245.

49. For recent discussions of Donne's attempts at preferment, see John Carey, John Donne, Life, Mind, and Art (New York: Oxford University Press, 1981), 60–93; Lewalski, Donne's "Anniversaries," 42–72; and "Lucy, Countess of Bedford: Images of a Jacobean Courtier and Patroness," in Politics of Discourse: The Literature and History of Seventeenth-Century England, edited by Kevin Sharpe and Steven N. Zwicker (Berkeley and Los Angeles: University of California Press, 1987), 52–77; and Arthur F. Marotti, "John Donne and the Rewards of Patronage," in Patronage in the Renaissance, edited by Guy Fitch Lytle and Stephen Orgel (Princeton: Princeton University Press, 1981), 207–34.

=

50. Citations are from John Donne, *Essayes in Divinity*, edited by Evelyn M. Simpson (Oxford: Oxford University Press, 1952).

51. Francis Bacon, *The Works of Francis Bacon*, edited by James Spedding, Robert L. Ellis, and Douglas D. Heath, 15 vols. (London: Longmans, 1883), 4:26–27.

52. Several of these are translated by Benjamin Farringdon, *The Philosophy of Francis Bacon* (Chicago: University of Chicago Press, 1964). On the resolve, see John L. Lievsay, *The Seventeenth-Century Resolve: A Historical Anthology of a Literary Form* (Lexington: University of Kentucky Press, 1980), 1–9.

53. On the several kinds of method Bacon employs, see Jardine, *Francis Bacon*, 169–78.

54. Hall, *The Arte of Divine Meditation*, 96, 72.

55. On Donne's position, see Joseph A. Mazzeo, "St. Augustine's Rhetoric of Silence: Truth vs. Eloquence and Things vs. Signs," *Renaissance and Seventeenth-Century Studies* (New York: Columbia University Press, 1964), 1–28.

56. Donne, *The Progres of the Soule*, 291–300.

57. Letter to Sir G. F., in Hardison, *The Enduring Monument*, 166.

58. John Stoughton, *XIII Sermons, Preached in the Church of Aldermanbury, London . . . To Which is Added, An Exact and Learned Discourse, Perfected by the Author, Concerning the Definition and Distribution of Divinity: And the Happiness of Man* (London, 1640). On Stoughton, see Paul S. Seaver, *The Puritan Lectureships* (Stanford: Stanford University Press, 1970), 257.

59. For analogous procedures, see Joseph Hall, *Contemplations Upon the Principal Passages of the Holy Story* (London, 1612; there are many later editions). Hall's effusive commentaries, like Donne's, are a far remove from Calvin's.

60. In Stoughton, *XIII Sermons*. Hall was attacked on much the same ground by Henry Burton: "It [is] a matter to be maintained by fineness of wit, or quaint rhetorical discourse, but upon sound ground and substantial demonstration," cited in Kranidas, "Style and Rectitude," 240. Kranidas argues that style and politics were becoming inseparable in Protestant polemics.

61. Donne, *An Anatomy of the World*, 461–68.

Chapter Two. Seventeenth-Century Georgic

1. Anthony Ashley Cooper, Lord Shaftesbury, *Characteristics of Men, Manners, Opinions, Times*, edited by John M. Robertson (rpt. 2 vols. in 1, Indianapolis: Bobbs Merrill, 1964), 1:46.

2. On Denham's life, see Brendan O Hehir, *Harmony from Discords: A Life of Sir John Denham* (Berkeley and Los Angeles: University of California Press, 1968). Maren-Sofie Rostwig discusses midcentury poetry in *The Happy Man: Studies in the Metamorphosis of a Classical Ideal*, 2d ed. (Trondheim: Norwegian Universities Press, 1962), 119–227.

3. Earl R. Wasserman, *The Subtler Language: Critical Readings of Neoclassic*

and Romantic Poems (Baltimore: Johns Hopkins University Press, 1959), 49, 58. Further citations are given in the text.

4. James Turner, *The Politics of Landscape: Rural Scenery and Society in English Poetry, 1630–1660* (Cambridge: Harvard University Press, 1979), 57, 56, 53. Further citations are given in the text.

5. Citations are from the 1642 version of *Coopers Hill*, reprinted in Brendan O Hehir, *Expans'd Hieroglyphics: A Study of Sir John Denham's "Coopers Hill" with a Critical Edition of the Poem* (Berkeley and Los Angeles: University of California Press, 1969). Further references are given in the text.

6. M. H. Abrams, "Structure and Style in the Greater Romantic Lyric," in *From Sensibility to Romanticism: Essays Presented to Frederick A. Pottle* (Oxford: Oxford University Press, 1965), 527–60, 547, 538–39.

7. Wasserman, *The Subtler Language*, 46. This passage is quoted from Johnson in Sherburn, "Life of Denham."

8. Abrams, "Structure and Style," 528, 535.

9. Alastair Fowler, *Kinds of Literature: An Introduction to the Theory of Genres and Modes* (Cambridge: Harvard University Press, 1982), 200.

10. See John L. Lievsay, *The Seventeenth-Century Resolve: A Historical Anthology of a Literary Form* (Lexington: University of Kentucky Press, 1980).

11. Thomas Fuller, *Thoughts and Contemplations*, edited by James O. Wood (London: SPCK, 1964), 47.

12. In Frank Livingstone Huntley, *Bishop Hall and Protestant Meditation in Seventeenth-Century England* (Binghampton: Center for Medieval and Renaissance Studies, 1981), 76.

13. Francis Quarles, *Works*, edited by Alexander B. Grosart, 3 vols. (rpt., New York: AMS Press, 1967), 1:57.

14. Robert Herrick, *Hesperides: or, The Works both Humane and Divine of Robert Herrick, Esq.* (London, 1648, rpt., Menston: Scolar, 1969, 1973), 1.

15. Edmund Spenser, *The Faerie Queene*, edited by A. C. Hamilton (London: Longmans, 1977), 5.2.36, ll. 5–9. But Spenser's arguments were still being made during the 1640s, indeed, citing this very episode. See *The Faerie Leveller; or, King Charles his Leveller Descried and Deciphered in Queene Elizabeths Dayes. By her Poet Laureat Edmond Spenser, in his Unparaleld Poem, Entituled The Faire Queene. A Lively Representation of our Times* (London, 1648).

16. Virgil, "The Second Book of the Georgics," in John Dryden, *Works of Dryden*, edited by William Frost (Berkeley and Los Angeles: University of California Press, 1987), 5:673–80.

17. Ralph Cohen, "Innovation and Variation: Literary Change and Georgic Poetry," in *Literature and History, Papers Read at a Clark Library Seminar, March 3, 1973* (Los Angeles: William Andrews Clark Memorial Library, 1974), 16–17.

18. The literary, historical, and philosophical basis of English georgics have been most thoroughly studied by Geoffrey Tillotson, *Augustan Studies* (London:

=

Athlone, 1961); Ralph Cohen, *The Art of Discrimination: Thomson's Seasons and the Language of Criticism* (Berkeley and Los Angeles: University of California Press, 1964); and Ralph Cohen, *The Unfolding of the Seasons* (Baltimore: Johns Hopkins Press, 1970). See also Ralph Cohen, "On the Interrelation of Eighteenth-Century Literary Forms," *English Institute Annual* (New York: Columbia University Press, 1974). Eric Rothstein, *Restoration and Eighteenth-Century Poetry 1660–1780* (Boston: Routledge and Kegan Paul, 1981), is also a good introduction. Anthony Low, *The Georgic Revolution* (Princeton: Princeton University Press, 1985), takes a narrowly thematic approach to georgic that leads him to conclude that *Coopers Hill* "lacks a georgic spirit or georgic subject matter," 73. General surveys are offered by Dwight L. Durling, *Georgic Tradition in English Poetry* (New York: Columbia University Press, 1935), and John Chalker, *The English Georgic: A Study in the Development of a Form* (Baltimore: Johns Hopkins University Press, 1969).

19. Joseph Addison, "Essay on the Georgics," in Dryden, *Works,* 5:148. Further references are to this edition.

20. J. G. A. Pocock, *The Machiavellian Moment: Florentine Political Thought and the Atlantic Republican Tradition* (Princeton: Princeton University Press, 1975), 3.

21. Cited in ibid., 362.

22. On the political allegory, see John Wallace, "*Coopers Hill,* the Manifesto of Parliamentary Royalism," *ELH* 61 (1974): 516ff.

23. John Barrell and Harriet Guest, "On the Use of Contradiction: Economics and Morality in the Eighteenth-Century Long Poem," in *The New Eighteenth Century: Theory, Politics, English Literature,* edited by Felicity Nussbaum and Laura Brown (New York: Methuen, 1987), 121–43.

24. Other instances of the genre include Henry Peacham's *Complete Gentleman* (1622), Gervase Markham's *Complete Farrier* (1639), Dudley Digges's *Compleat Ambassador* (1655), and John Evelyn's *Complete Gard'ner* (1693). On Walton's use of the instructional dialogue, see H. J. Oliver, "The Composition and Revisions of *The Complete Angler,*" *Modern Language Review* 42 (1947): 297–98, and John R. Cooper, *The Art of the Complete Angler* (Durham: Duke University Press, 1968), chap. 3.

25. Citations are from the 1653 version, in Izaak Walton, *The Compleat Angler: or, the Contemplative Man's Recreation,* edited by Jonquil Bevan (Oxford: Clarendon, 1983). Later editions substituted "Venator" for "Viator" and make considerable additions.

26. See Eugene P. Kirk, *Menippean Satire, An Annotated Catalogue of Texts and Criticism* (New York: Garland, 1980). Kirk's critical introduction is far and away the best account of the genre; other references may be found in his bibliography. John Dryden is the most insightful seventeenth-century commentator; see his *Essays,* edited by George Watson (London: Dent, 1962), 2:113ff.

≡

27. Izaak Walton, *Life of Sanderson* (London, 1678), sig. g2v–g3v.

28. This parenthetical remark was dropped in later editions. Walton also omits references to drinking or changes "ale" to "barley wine." Self-censorship in such small matters indicates how sensitive readers might be to the issue of pleasure. On revisions generally, see Oliver, "Composition of *The Angler*," 310.

29. On manners in relation to republican thought, see J. G. A. Pocock, "Virtues, Rights, and Manners: A Model for Historians of Political Thought," *Virtue, Commerce, and History: Essays on Political Thought and History, Chiefly in the Seventeenth-Century* (Cambridge: Cambridge University Press, 1985), 37–50.

30. See Joseph Hall, *Occasional Meditations* (London, 1633), reprinted in Huntley, *Bishop Hall and Protestant Meditation*. Simultaneously with Walton, the chemist Robert Boyle was using a fishing expedition as the occasion for devotional recreation. His "Discourse touching on Occasional Meditations" underscores the complementary relation of this irregular form to "lectures" on ethics and theology: "He that is versed in making reflections upon what occurs to him . . . can make the little accidents of his life, and the very flowers of his garden, read him lectures of ethicks or divinity," Boyle, *Works* (London, 1744), 2:162.

31. Addison, "Essay on the Georgics," 146. On Walton's georgic sources, see Cooper, *Art of the Complete Angler*, 30–58.

32. See Annabel Patterson, "Fables of Power," in *Politics of Discourse*, edited by Kevin Sharp and Steven N. Zwicker (Berkeley and Los Angeles: University of California Press, 1987), 271–96.

33. On Walton's pastoral sources, see Cooper, *Art of the Complete Angler*, 59–76. Annabel Patterson describes how "fragments of the *Eclogues* became nodes of political theory" in Caroline England, "Pastoral versus Georgic: The Politics of Virgilian Quotation," in *Renaissance Genres: Essays on Theory, History, and Interpretation*, edited by Barbara Keifer Lewalski (Cambridge: Harvard University Press, 1986), 241–67, 249.

34. Anna K. Nardo, "'A recreation of a recreation': Reading *The Compleat Angler*," *South Atlantic Quarterly* 79 (1980): 311.

35. Reprinted in *Profession 89* (New York: Modern Language Association, 1989), 15–31, 20.

36. For a similar kind of analysis, see the discussion of "the sociology of genres" in Tony Bennett, *Outside Literature* (London: Routledge, 1990), 78–114.

37. Ben Jonson, *Works*, edited by C. H. Herford, Percy Simpson, and Evelyn Simpson (Oxford: Oxford University Press, 1947), 8:126. For useful discussions of the genre, see Alastair Fowler, "The Silva Tradition in Jonson's *The Forrest*," *Poetic Traditions of the Renaissance*, edited by Maynard Mack (New Haven: Yale University Press, 1981), 163–80; Annabel Patterson, "Jonson, Marvell, and Miscellaneity?" in *Poems in their Places*, edited by Neil Fraistat (Chapel Hill: University of North Carolina Press, 1986); and Robert Cummings, "*Windsor Forest* as

a Silvan Poem," *ELH* 54 (1987): 63–80). In addition to Ben Jonson's *The Forrest*, *Under-woods*, and *Timber*, members of the genre include Abraham Cowley's *Sylvae*, *Libri Plantaram*, and *Essays*, Phineas Fletcher's *Sylva poetica*, George Herbert's *Lucus*, Robert Herrick's *Hesperides*, and John Dryden's *Sylvae: or, the Second Part of Poetical Miscellanies*.

38. The translation is from the edition by Israel Gollancz, *Timber: or, Discoveries: Made upon Men and Matter: as they have flowed out of his daily Readings; or had their reflux to his peculiar Notion of the Times* (London: Dent, 1902).

39. On the importance of sequence, see Fowler, "The Silva Tradition," 171–75.

40. Abraham Cowley, "Of Liberty," in *Several Discourses by way of Essays, in Verse and Prose*, in *Works*, edited by A. R. Waller (Cambridge: Cambridge University Press, 1906), 2:377–86.

41. On the tradition of retirement poetry, see Rostwig, *The Happy Man*. Cowley's *Essays* are discussed in 1:212–21, curiously out of sequence, since this is a Restoration and not an interregnum work.

42. On Cowley's straitened circumstances and difficulties with the court, see A. H. Nethercott, *The Muse's Hannibal* (Oxford: Clarendon, 1931), 179–250.

43. On the opposition between court and country, see Derek Hirst, "Court, Country, and Politics before 1629," in *Faction and Parliament: Essays on Early Stuart History*, edited by Kevin Sharp (Oxford: Clarendon, 1978), 105–38. Hirst's essay is especially useful since it describes the mixture and interpenetration of court and country politics that one finds in Jonson's *Forrest* and many seventeenth-century georgics. Cowley's stance of "self-exile" can thus be seen as a departure from the norm.

44. But not necessarily, since some vestiges of feudalism continued into the seventeenth century, and Stuart policy encouraged the reintroduction of others. Idealizations in estate poems do not necessarily falsify real relations of exchange, as Raymond Williams argues, *The Country and the City* (New York: Oxford University Press, 1973), 35–54. See Alastair Fowler, "Country House Poems: The Politics of a Genre," in *Seventeenth Century* 1:1 (1986): 1–13; and Kevin Sharp, "Cavalier Critic? The Ethics and Politics of Thomas Carew's Poetry," in *Politics of Discourse: The Literature and History of Seventeenth-Century England*, edited by Kevin Sharp and Steven N. Zwicker (Berkeley and Los Angeles: University of California Press, 1987), 117–46. On the "Gothic revival," see Don E. Wayne, *Penshurst: The Semiotics of Place and the Poetics of History* (Madison: University of Wisconsin Press, 1984), 86ff.

45. See Malcolm Smuts, "The Political Failure of Stuart Cultural Patronage," in *Patronage in the Renaissance*, edited Guy Fitch Lytle and Stephen Orgel (Princeton: Princeton University Press, 1981), 165–90.

46. Fowler, "The Silva Tradition," 173.

47. An instructive contrast here is Henry Vaughan, *The Praise and Happi-*

=

nesse of the Countrie-Life (1651), in *Works*, edited by L. C. Martin (Oxford: Clarendon, 1957), 123–36, in which similar arguments are presented in an even lower stylistic register.

48. *Epistle to Augustus*, 11.75–78, quoted in Maynard Mack, "A Poet in His Landscape: Pope at Twickenham," in *From Sensibility to Romanticism: Essays Presented to Frederick A. Pottle* (Oxford: Oxford University Press, 1965), 3–29.

Chapter Three. Providence or Prudence?

1. *Crusoe* criticism is usefully summarized by Pat Rogers in *Robinson Crusoe* (London: Allen and Unwin, 1979). Since 1980, critics have concentrated on relating Defoe's concept of fiction to our own changing understandings of discourse and ideology. See, for example, Timothy J. Reiss, *The Discourse of Modernism* (Ithaca: Cornell University Press, 1982); and Lennard J. Davis, *Factual Fictions: The Origins of the English Novel* (New York: Columbia University Press, 1983).

2. Charles Gildon, *The Life and Strange Surprizing Adventures of Mr. D.——, DeF——, of London, Hosier*, edited by Paul Dottin (London: Dent, 1923), iv. Further citations are from this edition.

3. Ian Watt, *The Rise of the Novel* (Berkeley and Los Angeles: University of California Press, 1957), 89. Paul Hunter, *The Reluctant Pilgrim: Defoe's Emblematic Method and Quest for Form in Robinson Crusoe* (Baltimore: Johns Hopkins University Press, 1966), x.

4. *Serious Reflections* and *Vision of the Angelic World* were not reprinted in their entirety before 1790. They were, however, translated into French (1721), German (1721), and Dutch (1722) and appeared (where one might least expect) in abridgments of *Crusoe* in 1722, 1726, 1733, 1734, and in many later editions. Defoe's demonology must have been more popular with less-educated readers. *Serious Reflections* has not been edited since 1904. On the publication history of *Robinson Crusoe*, see Rogers, *Robinson Crusoe*, 4–16. As Maximillian Novak notes, "In approaching Defoe's ideas on fiction we must remember that his remarks are addressed to different reading audiences for different effects," "Defoe's Theory of Fiction," *Studies in Philology* 61:3 (1964): 650–68, 651.

5. Daniel Defoe, *Serious Reflections of Robinson Crusoe*, edited by George A. Aiken (London: Dent, 1896), ix. Further citations are from this edition.

6. While early sales of *Crusoe* were good, they were not unprecedented: "Defoe does not appear to have been especially impressed with his milestone in literary history. Several of his secret histories and a few of his works on the Jacobite rebels had begun as well or nearly as well, and the 1715 *Family Instructor* was in its seventh edition by then," Paula Backscheider, *Daniel Defoe, His Life* (Baltimore: Johns Hopkins University Press, 1989), 412.

7. Daniel Defoe, *Robinson Crusoe* (Oxford: Basil Blackwell, 1927; rpt. London: William Clowes and Sons, 1974), 1:ix.

=

8. Michael McKeon, *The Origins of the English Novel, 1600–1740* (Baltimore: Johns Hopkins University Press, 1987), 319.

9. On probability as a rhetorical concept, see Douglas Lane Patey, *Probability and Literary Form: Philosophic Theory and Literary Practice in the Augustan Age* (Cambridge: Cambridge University Press, 1984), 3–34.

10. James Beattie, "On Fable and Romance," in *Dissertations Moral and Critical* (Philadelphia: Hopkins and Earle, 1809), 3:22. Beattie's notion of a "poetical prose fable" is an early attempt to define imaginative writing as a "species" in its own right, a procedure that would lead the notion of "mixed kinds" to fall into disuse.

11. Paul J. Korshin, *Typologies in England, 1650–1820* (Princeton: Princeton University Press, 1982).

12. Hans W. Frei, *The Eclipse of Biblical Narrative: A Study in Eighteenth- and Nineteenth-Century Hermeneutics* (New Haven: Yale University Press, 1974), 63. See also McKeon, *The Origins of the English Novel:* "Frei's formulation permits us to see that it is not enough to treat the 'questions of truth' which are our present concern as significant of a revolution in epistemology. For what is most important about this revolution is that it entails a transformation *from* metaphysics and theology *to* epistemology," 83 (emphasis in original). Frei, however, describes a transformation of theology.

13. See Rodney M. Baine, *Daniel Defoe and the Supernatural* (Athens: University of Georgia Press, 1968), 31.

14. David Marshall, *The Figure of Theater: Shaftesbury, Defoe, Adam Smith, and George Eliot* (New York: Columbia University Press, 1986), 99.

15. U. Milo Kaufmann, *The Pilgrim's Progress and Traditions in Puritan Meditation* (New Haven: Yale University Press, 1966), 62, 67. John Bunyan, *The Pilgrim's Progress*, edited by James Blanton Wharey and Roger Sharrock, 2d ed. (Oxford: Clarendon, 1960, 1975): 316n. Further citations are from this edition.

16. See Frances A. Yates, *The Art of Memory* (Chicago: University of Chicago Press, 1966), 3, passim. While artificial memory and probabilistic interpretation serve different functions, they both originate in classical rhetoric.

17. Leopold Damrosch, Jr., *God's Plot and Man's Stories: Studies in the Fictional Imagination from Milton to Fielding* (Chicago: University of Chicago Press, 1985), 175; see also Stanley E. Fish's analysis of seemings in Bunyan's allegory: "*The Pilgrim's Progress* is the ultimate self-consuming artifact, for the insights it yields are inseparable from the demonstration of the inadequacy of its own forms, which are also the forms of the reader's understanding," *Self-Consuming Artifacts: The Experience of Seventeenth-Century Literature* (Berkeley and Los Angeles: University of California Press, 1972), 264.

18. *Paradise Lost* allusions are dotted throughout *Serious Reflections*; Gildon, *The Life and Strange Surprizing Adventures*, who divined the literary provenance

of Crusoe's fortunate fall, parodies Defoe, Crusoe, and Friday in the persons of Satan, Sin, and Death.

19. See Douglas Brooks, *Number and Pattern in the Eighteenth-Century Novel* (London: 1973), 18–26; and Paul Alkon, *Defoe and Fictional Time* (Athens: University of Georgia Press, 1979), 61. Defoe's application of probability to improbable circumstances conforms to the formula McKeon, *The Origins of the English Novel*, describes as "strange, therefore true," 46–47. That this was a chapbook and ballad formula might explain why the providential narratives of *Serious Reflections* found their way into the abridgments of *Robinson Crusoe* when they were not reprinted for polite readers.

20. They roll two sixes, two fives, two fours; see Francis Hutcheson, "The recurring of any Effect oftner than the laws of Hazard determine, gives the Presumption of Design . . . and that with superior probability, as the multitude of Cases in which the contrary might happen, surpass all the Cases in which this could happen," quoted in Patey, *Probability and Literary Form*, 68.

21. Defoe's phrase, putting "a name . . . upon the medium," aptly describes allegories in which language acquires a life of its own, as it tends to do in Milton's more Spenserian characters. While Milton's own allegory is historical and probabilistic, Sin, Death, and especially Chaos reveal their own inconsistencies. Damrosch, *God's Plot and Man's Stories*, contrasts Milton's allegory with Bunyan's: "Bunyan operates in a humbler tradition which, paradoxically, launches him into deeper waters that Milton avoids. Since he takes every text to be independently decisive, the texts tend to develop their own *unpredictable* connections instead of conforming to authorial *design*" 156 (emphasis added). *Paradise Lost* was an important model for Defoe's use of probabilism in "allusive allegorical history."

22. An obvious case in point is Locke's famous *Essay Concerning Human Understanding*. In the eighteenth century, essays assimilate qualities of many genres. As Patey, *Probability and Literary Form*, remarks, "That the essay could become the vehicle for physicists as well as historians, politicians, and moralists is itself a product of the Augustan redirection of rhetoric from the vulgar to the learned—the learned now comprising an enlarged reading public interested to follow the reasonings of a Locke or a Boyle. At the same time, the repertory of literary devices open to the essayist widens. The most striking feature of the Augustan essay—aside from its broad appeal—is not probable argument but its endless variety and flexibility, its capacity to assimilate nearly all literary devices," 172. Other probabilistic genres were undergoing similar extensions, notably georgic and prose fiction.

23. Geoffry M. Sill, *Defoe and the Idea of Fiction, 1713–1719* (Newark: University of Delaware Press, 1983), 25.

24. Tony Bennett, *Outside Literature* (London: Routledge, 1990), 67.

25. G. A. Starr supplies contemporary analogues for Defoe's remarks on honesty in his appendix, "Fiction and Mendacity," to *Defoe and Casuistry* (Princeton:

=

Princeton University Press, 1971). "Of Honesty" is cited but not discussed.

26. See Fish's discussion of this episode, *Self-Consuming Artifacts*, 227–29.

27. David B. Morris, *Alexander Pope: The Genius of Sense* (Cambridge: Harvard University Press, 1984), 194.

28. *Serious Reflections* appeared at a time when many were learning the mysteries of probability the hard way: "'Our estate is an imaginary one only,' Pope wrote in a letter of 1720 referring to the modest investment he made with Martha and Theresa Blount in South Sea Stock: 'One day we were worth two or three thousand, and the next not 3 parts of the sum.' The source of such fluctuating wealth, Pope correctly implies, is illusion, passion, rumor, and credit," Morris, *Alexander Pope*, 185.

29. Bernard Mandeville, *The Fable of the Bees*, edited by F. B. Kaye (Oxford: Clarendon, 1924), 1:27. All references are to this edition.

30. Another good instance of a self-reflexive economic fable is Addison's famous allegory of public credit in the third *Spectator*. The meditator falls "insensibly into a kind of Methodical dream" of a Public Credit who is herself haunted by the phantoms and fictions hovering about her chamber. Addison dresses out his fable in all the paraphernalia of probable reasoning, so that the "vapours" of Credit become comprehensible and even methodical to those interpreting the fiction. Donald F. Bond, editor, *The Spectator* (Oxford: Clarendon, 1965).

31. Lennard Davis, *Factural Fictions*, 161. Here, as elsewhere, Defoe cannot bring himself to describe his work as a fiction. This is not because he was unaware (as has been claimed) of differences between fact and fiction, but because he does not want his work associated with purely imaginative creation. His use of the term *history* conforms to contemporary usage, which included what we now call realistic fiction. See William Nelson, *Fact or Fiction: The Dilemma of the Renaissance Storyteller* (Cambridge: Harvard University Press, 1973), and McKeon, *The Origins of the English Novel*, 52–54.

32. Many of the inset stories in *Serious Reflections* begin with one or the other of these formulas. Since the stories are told by a character whose own status is in doubt, we are left to make such "honest" uses of them as we can. Shifting the onus of interpretation to the reader would appear to be part of Defoe's didactic strategy.

33. McKeon, *The Origins of the English Novel*, offers insightful remarks on the impact of print on late Renaissance attitudes toward history and representation, 39–45 and passim.

34. Surveying earlier discussions of lying, Starr, "Fiction and Mendacity," concludes that "Defoe's stress on injurious intent is therefore distinctive but not unique," 198.

35. Once again, I'm in disagreement with McKeon, *The Origins of the English Novel*, who argues that "the very rigor of providential argument, the polemical urgency and extremity of its presentation, signifies not faith but a crisis

of faith. Indeed, it is the nature of such a crisis to evoke not only a straightforward skepticism, but also a contradictory effort to employ the tools of skepticism—the claim to historicity—to justify what hitherto might have been 'taken on faith' and tacitly assumed to be true," 124. By this logic, Christianity has been secularizing all along: Bunyan's equally urgent turn toward the inner light implies a lack of faith in expositions of Scripture, which in turn reflect a lack of faith in the authority of tradition, which in turn reflects a lack of faith in textual transmission, and so on back to Doubting Thomas himself. Defoe understood doubt as the condition of true belief, as Christians have ever since Jesus first declared his divinity.

36. I owe this observation to Marshall, *The Figure of Theater*, 102–4.

37. Richard Baxter, *The Saint's Everlasting Rest*, 11th ed. (London, 1677), 4.2.2:752.

Chapter Four. Eighteenth-Century Georgic

1. David Hume, *Essays Moral, Political, and Literary*, edited by Eugene F. Miller (Indianapolis: Liberty Classics, 1985), 536. Originally published from 1753 to 1756.

2. Margaret, Duchess of Newcastle, *Life of the Duke, Memoirs of Her Own Life and Certain Sociable Letters* (London: Dent, nd), 225–26.

3. Donald F. Bond, editor, *The Spectator*, 5 vols. (Oxford: Clarendon, 1965), 1:167–68. On the importance of manners and femininity in Whig politics, see J. G. A. Pocock, "Virtues, Rights, and Manners: A Model for Historians of Eighteenth-Century Political Thought," and "The Mobility of Property and the Rise of Eighteenth-Century Sociology," in *Virtue, Commerce, and History: Essays on Political Thought and History, Chiefly in the Eighteenth Century* (Cambridge: Cambridge University Press, 1985), 48–50, 114–15.

4. On Frances Thynne Seymour, see "Lady Hertford and Lady Pomfret," in George Paston, *Little Memoirs of the Eighteenth Century* (London: Grant Richards, 1901), 3–56, notable for its extreme condescension; and Helen Sard Hughes, *The Gentle Hertford: Her Life and Letters* (New York: Macmillan, 1940), which runs to the opposite extreme. Hughes's book, which gives the texts of several hundred letters, will hereafter be cited in the text as *TGH*. Hughes also published a series of articles on the Hertford circle drawing on manuscript material now at Alnwick Castle: "Thomson and the Countess of Hertford," *Modern Philology* 25 (1928): 439–68; "Thomson and Lady Hertford Again," *Modern Philology* 28 (1931): 468–70; "John Dyer and the Countess of Hertford," *Modern Philology* 27 (1930): 311–20; "Shenstone and the Countess of Hertford," *PMLA* 46 (1931): 1113–27; "Mr. Cowslade's Memoirs," *Yale Review* 28 (1939): 861–64; "A Romantic Correspondence of the Year 1729," *Modern Philology* 37 (1939): 187–200; "Elizabeth Rowe and the Countess of Hertford," *PMLA* 49 (1944): 726–46.

5. See John Locke, *Some Thoughts Concerning Education*: "Occasions will

daily force [the gentleman] to make use of his Pen, which, besides the Conse-quences, that, in his Affairs, his well or ill managing of it often draws after it, always lays him open to a severer Examination of his Breeding, Sense, and Abil-ities, than oral Discourses," cited in William Henry Irving, *The Providence of Wit in the English Letter Writers* (1955; rpt., New York: Octagon, 1975), 15. Defoe ridicules illiteracy among the gentry: "Gentleman: 'I write indifferently. I can set my name, and that's enough for a gentleman,'" *The Complete English Gentleman* (London: David Nutt, 1890), 128. Whig writers emphasize literacy as part of their general program of progress through commerce.

6. These skills are documented in a journal kept by the countess of the dark days following the demise of Walpole, Hertford's patron (*TGH*, 185–211).

7. On the proud duke, see the entry in the *Dictionary of National Biography*. Mark Girouard illustrates the relation of place to space by describing the king of Spain's visit to the old duke's Petworth estate in 1703: "As the king arrived he was welcomed at the door by the prince [of Denmark; the queen's husband, outrank-ing the duke, acted as host] and escorted to the entrance of his apartment on the first floor. After a decent interval to allow the king to settle in, a series of state vis-its were paid between the various great people. First, the prince sent a message to the king to ask if he could call on him. Permission being given, the prince emerged from his apartment, and proceeded through the ante-room and with-drawing room of the king's apartment to the door of his bedchamber. The king, who was sitting in an armchair in his bedchamber, came to the door—but no farther—to welcome him, and sat him in an armchair opposite him—an armchair being a rank above a chair without arms, and two ranks above a stool. . . . After they had passed the time of day for a few minutes, the prince returned to his apartment. Shortly afterwards the king sent a message to ask if he could call on the prince. Permission being given, the king emerged from his apartment and was met by the prince who, being of an inferior grade of royalty, came out of his own apartment to the top of the stairs to greet him. He was then conveyed to the prince's bedchamber, where he passed the time of day for a few minutes." And so on. This was the household in which Algernon Seymour grew up. *Life in the English Country House* (New Haven: Yale University Press, 1978), 147.

8. James Thomson, *The Seasons*, edited by James Sambrook (Oxford: Claren-don, 1981), 2.

9. Isaac Watts, *Reliquiae Junvenile: Miscellaneous Thoughts in Prose and Verse, on Natural, Moral, and Divine Subjects* (1734) (rpt., New York: Garland, 1972), iii–iv. References to this edition are cited in the text.

10. The epistolary device for asserting veracity was of course familiar to read-ers of restoration fiction. See Robert Adams Day, *Told in Letters: Epistolary Fic-tion Before Richardson* (Ann Arbor: University of Michigan Press, 1966).

11. Elizabeth Rowe, *Letters Moral and Entertaining, appended to her famous*

Friendship in Death (rpt., New York: Garland, 1972). References to this edition are cited in the text.

12. Hume, *Essays*, 537. On religion and romance, see also Day, *Told in Letters*, 113.

13. Elizabeth Rowe, *Miscellaneous Works, in Prose and Verse, the greater Part Now First Published*, 2 vols. (London, 1739), 2:119–20. Cited in the text as *Works*.

14. Nancy Armstrong, *Desire and Domestic Fiction: A Political History of the Novel* (New York: Oxford University Press, 1987).

15. "Song: Hard is the Fate" (ll. 13–16); in James Thomson, *Liberty, The Castle of Indolence, and Other Poems*, edited by James Sambrook (Oxford: Clarendon, 1986), 296. On Frances Seymour's exchange with Thomson, see Hilbert H. Campbell, "Thomson and the Countess of Hertford Yet Again," *Modern Philology* 67:4 (1970): 367–69.

16. On the more libertine strains in retirement writing, see Maren-Sofie Rostwig's chapter, "The Innocent Epicurean," in *The Happy Man: Studies in the Metamorphosis of a Classical Ideal* (Oslo: Norwegian Universities Press, 1962), 1:227–310.

17. Nor was the youthful Elizabeth Rowe, who carried on at least three Platonic affairs—in print—including one with a married man. For the details of Rowe's commerce with John Dunton, Matthew Prior, and Isaac Watts, see Henry F. Stecher, *Elizabeth Rowe, the Poetess of Frome: A Study in Eighteenth-Century English Pietism* (Bern: Herbert Lang, 1973).

18. Lord Warncliff and W. Moy Thomas, eds., *The Letters and Works of Lady Mary Wortley Montagu*, 2 vols. (New York: Macmillan, 1893), 2:345. Frances Seymour's poem, and the nasty reply Lady Mary penned for Hamilton, are reprinted at 2:477. Lady Mary's poem, edited by Robert Halsband and Isobel Grundy, may be found in Lady Mary Wortley Montagu, *Essays and Poems and Simplicity: A Comedy* (Oxford: Clarendon, 1977), 263.

19. Horace Walpole to the Countess of Upper Ossory, Dec. 20, 1775, in *The Yale Edition of Horace Walpole's Correspondence*, edited by W. S. Lewis et al., 48 vols. (New Haven: Yale University Press, 1937–83), 32:283. In a letter to her son, Frances Seymour asserted the innocence of "an old friend who has been so long a prisoner, and I am convinced upon a false accusation." She refused, however, to defend Lady Luxborough's manners: "She is the same person she was ten, nay twenty years ago, her dress as French, her manner as thoughtless" (*TGH*, 277). On the whole affair, see Walter Sichel, *Bolingbroke and His Times, the Sequel* (1902; rpt., New York: Greenwood, 1968), 356–58.

20. On these works, see Irving, *Providence of Wit*, 138–63.

21. See Douglas Grant, *James Thomson, Poet of the Seasons* (London: Cresset, 1951), 90.

22. William Bingley, ed., *Correspondence Between Frances, Countess of Hart-*

ford, (Afterwards Duchess of Somerset,) and Henrietta Louisa, Countess of Pomfret, Between the Years 1738 and 1741, 3 vols. (London, 1805). A second edition was printed the following year. Cited in the text as *CHP.*

23. On Pope and retirement, see Maynard Mack, *The Garden and the City: Retirement and Politics in the Later Poetry of Pope* (Toronto: University of Toronto Press, 1969); and Morris R. Brownell, *Alexander Pope and the Arts of Georgian England* (Oxford: Clarendon, 1978). Pope's relation to Riskings is discussed in Peter Martin, *Pursuing Innocent Pleasures: The Gardening World of Alexander Pope* (Hamden: Archon, 1984), 66–78. Apart from the Moses Browne poem discussed below, Martin offers the best description of the estate.

24. On changing attitudes toward Gothicism, see Kenneth Clark, *The Gothic Revival: An Essay in the History of Taste* (1928, rpt., London: John Murray, 1973). On gardening, poetry, and devotion, see Stephen Switzer, *Ichonographia Rustica; or, The Nobleman, Gentleman, and Gardener's Recreation*, 3 vols. (1718; rpt., New York: Garland, 1982), 1:50, 3:8. Switzer includes devotional writing in his handbook: "And 'tis from the Admiration of these that the Soul is elevated to unlimited Heights above, and modell'd and prepar'd for the sweet Reception and happy Enjoyment of Felicities, the durablest as well as happiest that Omniscience has created" (1:v). Switzer, who apparently worked at Riskings, supplies a diagram of the estate in the second edition.

25. John Dixon Hunt describes the devotional paraphernalia of eighteenth-century parks as mere "tokens of the contemplative life." *The Figure in the Landscape: Poetry, Painting, and Gardening during the Eighteenth Century* (Baltimore: Johns Hopkins University Press, 1976), 3. No doubt some of it was, but parks and hermitages were sometimes more than toys. James Hervey, a favorite author at Percy Lodge, was not unusual in combining discussions of theology and taste, as in the headings of one of his dialogues: "Park and romantic mount. Christ's death farther considered, as the very punishment which our sins deserved," "Elegant arbour in the flower-garden. Imputation of CHRIST's righteousness," "Gallery of pictures. Library and its furniture. A sordid taste in painting censured; a more graceful manner displayed. Imputation of CHRIST's righteousness resumed." *Theron and Aspasia; or, A Series of Dialogues and Letters*, 3 vols. (London, 1755); in *Works* 6 vols. (Pontefract, 1805), 2:xi–xii.

26. The country-house poem has been the subject of a great deal of scholarship in recent years, most of it devoted to seventeenth-century instances of the genre. See G. R. Hibbard, "The Country House Poem of the Seventeenth Century," *Journal of the Warburg and Courtauld Institutes* 19 (1956), 159–74; Raymond Williams, *The Country and the City* (New York: Oxford University Press, 1973), 13–59; William McClung, *The Country House in English Renaissance Poetry* (Berkeley and Los Angeles: University of California Press, 1977); Virginia C. Kinny, *The Country-House Ethos in Literature, 1688–1750: Themes of Personal Retreat and National Expansion* (Sussex: Harvester, 1985); Don E. Wayne,

=

Penshurst: The Semeiotics of Place and the Poetics of History (Madison: University of Wisconsin Press, 1984); and Alastair Fowler, "Country House Poems: The Politics of a Genre," *Seventeenth Century* 1 (1986): 1–13. On the much larger number of eighteenth-century house poems, see Robert Arnold Aubin, *Topographical Poetry in Eighteenth-Century England* (New York: Modern Language Association of America, 1936). Aubin supplies an extensive bibliography of estate poems, including ten examples written before 1700 and some 350 written in the following century. Morris Brownell argues that the Jonsonian house poem "virtually disappear[s] from the poetry of the period 1700 to 1750, but that its ideals survive in the satire of Pope and Swift about the villa." "Poetical Villas: English Verse Satire of the Country House 1700–1750," in *Satire in the Eighteenth Century*, edited by J. D. Browning (New York: Garland, 1983), 9–52.

27. This is a perennial theme of her correspondence. Of the several accounts, the most detailed is in a letter of 1742 to Mrs. Mary Rich (*TGH*, 149–50). Although she was an avid romance reader, it is doubtful that Lady Hertford saw fiction as an escape from, or a metaphor for, "the reality of married women experiencing living death in the wasteland of domestic life," Ellen Pollak, *The Poetics of Sexual Myth* (Chicago: University of Chicago Press, 1985), 75.

28. First published in *Two Epistles . . . by the Rev'd Mr. Dalton* (London, 1745). Citations, by page number, are from *Bell's Classical Arrangement of Fugitive Poetry* (London, 1789).

29. Samuel Garth, *Claremont* (London, 1715).

30. The departure from Renaissance ideas of nobility can be made even more obvious by comparing Cotton's "Belvoir: Being a Pindarick Ode upon Belvoir Castle" (1679):

See with what Beauty 'tis o'erspread;
How the exalted Head
Looks down with Scorn on Hills below,
So high and fair, that it a Piece of Heav'n doth show.

Cited from Aubin, *Topographical Poetry*, 118; on the prospect view see also John Barrell, "An Unerring Gaze: The Prospect of Society in the Poetry of James Thomson and John Dyer," in *English Literature in History 1730–80: An Equal, Wide Survey* (London: Hutchinson, 1983); David H. Solkin, *Richard Wilson: The Landscape of Reaction* (London: Tate Gallery, 1982), 22–35; Carol Fabricant, "The Aesthetics and Politics of Landscape in the Eighteenth-Century," in *Studies in Eighteenth-Century British Art and Aesthetics*, edited by Ralph Cohen (Berkeley and Los Angeles: University of California Press, 1985), 49–81; and Ann Bermingham, *Landscape and Ideology: The English Rustic Tradition, 1740–1850* (Berkeley and Los Angeles: University of California Press, 1986).

31. On the relation of aesthetic to political disinterestedness, see John Barrell's chapter, "A Republic of Taste," in *The Political Theory of Painting from*

Reynolds to Hazlitt (New Haven: Yale University Press, 1986), 1–68.

32. A selection of these letters is printed in *TGH*, 212–348.

33. Moses Browne, *Percy Lodge, A Seat of The Duke and Duchess of Somerset, A Poem Written by Command of their Late Graces, (in the Year 1749) And Inscribed to the Right Honourable The (present) Countess of Northumberland. By the Rev. Mr. Moses Browne, Vicar of Olney, Bucks; Author of Sunday Thoughts, Essay on the Universe, etc.* (London, 1755). Citations are by page number.

34. On the gothic poetry of the 1740s, see Amy Louise Reed, *The Background of Gray's Elegy: A Study in the Taste for Melancholy Poetry 1700–1751* (New York: Columbia University Press, 1924); on the Spenserian idiom, see Earl R. Wasserman, *Elizabethan Poetry in the Eighteenth Century* (Bloomington: University of Indiana Press, 1947); on imitations of Milton, see Raymond Dexter Havens, *The Influence of Milton on English Poetry* (1922; rpt. New York: Russell and Russell, 1961), 439–78.

35. As matters turned out, the broken line of descent was restored through the female branch. The countess's daughter became the countess of Northumberland; she and her husband, Hugh Smithson, became important patrons in their own right.

36. Joseph Trapp, *Aedes Badmintoniae, A Poem* (London, 1701), cited in Aubin, *Topographical Poetry*, 117–18.

37. See Hughes, "Shenstone and the Countess of Hertford." She does not report variations between the manuscript of "Rural Elegance" and the published versions. Citations, by stanza number, are from *A Collection of Poems in Six Volumes* (London, 1770), edited by Robert Dodsley.

38. *The Letters of William Shenstone*, edited by Marjorie Williams (Oxford: Basil Blackwell, 1939), 63. Cited in the text as *LWS*.

39. In 1739 the countess rejected a dedication from Elizabeth Carter, noting "I have been obliged to refuse the same honour both from Dr. Watts and Mr. Rowe, within these twelve months, for reasons which (if they were not too long to trouble you with) I am sure you would not disapprove," *Memoirs of the Life of Mrs. Elizabeth Carter*, edited by Montague Pennington (London, 1816), 1:51–52. The countess preferred friends to clients, and worked actively to promote their interests through private correspondence with her influential acquaintances. On her later life as a religious devotee, see *TGH*, 349–417.

40. For Shenstone, like Shaftesbury, the Venetian republic was seen as the archetypal commercial state. The danger was always that such an economy would lead to luxury and "interested" factionalism; Shenstone's notion of aesthetic disinterestedness seeks to avoid these pitfalls. His story is adapted from Shaftesbury's "Moralists," in *Characteristics of Men, Manners, Opinions, and Times*, edited by John M. Robertson (Indianapolis: Bobbs-Merrill, 1964), 2:127. On commerce and republicanism, see J. G. A. Pocock, *The Machiavellian Moment:*

≡

Florentine Political Thought and the Atlantic Republican Tradition (Princeton: Princeton University Press, 1975), 401–505.

41. Hughes, "Shenstone and the Countess of Hertford," 1121.

Chapter Five. Cultivation into Culture

1. R. L. Brett, *The Third Earl of Shaftesbury: A Study in Eighteenth-Century Literary Theory* (London: Hutchinson's University Library, 1951), 116; Ernest Tuveson, "The Importance of Shaftesbury," *ELH* 20 (1953): 267, 298; Robert Marsh, *Four Dialectical Theories of Poetry* (Chicago: University of Chicago Press, 1965), 4, 189. Marsh, a neo-Aristotelian, is concerned with types of theories, rather than the genres in which theorists write.

2. Citations are from *Characteristics of Men, Manners, Opinions, Times*, edited by John M. Robertson, 2 vols. (1900; rpt., Indianapolis: Bobbs-Merrill, 1964), 1:155. Also see Samuel Taylor Coleridge, *The Friend*, 2 vols., in *Collected Works*, vol. 4, edited by Barbara E. Rooke (Princeton: Princeton University Press, 1969). I have altered spelling and punctuation to correspond to the 1727 edition of *Characteristicks*.

3. Coleridge, *Collected Works*, 2:85.

4. James W. Davidson summarizes Shaftesbury's position: "A disaffected group of writers supporting the Tories could inflame the public to disorder, especially during time of war; and an unstable self could easily be excited to participate in a 'panic'—of the kind, say, that occurred in 1708 when the Jacobites attempted to invade the country," "Criticism and Self-Knowledge in Shaftesbury's Soliloquy," *Enlightenment Essays* 5:2 (1974): 50–61, 61. On Shaftesbury's aesthetics and politics generally, see Michael Meehan, *Liberty and Poetics in Eighteenth-Century England* (London: Croom Helm, 1986), 25–41. On Coleridge's republicanism, see Nigel Leask, *The Politics of Imagination in Coleridge's Critical Thought* (New York: St. Martin's, 1988): "The 'One Life' ideal should be . . . identified with an older from of radicalism partaking of many of the political, theological and cosmological ideas of the 'Commonwealth' tradition, which had its origins in the previous century, and which by the end of the eighteenth was being modified, dispersed, or assimilated," 18. Leask does not discuss *The Friend*.

5. On the relation of commerce to republicanism, see J. G. A. Pocock, *The Machiavellian Moment: Florentine Political Thought and the Atlantic Republican Tradition* (Princeton: Princeton University Press, 1975), chaps. 13 and 14, and *Virtue, Commerce, and History: Essays on Political Thought and History, Chiefly in the Seventeenth Century* (Cambridge: Cambridge University Press, 1985), 37–50. See also Lawrence Klein's groundbreaking article, "The Third Earl of Shaftesbury and the Progress of Politeness," *Eighteenth-Century Studies* 18:2 (1984–85): 186–214: "We see not only a highly enriched notion of 'politeness,' but its deployment in an attempt to perform the delicate negotiations

=

between traditional and classical notions of virtue and the commercial society," 188–89. Thomas Woodman brings a wide range of primary and secondary works to bear on these issues in *Politeness and Poetry in the Age of Pope* (Rutherford: Fairleigh Dickinson University Press, 1989), 17–29 and passim; Susan Staves considers the relationship between politeness and commerce in "Pope's Refinement," *Eighteenth Century* 29:2 (1988): 145–163: "Pope is often described as having struggled to resist 'the new commercial spirit of the nation'— to borrow the formulation of the Norton Anthology—but in important ways he was very much a participant in that commercial spirit," 146.

6. Klein, "Progress of Politeness," suggests the following as a list of suspects: Henry Tubbe, *Meditations Divine and Morall* (1659); Joseph Henshaw, *Meditations, Miscellaneous, Holy, and Humane* (1658); Sir Matthew Hale, *Contemplations, Moral and Divine* (1682); Sir William Killigrew, *Mid-Night Thoughts* (1682); and Sir Thomas Culpeper, *Essays or Subjects* (1665).

7. On Shaftesbury's theatrical metaphors, see David Marshall, *The Figure of Theater: Shaftesbury, Defoe, Adam Smith, and George Eliot* (New York: Columbia University Press, 1986), especially the discussion of "character": "Character means at once the aggregate of the distinctive features of something, its essential peculiarity or nature, the moral or mental qualities which distinguish one as an individual, individuality itself; *and* the face or features of something or someone, a personality invented by a novelist or a dramatist, the part assumed and played by an actor on the stage. *Character* is also writing itself: from its Greek etymology meaning to mark, stamp, or engrave to an alphabetic mark, a graphic symbol, or sign, a figure, an expression, or direct representation. Is the character of a person something essential and individual or a role to be enacted, a figure that represents a self?" 41.

8. Jerome Stolnitz, "On the Origins of 'Aesthetic Disinterestedness,'" *Journal of Aesthetics and Art Criticism* 20:1 (1961–62): 131–43, 133. See also Dabney Townsend, "From Shaftesbury to Kant: The Development of the Concept of Aesthetic Experience," *Journal of the History of Ideas* 48:2 (1987): 287–305. On the dialogue, see Eugene R. Purpose, "The 'Plain, Easy, and Familiar Way': The Dialogue in English Literature, 1660–1725," *ELH* 17:1 (1950): 47–58.

9. Robert Markley, "Style as Philosophical Structure: The Contexts of Shaftesbury's *Characteristicks*," in *The Philosopher as Writer: The Eighteenth-Century*, edited by Robert Ginsberg (Selinsgrove: Susquehanna University Press, 1987): 140–154, 141.

10. Klein, "Progress of Politeness," 186–87.

11. Robert Markley, "Sentimentality as Performance: Shaftesbury, Sterne, and the Theatrics of Virtue," in *The New Eighteenth Century: Theory, Politics, English Literature*, edited by Felicity Nussbaum and Laura Brown (New York: Methuen, 1987), 210–30, 305n.

12. Markley, "Style as Philosophical Structure," 153.

13. See Lawrence Stone and Jeanne C. Fawtier Stone, *An Open Elite? England, 1540–1880* (Oxford: Clarendon, 1984), which concludes that the peerage, at least, was relatively closed; Roy Porter splits the difference: "Partly because the crevasses between the ranks were at least in theory bridgeable, personal mobility upwards and downwards acted as a safety valve, preserving the overall profile of society" *English Society in the Eighteenth Century* (London: Penguin, 1981), 65. Thomas Woodman argues that "politeness thus represents the modification of traditional aristocratic attitudes and the coopting of a wider polite elite through subtle instructions in such values"; he also suggests that politeness was "exclusionary." *Politeness and Poetry*, 22.

14. Christopher Hill notes: "Milton praised equality, but opposed 'the absurdity of equalling the unequal. . . . Each person should be cared for according to his rank and eminence.' He no more shared the Leveller confidence in democracy than he shared the Digger distrust of private property." *Milton and the English Revolution* (New York: Viking, 1977), 114.

15. Coleridge, *The Friend*, 1:93. Barbara Rooke suggests that *The Friend* was intended as a response to William Cobbett's less expensive *Political Register,* Coleridge, *Collected Works,* 1:xlii. Deirdre Coleman also notes Coleridge's antipathy toward Cobbett: "To prospective subscribers, he proudly declared that he had no intention of writing 'for the Multitude; but for those, who by Rank, or Fortune, or official Situation, or Talents and habits of Reflection, are to influence the Multitude.'" *Coleridge and The Friend* (Oxford: Clarendon, 1988), 42.

16. Donald F. Bond, ed., *The Spectator* (Oxford: Clarendon, 1965), 1:44. Jerome R. Nabholtz supplies a useful explication of these arguments in *"My Reader, My Fellow-Labourer": A Study of English Romantic Prose* (Columbia: University of Missouri Press, 1986), 107–17. See also Victoria Myers, "Coleridge's *The Friend*: An Experiment in Rhetorical Theory," *JEGP* 86:1 (1987): 9–32, which locates Coleridge's "experiment" in the context of contemporary theories of rhetoric.

17. See Maynard Mack's discussion of Pope's personae in *The Garden and the City: Retirement and Politics in the Later Poetry of Pope* (Toronto: University of Toronto Press, 1969): Shaftesbury includes both town and country personae in *Characteristicks.* See also John G. Hayman, "Shaftesbury and the Search for a Persona," *SEL* 10 (1970): 491–504, which (in my view) oversimplifies the question by assuming that, in advancing "a *systematic* body of thought," Shaftesbury attempts to resolve the problem of identity by "the use of an artificial persona," 491, 497 (emphasis added).

18. See Bond, *The Spectator,* introduction. For an acute analysis of the genre, see Charles A. Knight, "Bibliography and the Shape of the Literary Periodical in the Early Eighteenth Century," *Library* 8:3 (1986): 232–248.

19. On the managerial problems, which were formidable, see Rooke's intro-

=

duction to Coleridge: *Collected Works*. On the unhappy domestic situation, see Coleman, *Coleridge*, 21–40.

20. Coleridge, *The Friend*, 2:17.

21. In J. R. de J. Jackson, editor, *Coleridge: The Critical Heritage* (London: Routledge and Kegan Paul, 1970), 428. On difficulty as an aid to reflection, see Myers, "Coleridge's *The Friend*," 14. Jerome Christensen wittily compares the deferral of meaning in difficult arguments to Coleridge's remarks on credit and the national debt in *Coleridge's Blessed Machine of Language* (Ithaca: Cornell University Press, 1981), 204–20.

22. See Knight, "Bibliography": "The folio format emphasized the immediate interest of each essay and tended to define the given periodical series as a collection of discrete essays, on diverse subjects, to be successively and independently read; the printed volumes, on the other hand, seemed to mark the series as an identifiable if not coherent work of art, with some commonality of approach, concern, and interest, written with a sense of enduring values, and hence worth re-reading," 236.

23. On eighteenth-century attitudes toward Augustus and patronage, see Howard Weinbrot, *Augustus Caesar in "Augustan" England: The Decline of a Classical Norm* (Princeton: Princeton University Press, 1978). Shaftesbury is discussed on 160.

24. Markley, "Style as Philosophical Structure," 152–53.

25. See Leask, "History-Writing, Higher Criticism and the Mystery Cults," in *Politics of Imagination*, 165–83.

26. Rooke, in Coleridge's *Collected Works*, identifies Mathetes as John Wilson and Alexander Blair (1:377).

27. Coleridge, *The Friend*, 2:262. Shaftesbury added *A Notion of the Historical Draught or Tablature of the Judgement of Hercules* to later editions of *Characteristicks*. It is reprinted in Stephen Orgel, ed., *Cebes in England: English Translations of the Tablet of Cebes from Three Centuries with Related Materials* (New York: Garland, 1980).

28. On the relation of Kantian philosophy to *The Friend*, which runs deep, see Coleman, *Coleridge*, 132–64 and passim.

29. The opposition to political engagement accords with Jerome K. Chandler's assessment that "Wordsworth's major work, his programmatic poetry of second nature, is conservative from the start," *Wordsworth's Second Nature: A Study of the Poetry and Politics* (Chicago: University of Chicago Press, 1984), xviii.

30. This diversity of Shaftesbury's structure, not surprisingly, has led to a diversity of opinion about its principles of order. Brett, *Third Earl of Shaftesbury*, says that "one must recognize at the start that there is no coherent or comprehensive system in his writings," 59; Tuveson, *Importance of Shaftesbury*, that "he constructed of many elements a complete and artistically consistent whole," 268; Marsh, *Four Dialectical Theories of Poetry*, describes "a collection of loosely orga-

nized and 'familiar' dialogues, conversational epistles, and 'soliloquies,' which bear closer resemblance to the Horatian mode of satire than to the literary modes of any essentially philosophical school," 26; Markley, "Style as Structure," finds "three basic forms of prose style" (satirical, philosophical, rhapsodic) that "are different strategies to the same or similar ends," 143; Marshall, *The Figure of Theater*, describes "the realm of Shaftesbury's texts" as a "world of theater," 67.

31. See Coleridge, *Collected Works*, lxxvii–lxxxv and xcii–xcvii.

32. For a useful explication of the essays on method, see J. R. deJ. Jackson, *Method and Imagination in Coleridge's Criticism* (Cambridge: Harvard University Press, 1969), 21–47.

33. On the consequences of the ancient-moderns debate for the redefinition of literature as belles lettres, see Douglas Lane Patey, "The Eighteenth-Century Invents the Canon," *Modern Language Studies* 18:1 (Winter 1988): 17–37.

34. Clifford Siskin supplies a number of instances illustrating the ways in which Coleridgean procedures for writing cultural history are alive and well in current literary criticism: "We begin with a poet such as Keats, who . . . writes up himself and his work in terms of a biological development thematized as a development of forms. We then 'interpret' him and his works by using those same procedures to reproduce the identical kind of order that his own texts first imposed on themselves. Then we document the truth of our 'findings' by transforming all of the past into a developmental prelude to our present." *The Historicity of Romantic Discourse* (New York: Oxford University Press, 1988), 45.

35. Arthur Friedman, editor, *Collected Works of Oliver Goldsmith*, 5 vols. (Oxford: Clarendon, 1966), 1:4.

36. Terry Eagleton, *The Function of Criticism from the Spectator to Post-Structuralism* (London: Verso, 1984): 123.

37. David Kaufmann, "The Profession of Theory," *PMLA* 105:3 (1990): 519–30, 524.

38. Leask, *Politics of Imagination*, 2 (emphasis added).

Index

Abrams, M. H., 46, 47
Addison, Joseph, 146; on georgic, 53, 56, 66; *Spectator*, 122–23, 126, 173–74, 177, 178
Alkon, Paul, 214n
Allegory: in *Compleat Angler*, 68; in *The Friend*, 176; in *Paradise Lost*, 52, 214n; in *Percy Lodge*, 153–55; in *Pilgrim's Progress*, 95–97; in *Robinson Crusoe*, 81, 85–86, 88–91, 92, 101, 104, 111–12; in *Faerie Queene*, 52
Anatomy genre: in Coleridge, 194; in Donne, 15–16; in Shaftesbury, 167
Arac, Jonathan, 206n
Armstrong, Nancy, 133–37, 162
Arnold, Matthew, 201
Aubin, Robert Arnold, 220n

Backscheider, Paula, 212n
Bacon, Francis *Cogitata et Visa*, 31; Coleridge on, 175, 196; *Essayes*, 31; *Great Instauration*, 31–33, 190
Baine, Rodney, 112
Ballads, 105; in *Compleat Angler*, 66
Barrell, John, 58–59, 220nn
Baxter, Richard, *Saint's Everlasting Rest*, 117
Beattie, James, 88, 91, 213n
Behn, Aphra, 86, 141

Bennet, Tony, 103, 150
Bermingham, Ann, 220n
Booty, John, 204n
Boyle, Robert, 214n; on occasional meditation, 210n
Brett, R. L., 165
Brooks, Douglas, 214n
Browne, Moses, 124; *Percy Lodge*, 153–55, 163
Brownell, Morris R., 219n, 220n
Bunyan, John, *Pilgrim's Progress*, 85, 86, 92–98, 102, 106–7
Burton, Henry, 207n

Campbell, Hilbert H., 218n
Carey, John, 206n
Carter, Elizabeth, 124, 149, 221n
Cavendish, Margaret, *Sociable Letters*, 122–23
Chalker, John, 209n
Chandler, Jerome K., 225n
Character genre: in *Characteristicks*, 189; in *Compleat Angler*, 67; in *The Friend*, 187; in *Robinson Crusoe*, 88, 97
Christensen, Jerome, 225n
Clark, Kenneth, 219n
Cobbett, William, 224n
Cohen, Ralph, 53, 208n, 209n
Coleman, Deirdre, 224n

227

=

Index

228

≡

Index